REFLECTIONS ON
FRANCIS SCHAEFFER

REFLECTIONS ON
FRANCIS SCHAEFFER

Ronald W. Ruegsegger, Editor

Academie
Books Grand Rapids,
Michigan
Zondervan Publishing House

Reflections on Francis Schaeffer

Academie Books are published by the Zondervan Publishing House
1415 Lake Drive, S.E., Grand Rapids, Michigan 49506

Library of Congress Cataloging in Publication Data

Reflections on Francis Schaeffer.

"Academie books."
Bibliography: p.
Includes index.
1. Schaeffer, Francis A. (Francis August) 2. Evangelicalism. I. Ruegsegger, Ronald W.
BR1643.S33R43   1986   230'.092'4   86-7777
ISBN 0-310-37091-4

Edited by James E. Ruark
Designed by Louise Bauer

Printed in the United States of America

86   87   88   89   90   91 / 10   9   8   7   6   5   4   3   2   1

CONTENTS

Foreword
NO LITTLE PERSON

JAMES I. PACKER

He was physically small, with a bulging forehead, furrowed brow, and goatee beard. Alpine knee-breeches housed his American legs, his head sank into his shoulders, and his face bore a look of bright abstraction. Nothing special there, you would think; a serious, resolute man, no doubt, maybe a bit eccentric, but hardly unique on that account. When he spoke, his English though clear was not elegant, and his voice had no special charm; British ears found it harsh, and if stirred he would screech from the podium in a way that was hard to enjoy. Nevertheless, what he said was arresting, however he might look or sound while saying it. It had firmness, arguing vision; gentleness, arguing strength; simple clarity, arguing mental mastery; and compassion, arguing an honest and good heart. There was no guile in it, no party narrowness, no manipulation, only the passionate persuasiveness of the prophet who hurries in to share with others what he himself sees.

I knew him slightly, and admired him tremendously. I remember him as a great man, and wish I could have spent

James I. Packer is Professor of Systematic and Historical Theology at Regent College, Vancouver, British Columbia, Canada. He hold degrees in classics and theology from Oxford University, where he was awarded the D.Phil. Among his writings are Fundamentalism and the Word of God, Evangelism and the Sovereignty of God, Knowing God, Keep in Step With the Spirit *(with Thomas Howard),* New Bible Dictionary *(ed.), and* The Bible Almanac.

more time in his company. Yet anyone who reads his books ends up knowing him pretty well, and that at least I have done.

Francis Schaeffer was an important evangelical: that is, an evangelical of importance to evangelicals, as well as to others. He saw himself, so he tells us, as an evangelist. He has been accused (I think, unjustly) of trying to be a pioneer theoretician in philosophy and apologetics. He has been applauded (again, I think, unjustly) for trying to foster a Christian renewal of the fine arts, as if a program in aesthetics was the heart of his work. But his concern under God, it seems to me, was for people as people rather than for procedures or products. Therefore I think it is truest to call him a prophet-pastor, a well-informed Bible-based visionary who by the light of his vision sought out and shepherded the Lord's sheep.

In that role he had influence. Under God, he changed people. Among evangelicals he became an opinion-maker, a consciousness-raiser, and a conscience-stirrer, particularly regarding abortion on demand, for which the *Roe v. Wade* decision laid the foundation in 1973. More than three million copies of his twenty-two books have been sold, and his complete works in five volumes, first published in 1982, have gone through five printings in three years. L'Abri (French for "the shelter"), the international study center that he founded in Switzerland, has replicated itself in England, France, Sweden, the Netherlands, and the United States, and L'Abri seminars and conferences, plus the showing of L'Abri films made by his son Franky, have become a regular part of today's Christian scene. Schaeffer himself spoke frequently to prestigious gatherings in prestigious places, and was noticed outside evangelical circles as an evangelical leader.

What gave Schaeffer his importance among evangelicals? The brief answer is that he embodied to an outstanding degree qualities of which mid-twentieth-century English-speaking evangelicalism was very short, and so brought a measure of depth to themes on which in that era of English-speaking evangelicalism was very shallow. He was not original in any far-reaching sense; he was a conservative Presbyterian who professed what was in essence the old-Princeton system of theology, with some garnishings of detail from Gordon Clark and Cornelius Van Til, and he had no fault to find with any part of this doctrinal heritage.

But Schaeffer was felt to be original because he did seven things (at least) that other evangelicals, by and large, were not doing.

First, with his flair for didactic communication he coined some new and pointed ways of expressing old thoughts (the "true truth" or revelation, the "mannishness" of human beings, the "upper story" and "lower story" of the divided Western mind, etc.).

Second, with his gift of empathy he listened to and dialogued with the modern secular world as it expressed itself in literature and art, which most evangelicals were too co-cooned in their own subculture to do.

Third, he threw light on the things that today's secularists take for granted by tracing them, however sketchily, to their source in the history of thought, a task for which few evangelicals outside the seminaries had the skill.

Fourth, he cherished a vivid sense of the ongoing historical process of which we are all part, and offered shrewd analysis of the *Megatrends–Future Shock* type concerning the likely effect of current Christian and secular developments.

Fifth, he felt, focused, and dwelt on the dignity and tragedy of sinful human beings rather than their grossness and nastiness.

Sixth, he linked the passion for orthodoxy with a life of love to others as the necessary expression of gospel truth, and censured the all-too-common unlovingness of front-line fighters for that truth, including the Presbyterian separatists with whom in the thirties he had thrown in his lot.

Seventh, he celebrated the wholeness of created reality under God and stressed that the Christian life must be a corresponding whole–that is, a life in which truth, goodness, and beauty are valued together and sought with equal zeal. Having these emphases institutionally incarnated at L'Abri, his ministry understandably attracted attention. For it was intrinsically masterful, and it was also badly needed.

Evangelicalism (by which I mean the position of all Protestants, of whatever stripe, who combine belief in the divine truth and authority of Holy Scripture with the Reformational-Puritan-Pietist understanding of justification by faith and the new birth) reached the mid-twentieth century in a somewhat battered condition. Liberal bureaucrats and boards in most major denominations and older educational institutions had given evangelicals a bad beating, leaving them sore and suspicious, anti-intellectual and defensive, backward-looking and culturally negative, enmeshed in ideological isolationism with regard to the world of thought, and lacking all vision for the future of the church save the defiant hope that a faithful remnant would survive somewhere. Evangelism, nurture, and evangelical church life were set in a distinctly old-fashioned mold.

Evangelicals as a body seemed to their peers to be superficial, sentimental, and sometimes smug, certainly strong-minded but often shallow, apathetic on social issues, pharisaic on personal morality, philistine toward the arts, and apt to regard religion as one compartment of life rather than as a way of living it all. Young people were conditioned to believe that only overseas missionary service and full-time pastoral ministry were fully worthwhile vocations; the value of other employments was merely that the money you made could be used to support missions and churches. Beyond this, let the world go by! Separation, understood as uninterested detachment, was the only proper Christian stance in relation to it.

The upshot of all this, not surprisingly, was that young people were rebelling, congregations were aging, and despite some impressive evangelistic efforts, evangelical credibility was diminishing overall. The crude conversionist folk-religion of America, especially of its Bible Belt, and the simplistic Moody-esque pietism of England, seemed to have had their day. As a significant force in the community, evangelicalism, so it seemed, was finished.

The funeral orations that some meditated and others actually delivered proved, however, to be premature. Into this degenerate situation God sent renewers of evangelicalism, men like Martyn Lloyd-Jones and John Stott in Britain, Carl Henry and Harold Ockenga in the United States, and with them, operating from his Swiss base, Francis Schaeffer.

Schaeffer was a reading, listening, thinking man who lived in the present, learned from the past, and looked to the future, and who had an unusual gift for communicating ideas at a nontechnical level. His communicative style was not that of the cautious academic who labors for a complete coverage that never exaggerates or gets proportions wrong. It was rather that of the crusading "cartoonist" whose simple sketches leave behind photographic rectitude and embrace a measure of the grotesque in order to ram home a judgment. Academics censured Schaeffer for communicating this way, but his informal cartoonist's style was apt enough for what he was trying to do.

His complete works are subtitled "A Christian Worldview," and the title of each separate volume is "A Christian View of" some great reality—(1) Philosophy and Culture; (2) the Bible as Truth; (3) Spirituality; (4) the Church; (5) the West. All of them offer genetic and homiletic analyses of the relativism, irrationalism, fragmentation, and incipient nihilism of our culture and community today, with an equally comprehensive recall to the absolutes of God's revealed truth as the only road to rationality. In these volumes Schaeffer the prophet-pastor is preaching to the post-Christian Protestant West, diagnosing its deep existential questions, detecting its drift from its former creedal moorings, and delineating the desert lands into which today's trends have led us; after which he points up in each area the true way back—belief of the biblical system, commitment to the biblical Christ, and the hallowing of all relationships and life-activities by the light of the value-pattern revealed in creation and reinforced by redemption. It is all-compassionate, well-informed, popularly phrased pastoral evangelism, with a remarkably wide range and a very probing thrust.

Determining the shape of this one-man literary mission to the Western world was a set of perceptions which it may be helpful to list at this point.

First, Schaeffer vividly perceived the wholeness of created reality, of human life, of each person's thinking, and of God's revealed truth. He had a mind for first principles, for systems, and for totalities, and he would never discuss issues in isolation or let a viewpoint go till he had explored and tested its implications as a total account of reality and life. He saw fundamental analysis of this kind as clarifying, for, as he often pointed out, there are not many basic world views, and we all need to realize how much our haphazard, surface-level thoughts are actually taking for granted. Exposure of presuppositions was thus central to Schaeffer's method of encounter with all opinions on any subject, and he always presented Christianity in terms of its own presuppositions and in theologically systematic form, as the revealed good news of our rational and holy Creator becoming our gracious and merciful redeemer within the space-time continuum of this world's history and life.

Second, Schaeffer perceived the primacy of reason in each individual's makeup and hence the potency of ideas in the human mind. He saw that, as it has been put, ideas have legs, so that how we think determines what we are. So the first task in evangelism, in the modern West or anywhere else, is to persuade the other person that he ought to embrace the Christian view of reality; and the first step in doing this would be to convince him of the nonviability of all other views, including whatever form of non-Christianity is implicit in his own thinking up to this point. This is to treat him, not as an intellectual in the sociocultural sense (he might or might not be that), but as the human being that he undoubtedly is. To address his mind in this way is to show respect for him as a human being, made for truth because he is made in God's image.

At this point Schaeffer's enterprise was in direct continuity with the lesson in basic theism that was Paul's first move in his attempt to evangelize the Athenian Areopagites, before they howled him down (Acts 17:22–34). For only when a theistic frame of reference has been established can words like *sin, guilt, redemption, faith, repentance, creativity,* and *love* bear their authentic Christian meaning. One must begin at the beginning.

Third, Schaeffer perceived the Western mind as adrift on a trackless sea of relativism and irrationalism just because the notion of truth as involving exclusion of untruth, and of value as involving exclusion of dysvalue, had perished in both sophisticated and popular thinking. Into its place had crept the idea of ongoing synthesis, the idea, that is, that anything may eventually prove to be an aspect of anything else to which at present it seems to be opposed, so that infinite openness to everything, with negation of nothing and no value judgments, is the only appropriate way for anyone to go.

Now, as a result most mainstream Westerners, religious and irreligious alike, whether intellectual, anti-intellectual, or merely conventional, were held more or less firmly in the grip of this category-less "pan-everythingism" (as Schaeffer called it), from which they need to be rescued. To make people realize how this viewpoint has victimized them across the board, and thus to free them from it, Schaeffer regularly introduced all topics by a genetic historical analysis showing how Western thought about it had reached its current state of delirium. The aim of these analyses was to reestablish the notion that there is an absolute antithesis between truth and error, good and evil, beauty and the obscenely ugly, and so to refurnish our ravaged and pillaged minds in a way that makes significant thinking about life, death, personhood, and God possible for us once more.

It is a fact that many younger thinkers and artists, whose "mannishness" (instinctual craving for the absolutes of personal reality, rationality, significance, and love) was in outraged agony at fashions in their professional fields that were tyrannizing them to destruction, have found in Schaeffer's analyses a lifeline to sanity without which they literally could not have gone on living. This fact should be borne in mind when academic criticisms of these nonacademic genetic "cartoons" are brought forward. Whether or not the cartoons satisfy the fastidious, they have in case after case spoken to the condition of real people in real trouble, and thus done the pastoral job that they were created to do. What more, one wonders, should one ask?

Fourth, Schaeffer perceived the importance of identifying in all apologetic and evangelistic discussion, and all teaching on what being a Christian involves, that which he called the antithesis and the point of tension. The antithesis is between truth and untruth, right and wrong, good and evil, the ·meaningful and the meaningless, Christian and non-Christian value systems, secular relativism and Christian absolutism; the point of tension is between clashing elements in incoherent world views and between the logical implications of non-Christian ontologies on the one hand and the demands of our inalienable "mannishness" on the other. He made it his business on every topic he handled to cover the "either-or" choices that have to be made (and, whether consciously or not, actually are made) at the level of first principles and to show that the biblical-Christian options for personal and community life are the only ones that are consistently rational and satisfyingly human. In this way he sought to remake disordered and disorderly minds, with regard both to ontological options facing the individual and to ethical options facing the contemporary West.

To him, as must now be evident, these two fields for persuasion ran into each other and belonged together, both historically (because, as he saw it, the West of today grew out of the Christian West as shaped by the Reformation, and the America of today grew out of Christian America as defined by the Constitution) and also theologically (because biblical truths and values derive from a single whole, a transcript of the declared thoughts of the infinite-personal, triune God).

Schaeffer's fiercest polemics were accordingly launched against professed Christians who seemed to him to have lost sight of the true antithesis between what God tells us in the Bible and the false alternatives developed by fanciedly autonomous man in the folly of his fallenness. He berated, for instance, liberal and neo-orthodox Protestants who, as he saw it, took faith out of the realm of "true truth" into that of blind mysticism and reduced "Christ" to a vacuous "connotation word." He was sharply critical of non-inerrantist students of Scripture who, as he thought, claimed to believe biblically while evading part of the Bible's witness to space-time realities, thus in principle disjoining the "upper story" of faith from the "lower story" of fact just as ruinously as the liberals and neo-orthodox did. He assailed evangelicals who in his view compromised truth by declining to apply and obey it in a radical way, but instead accommodated themselves to craven unfaithfulness on the ecclesiastical front and to the cruel and callous lifestyle of the secular world.

Settling for peace at any price was never to Schaeffer's mind a Christian way to go. The prophet-pastor could find in himself much compassion for victims of modern madness who had never encountered anything else, but little for those who, having been shown the light, dehumanized themselves to a degree by backing off from it into mental or moral semi-darkness. In his attempts to stir Christians to stand in particular for the sanctity of human life, and to pray and fight appropriately against the abortion industry, this became very plain. The broken-hearted scorn that marked his manner on these occasions made one think of Jeremiah: which statement (let my reader note) I mean as a compliment. For Schaeffer the most tragic—because the most anti-human—thing in life was willful refusal by a human being to face the antithesis, or rather the series of antitheses, with which God in Holy Scripture confronts us, and in this perception I think he was right.

Fifth, Schaeffer perceived the need to live truth as well as think it, and to demonstrate to the world through the transformed lifestyle of believing groups that—as he himself put it in the foreword to his wife Edith's narrative *L'Abri*—"the Personal-Infinite God is *really there* in our generation." Hence the emergence of the parent L'Abri in Huémoz, Switzerland, and of the satellite L'Abris around the Western world. Each L'Abri is study center, rescue mission, extended family, clinic, spiritual convalescent home, monastery, and local church rolled into one: a milieu where visitors learn to be both Christian and human through being part of a community that trusts God the Creator and worships him through Christ the Redeemer.

Ordinarily truth and love must combine for effective evangelism and nurture. The testimony of twenty years is that in the world of L'Abri they do, and lives have been transformed as a result. Schaeffer's varied books, as preaching on paper, show him as one who always remembered that the proof of the pudding is in the eating and that Christians living with God are the final proof of Christian truth about God. Here too his sense of wholeness and his refusal to separate what God has joined were in full evidence. Christian credibility, he saw, requires that truth be not merely defended, but practiced; not just debated, but done. The knowledge that God's truth was being done at L'Abri sustained his boldness as he called for that same truth to be done elsewhere.

Schaeffer has been criticized as a grandiose guru, but the criticism is inept. It assumes a degree of egoism and calculation that was simply not there. Schaeffer was no more, just as he was no less, than a sensitive man of God who sought to minister the everlasting gospel to twentieth-century people, showing what it means in our time to believe it, to think it through, and to live it out. There was no grand strategy in his ministry; everything developed in a relatively haphazard way as needs, applications, and insights became clear one after another. The needs of bemused young people in the 1950s and 1960s produced L'Abri and the first books; the needs of drifting America in the 1970s and 1980s produced the seminars recalling to spiritual roots and the later books and films.

Edith Schaeffer indicated this developing, responsive quality of her husband's ministry in 1968 as she answered the question, "Where did your husband get all this?" God, she affirmed, brought a variety of people to L'Abri not just for their own sakes but also

> as a training-ground and as a means of developing, in the arena of live conversation, that which Fran is giving in his apologetic today. Rather than studying volumes in an ivory tower separated from life, and developing a theory separated from the thinking and struggling of men, Fran has been talking for thirteen years now to men and women in the very midst of their struggles. He has talked to existentialists, logical positivists, Hindus, Buddhists, liberal Protestants, liberal Roman Catholics, Reformed Jews and atheistic Jews, Muslims, members of occult cults, and people of a wide variety of religions and philosophies, as well as atheists of a variety of types. He has talked to brilliant professors, brilliant

students, and brilliant drop-outs! He has talked to beatniks, hippies, drug addicts, homosexuals and psychologically disturbed people. He has talked to Africans, Indians, Chinese, Koreans, Japanese, South Americans, people from the islands of the sea, from Australia and New Zealand and from all the European countries as well as from America and Canada. He has talked to people of many different political colours. He has talked to doctors, lawyers, scientists, artists, writers, engineers, research men in many fields, philosophers, businessmen, newspapermen and actors, famous people and peasants. He has talked to both generations!

In it all God has been giving him an education which it is not possible for many people to have. The answers have been given, not out of academic research (although he does volumes of reading constantly to keep up) but out of this arena of live conversation. He answers real questions with carefully thought out answers which are the real answers. He gets excited himself as he comes to me often saying, "It really *is* the answer, Edith; it fits, it really fits. It really *is* truth, and because it is true it fits what is really there." The excitement is genuine. This is what I mean when I say that God has given him an education in addition to unfolding a work in these past thirteen years.[1]

What long-term significance has Schaeffer for the Christian cause? Neither this foreword nor the book that it introduces can answer that question; it is far too soon to tell. Schaeffer's basic books still sell and are presumably being read. He left a team of trained helpers who now run the various L'Abris and who publish on their own account within what might be called Schaefferian Christian-humanist parameters. His son Franky, a self-styled activist agitator, carries the torch, rather raucously it must be said, for a Schaefferian sociocultural shift in the United States; what will come of that remains to be seen.

Perhaps the clique for whom "Schaeffer says" has long been the last word in human wisdom will disperse; or perhaps its members will now labor to build the prophet's tomb, embalming into hallowed irrelevance thoughts that were once responses to the desperations of our time. We wait to see. The law of human fame will no doubt treat Schaeffer as it has treated others, eclipsing him temporarily now that he is dead and only allowing us to see his real stature ten or twenty years down the road; and probably then some of the things he said will seem more significant than others. My guess is that his verbal and visual cartoons, simplistic but brilliant as they appear to me to be, will outlive everything else, but I may be wrong. I am sure, however, that I shall not be at all wrong when I hail Francis Schaeffer, the little Presbyterian pastor who saw so much more of what he was looking at and agonized over it so much more tenderly than the rest of us do, as one of the truly great Christians of my time.

NOTES

[1] Edith Schaeffer, *L'Abri* (London: Norfolk, 1969), 226–27.

PREFACE

RONALD W. RUEGSEGGER

My introduction to Francis Schaeffer occurred at Westmont College. My parents were missionaries in Mexico, and I had come to college to prepare, like them, for the ministry. However, rather than majoring in theology, I thought that studying literature would provide me with the best background for seminary. Eventually I realized that the issues that interested me in literature were treated more rigorously and systematically by philosophers.

It was at this point in time that Francis Schaeffer came to Westmont. In the fall of 1965 he delivered a week-long series of lectures on "Historic Christianity and Twentieth-Century Man." Then a year later he delivered a second series of lectures on "Man, Love, and Science in the Twentieth Century." Although I did not comprehend much that Schaeffer was saying, I was impressed by his seriousness. Furthermore, he reinforced my growing appreciation of the importance of philosophy. As a result of these and other influences I decided to make philosophy my major course of study.

After a brief period in seminary and a mandatory two-year tour in the Army, I began graduate school at the University of Toronto. Several years later I had the opportunity to teach a class to some young adults at church. I wanted to discuss a book that showed the importance of philosophy for Christians and yet was readable for the average educated person. I picked Schaeffer's book *The God Who Is There*.

Now that I had had some training in philosophy, I began to have some reservations about Schaeffer's treatment of several philosophers and philosophical problems. This uneasiness was reinforced when I passed on a copy of Schaeffer's *Escape From Reason* to a fellow graduate student. This friend had been reading Kierkegaard, and she informed me that, contrary to what Schaeffer said, Kierkegaard was not irrationalistic.

At the time I was too busy studying perception and writing my dissertation to delve further into Schaeffer. However, when I assumed my first teaching position at Nyack College, Dr. Leslie Flynn, my pastor at Grace Conservative Baptist Church, told me that the church would be viewing the Schaeffers' film series *How Should We Then Live?* and he asked if I would lead the discussion. Shortly afterward, I needed a course for the Winterim session I was teaching at Nyack College. Naturally I decided to teach a course on Francis Schaeffer, incorporating material I had developed for previous classes on *The God Who Is There, Escape From Reason* and *How Should We Then Live?* As I taught this class over the next several years I found that it was a good way to help students see the relevance of philosophy to their Christian world view. Yet I also became increasingly convinced that Schaeffer's treatment of several philosophical issues was not completely accurate. Eventually these experiences prompted me to write an article about Schaeffer on philosophy, and it was published in *Christian Scholar's Review.*

The positive response to this article suggested to me that there was a need for others to evaluate Schaeffer's discussion of their disciplines just as I had done in terms of philosophy. Several other scholars agreed, and this book is the result of our reflections on Francis Schaeffer.

Looking back over the series of events I have sketched reminds me how much help I have received along the way from many people. First, I wish to thank those who have studied Schaeffer's thought with me in various classes. They have forced me to rethink my insights, clarify my ideas, and see angles I had not thought of before. I am also particularly grateful to Les Gilbert, Holly Hager, and Mike Grey for compiling a bibliography on Francis Schaeffer.

Second, I am grateful to the administration of Nyack College for its support of this project. In particular Paul Collord, the academic dean, has allowed me frequent access to a word processor, helped defray the cost of typing the manuscript, and offered sound advice all through the project. In addition, Mabel

Cherry has assisted me on many occasions by tracking down articles and books that are not available at our library. Also, I owe a big thank-you to Gwen Grey for typing the manuscript. She has not only done a careful job of typing, but has also mastered the many technicalities involved submitting a manuscript on diskettes. Finally, I am grateful to Elaine Letchworth for the many secretarial tasks she has performed in connection with the preparation of this book.

Several colleagues deserve a special word of thanks. Besides writing a chapter in the book, Dennis Hollinger has been a source of advice from the very beginning of the endeavor. Moreover, Dennis, Don Nilsson, and Glenn Koponen have read various chapters for me and offered their suggestions for improvement. Finally, Stan Obitts taught me philosophy at Westmont, encouraged me many times as I have pursued my career, and has often served me as a model of dedicated Christian scholarship. Most recently he read through my chapter on Schaeffer on philosophy, pointing out numerous ways in which it could be improved.

Fourth, this book on Francis Schaeffer would simply not be possible without the combined efforts of knowledgeable individuals from several fields. Not only do I appreciate the contributors' taking time from their busy schedules to share their insights on Schaeffer, but I am also grateful for their suggestions about ways to improve the book. Their expertise will be largely responsible for whatever success this volume achieves.

I would also like to express my appreciation to two members of the editorial staff at Zondervan Publishing House. Initially Ed van der Maas, editor for Academie Books, advised me as I sought contributors for the chapters and offered helpful suggestions about the general ordering of the book's contents. More recently James Ruark, senior editor for academic books, improved the book significantly by his adjustments of wording and organization of material.

Finally, my greatest debt is to my wife, Beverley. She has graciously taken care of the children many Saturdays while I was working at the word processor and has patiently listened to me as I talked about the book. Most of all, I value her companionship.

LIST OF ABBREVIATIONS

AB   *Art and the Bible*
BFD   *Back to Freedom and Dignity*
CBWW   *The Church Before the Watching World*
CETC   *The Church at the End of the Twentieth Century*
CM   *A Christian Manifesto*
DIC   *Death in the City*
EFR   *Escape From Reason*
GED   *The Great Evangelical Disaster*
GST   *Genesis in Space and Time*
GWIT   *The God Who Is There*
HIT   *He Is There and He Is Not Silent*
HSWTL   *How Should We Then Live?*
JFBH   *Joshua and the Flow of Biblical History*
NFC   *No Final Conflict*
NLP   *No Little People*
PDM   *Pollution and the Death of Man*
RE   "Race and Economics"
TS   *True Spirituality*
WHHR   *Whatever Happened to the Human Race?*
WIFP   *Who Is for Peace?*

ACKNOWLEDGMENTS

The publisher is grateful for permission to quote extensively from the following works of Francis A. Schaeffer:

The God Who Is There. Copyright © 1968 by L'Abri Fellowship, Switzerland, and used by permission of Inter-Varsity Press, Downers Grove, IL 60515.

The Great Evangelical Disaster. Copyright © 1984. Used by permission of Good News Publishers/Crossway Books, Westchester, IL 60153.

How Should We Then Live? Copyright © 1976. Used by permission of Good News Publishers/Crossway Books, Westchester, IL 60153.

Whatever Happened to the Human Race? by Francis A. Schaeffer and C. Everett Koop. Copyright © 1979. Used by permission of Good News Publishers/Crossway Books, Westchester, IL 60153.

The publisher is grateful for permission to reprint the following article:

"Francis Schaeffer on Philosophy," by Ronald W. Ruegsegger, in *Christian Scholar's Review*, vol. X, no. 3 (1981).

1

SCHAEFFER'S SYSTEM OF THOUGHT

RONALD W. RUEGSEGGER

INTRODUCTION

One evidence that North American evangelicalism is maturing is the growing interest in the influences that have shaped this movement. Not only have the roots of evangelicalism been studied,[1] but critical examinations of influential figures are appearing as well.[2]

The late Francis Schaeffer was one of the most familiar figures in the evangelical community. His home base was L'Abri, a study center in the Swiss mountains where he offered an analysis of modern man's thought and a critique of his culture from the Christian perspective.[3] During the sixties and seventies Schaeffer became known in academic circles through his lectures at Christian colleges across the United States. Then, as his L'Abri tapes and college lectures were published as books,[4] Schaeffer gained a wider hearing among more intellectually oriented Christians. Finally, with the appearance of Schaeffer's two film series, his views have become familiar to even the average layperson in the church.

Schaeffer has been not only a familiar figure, but also an

Ronald W. Ruegsegger is Professor of Philosophy at Nyack College, Nyack, New York. He holds the M.A. and Ph.D. degrees from the University of Toronto. His published articles include "The Propositional Attitude in Perception" and "Judging, Believing and Taking: Three Candidates for the Propositional Attitude in Perception."

influential one. In his foreword to this collection of essays, James Packer notes that as a result of battles with Liberals during previous decades, evangelicalism began the present century "sore and suspicious, anti-intellectual and defensive, backward-looking and culturally negative, enmeshed in ideological isolationism with regard to the world of thought and lacking all vision for the future of the church save the defiant hope that a faithful remnant would survive somewhere." Schaeffer was instrumental in bringing about the transformation of evangelicalism that we have witnessed in recent years.

As Packer explains more fully, Schaeffer exposed the weaknesses of secular thought and persuaded many inquiring Christians that their faith is intellectually defensible. Moreover, in a healthy balance to his emphasis on the intellectual merits of belief in Christ, Schaeffer also stressed the importance of love, both among Christians and to those without. In addition, Schaeffer convinced many Christians that they should have a positive attitude toward culture. Finally, with his attacks on materialism and racism and his criticism of abortion, infanticide, and euthanasia, Schaeffer has reminded Christians of their ethical obligations.

Schaeffer's renown and influence suggest that it is time to evaluate his teaching. To a certain extent this has already been done through numerous reviews[5] of his writings, several substantial articles,[6] and even a book analyzing his apologetic.[7] But while all these writings shed valuable light on different aspects of Schaeffer's views, there is not yet a systematic and sustained evaluation of his thought as a whole. The essays that are collected in this book, none of them having been published before, offer an analysis and critique of Schaeffer's wide-ranging writings. The chapters have three foci: Schaeffer's conceptual framework, his analysis of the disciplines, and his critique of culture.

We encounter several difficulties in reflecting on Francis Schaeffer. First, we must avoid the tendency either to accept completely or to reject completely what Schaeffer says. Evangelical Christians who read his works without a background knowledge of the particular discipline under discussion may easily accept Schaeffer's analysis at face value because they share his commitment to the faith. On the other hand, those who have a detailed knowledge of a particular discipline may become so disturbed by Schaeffer's handling of specific details that they lose sight of the value of his general train of thought.

Another difficulty is to determine the standard against which we should measure Schaeffer's thought. He did not work in an academic community, and it is unfair to expect him to have a detailed knowledge of all aspects of the many disciplines he discussed. Nevertheless, references to lectures Schaeffer gave at major universities and his promotion by others as "one of the world's most respected thinkers" raise fairly high expectations.

Third, it is hard to know how to assess Schaeffer's significance. He seems to have had a positive influence on the average church layperson. But many of the articles written about Schaeffer within the academic community are quite critical of his thought.

For these reasons, the assessments of Schaeffer in this book will doubtless not please everyone. But I do hope that this collection of essays will accomplish two things. First, the expositions provided in the various chapters should provide every reader with a better understanding of Schaeffer's system of thought. Second, the background that each contributor brings to his reflections should also produce a fuller understanding of the subjects Schaeffer discussed.

SURVEY OF SCHAEFFER'S WORKS

The rest of this chapter is a survey of Schaeffer's major works. There are several reasons for having this overview in mind as we approach the essays that comprise this volume. First, since each of the chapters focuses on a narrow aspect of Schaeffer's thought, it will be helpful to have a general background against which to locate the following essays. Second, Schaeffer's writings are highly repetitive, so having a general understanding of the way the books build on one another will save one from reading material that is already familiar. Finally, this review will provide a means to introduce the essays that examine each subject in detail.

Francis Schaeffer wrote more than twenty books. Most of these have recently been collected in the *The Complete Works of Francis A. Schaeffer*.[8] It is obviously impossible to critique all of Schaeffer's books in this collection of essays. Instead, the focus will be on the following seven major works: *The God Who Is There*, *Escape From Reason*, *He Is There and He Is Not Silent*, *How Should We Then Live?*, *Whatever Happened to the Human Race?*, *A Christian Manifesto*, and *The Great Evangelical Disaster*.[9]

Schaeffer refers to the first three of these books as a trilogy. These books are connected not only by complementary subject matter, but by the fact that the latter two are largely amplifications of certain parts of *The God Who Is There*. The next section of this chapter provides an overview of Schaeffer's trilogy.

How Shall We Then Live? gives the fullest statement in one book of Schaeffer's entire system of thought. On the one hand, it summarizes both *Escape From Reason* and *The God Who Is There*. On the other hand, it anticipates both *Whatever Happened to the Human Race?* and *A Christian Manifesto*. This important book will be summarized after the survey of the trilogy.

Whatever Happened to the Human Race? and *A Christian Manifesto* break new ground for Schaeffer. His previous books have an academic tone about them; these books are more practically and politically oriented. To them should be added a third book, *The Great Evangelical Disaster*, which was written after the publication of *The Complete Works*. These three books will be summarized in the last portion of this chapter.

SCHAEFFER'S TRILOGY

It will be convenient to consider Schaeffer's trilogy in the following fashion. We will begin by looking at the first two and a half chapters of *Escape From Reason*.[10] Next we will examine sections I and II of *The God Who Is There*. Then we will survey all of *He Is There and He Is Not Silent*, since this book is a more detailed treatment of section III of *The God Who Is There*. Finally, we will finish by discussing sections IV through VI of *The God Who Is There*.[11]

Escape From Reason

The historical figure Schaeffer discusses first in *Escape From Reason* is Thomas Aquinas. Schaeffer's main objection to Aquinas concerns the latter's view that although man's will is fallen, his reason is not. According to Schaeffer, to say that man's intellect is not fallen is to make it autonomous, or independent from God. Furthermore, Schaeffer claims that when man's reason is made autonomous three bad results follow: natural theology, philosophy, and the arts are allowed to develop independently from scripture (EFR: 11–12). It is the consequences of allowing art to be independent from Scripture that engage Schaeffer at this point, and he identifies two unfortunate results: "nature eats up grace" (EFR: 13), and a dichotomy arises between universals and particulars (EFR: 17).

The claim about nature eating up grace is perhaps the easier to understand. Schaeffer contends that once man's reason is made autonomous and earthly things are put on an equal footing with heavenly things, the inevitable result is that the natural begins to edge out the spiritual.

The other claim—that autonomous reason gives rise to a dichotomy between particulars and universals—is more difficult to follow.[12] Aquinas was a follower of Aristotle, and Aristotle emphasized particulars over against universals. Hence Schaeffer seems to see a link between Aquinas and particulars (EFR: 17). However, Schaeffer believes that particulars have no meaning apart from universals. Accordingly, he finishes the chapter by claiming that Leonardo da Vinci tried to paint the soul of various objects in order to arrive at the universal. He was not able to do this, and therefore Schaeffer concludes that Leonardo da Vinci, as well as the Renaissance that he typified, was never able to achieve a unity between particulars and universals.

However, in chapter 2 of *Escape From Reason* Schaeffer argues that what Leonardo da Vinci could not do, Reformation Christianity could. The Reformers held that the intellect as well as the will was fallen and hence not autonomous (EFR: 19). But if man is not autonomous, then the only being who is autonomous is God. And if God is autonomous, then there is no dichotomy between nature and grace, since the Scriptures give us knowledge of both God and man, that is, both grace and nature. Presumably, although he does not say so explicitly, Schaeffer holds that having only God autonomous also brings about a unity between particulars and universals.

In the first half of chapter 3 of *Escape From Reason,* Schaeffer discusses the relation of Christianity to science. His first contention is that the biblical conception of the universe favors the birth of science. He gives three reasons for this assertion. First, the biblical notion of creation explains why there is something rather than nothing. Second, since the universe is created by God, it is outside of him and hence objective. (In Eastern thought, by contrast, the universe is part of God.) Third, since the Bible says that a reasonable God made the universe, it follows that man, by the use of his reason, can hope to discover its nature (EFR: 30–31).

Another point Schaeffer makes regarding Christianity and science is that the early scientists thought that God could intervene in the causal relationships of nature. Schaeffer refers to this as the view that "the universe is a uniformity of natural causes in an *open* system." By this he means that nature is causally ordered, but open to miraculous acts by God and free acts by man. He holds that, by contrast, when man's reason was made autonomous he came to think of the universe as a "uniformity of natural causes in a *closed* system" (EFR: 36). This in turn means that the causal system of nature is not open to God's intervention and all man's acts are determined. The result is that man is no longer free; Schaeffer sees this as another instance in which "nature has eaten up grace."

Schaeffer develops this idea by claiming that by the time of Rousseau the nature-grace dichotomy was replaced by a nature-freedom dichotomy: Nature has eaten up so much of grace that all that is left of grace is the notion of freedom (EFR: 32–33). Because man is unwilling to give up his freedom, he rebels against science and its determinism and tries to make freedom completely autonomous (EFR: 34). But completely autonomous freedom is freedom without any restraint, including the restraint of rationality. In effect, then, man has given way to despair: he has abandoned reason, which tells him that his actions are determined, in favor of a blind leap of faith to the view that man is free. At this point Schaeffer begins to discuss Hegel and Kierkegaard and make observations that are stated in more detail in sections I and II of *The God Who Is There*.

The God Who Is There, Sections I and II

Schaeffer holds that until 1890 in Europe and 1935 in the United States, the common assumption prevailed that truth is absolute. After those dates Christians continued to maintain that truth is absolute, but non-Christians accepted the notion that truth is relative. Schaeffer calls the line that separates these two conceptions of truth "the line of despair" (GWIT: 13–15).

However, on closer inspection of Schaeffer's writings one discovers that he actually distinguishes *two* shifts and accordingly there must be two lines to cross. The first, as already indicated, involves *the nature of truth;* here the shift is *from absolutism to relativism*. The second, which occurs after the first shift, involves a shift *from reason to faith* and concerns *the way we know truth*. Let us call the first crossing *the line of relativism* and the second, *the line of despair*. See figure 1.1.

Figure 1.1. Tracing Schaeffer's "Line of Despair"

NATURE OF TRUTH	DISCIPLINE	PHILOSOPHY	ART	MUSIC	GENERAL CULTURE	THEOLOGY
A B S O L U T E →	PERSONAGE(S)	Hegel	Degas, Monet, Renoir	Debussy		Older Liberals like Schleiermacher
	ABSOLUTIST CONCEPT	Opposite beliefs are antithetical	Realism	?		Nature is causally ordered but open to miracles
LINE OF RELATIVISM						
R E L A T I V E	RELATIVIST CONCEPT	Opposite beliefs are included in synthesis	Impressionism	?		The causal system admits no miracles
		WAY KNOW TRUTH				
	DISCIPLINE	F A I T H ←	PHILOSOPHY	ART	MUSIC	GENERAL CULTURE	THEOLOGY
	PERSONAGE(S)		Kierkegaard	Van Gogh, Gauguin, Cézanne	?		Karl Barth
	POST-DESPAIR CONCEPT	Meaning can be found only through nonrational faith	Universals sought apart from particulars	?		Mystical belief in Jesus
LINE OF DESPAIR	R E A S O N					
	PRE-DESPAIR CONCEPTS	Meaning can be found through reason	Universals can be found in particulars	?		The historical Jesus is enough

The chart shows the relation between these two shifts. The first of the two horizontal lines is the line of relativism. Above this line truth is thought to be absolute; below this line truth is thought to be relative. Since the leap of faith is made after one enters the realm of relativism, I have located the line of despair—the second line—below the line of relativism. And since Schaeffer refers to the realm of faith as the "upper story," I have placed it above the line of despair. Thus the movement across the first line is from above to below, whereas the movement across the second line is from below to above.

Schaeffer also holds that the shift from the absolute to the relative conception of truth has spread in three ways: geographically, socially, and academically. On the academic scene, which is the only one that concerns us here, Schaeffer says the shift has passed through five steps in historical sequence as follows: philosophy, art, music, general culture, and theology. Schaeffer discusses philosophy in *The God Who Is There*, section I, chapter 2; art in chapter 3; music and general culture in chapter 4; and theology in section II, chapter 1. In each discipline Schaeffer mentions one or two key *personages* who were instrumental in causing the shift in question, and also certain basic *concepts* that define the shift. I have summarized Schaeffer's discussion of these chapters by inserting into the chart the key personages and concepts Schaeffer mentions in connection with each of the disciplines. (I am omitting "general culture," since it is not a discipline.)

The chart is incomplete because it is difficult to fit what Schaeffer says about music into this framework. It should also be noted that several of the concepts mentioned are inferences based on what Schaeffer does say. Although the chart is imperfect for these reasons, I think that it portrays fairly the pattern of Schaeffer's thought.

I provide a more detailed discussion of Schaeffer's treatment of philosophy in my essay (ch. 4). Harold Best evaluates Schaeffer's discussion of art and music in chapter 5. Finally, Clark Pinnock discusses the fifth step in the line of despair in his essay on Schaeffer on modern theology (ch. 6).

We have now seen how Schaeffer begins his argument in *Escape From Reason* and further develops it in sections I and II of *The God Who Is There*. The next step would naturally be to begin reviewing section III of the latter. However, as I pointed out in the introduction to this section, this material is covered in greater detail in *He Is There and He Is Not Silent*. Therefore, let us briefly examine that work.

He Is There and He Is Not Silent

He Is There and He Is Not Silent provides us with the heart of Schaeffer's apologetic system. Some of Schaeffer's observations suggest that he is a presuppositionalist. For one thing, he says toward the beginning of *The God Who Is There* that presuppositional apologetics would have stopped the slide from the absolute to the relative concept of truth (GWIT: 15). For another, Schaeffer's reasoning in *He Is There and He Is Not Silent* clearly follows the presuppositionalist pattern.

The basic Christian presupposition is this: There is an infinite, personal God. Schaeffer holds that there are two corollaries to this fundamental belief: first, that the universe has a personal beginning in Creation, and second, that nature is an open causal system. By contrast, the non-Christian holds the negation of these three presuppositions. In *He Is There and He Is Not Silent* Schaeffer compares the explanatory power of the Christian and the non-Christian presuppositions in three areas: metaphysics, morals, and epistemology. Schaeffer contends that Christian presuppositions answer several questions in these three areas better than non-Christian presuppositions do. These points can be summarized as shown in figure 1.2.

Christian Presuppositions	*Non-Christian Presuppositions*
1. There is an infinite, personal God.	1′ There is no infinite, personal God.
2. The universe has a personal beginning.	2′ The universe has an impersonal beginning.
3. Nature is an *open* causal system.	3′ Nature is a *closed* causal system.

Area of Concern	*Schaeffer's Argument*
A. Metaphysics	2 explains more than 2′
B. Morals	2 explains more than 2′
C. Epistemology	3 explains more than 3′

Figure 1.2. Comparison of Presuppositions

In light of the pattern of these arguments I think it is clear that there are some presuppositional elements in Schaeffer's apologetic. One source of this is doubtless Schaeffer's training under Van Til at Westminster Seminary. Forrest Baird explores this and other origins of Schaeffer's thought in his essay on Schaeffer's intellectual roots (ch. 2).

On the other hand, it would be a mistake to think that because Schaeffer uses the word "presupposition" and some of his arguments develop in a presuppositional pattern, he is a presuppositionalist in the Van Tilian sense. The key contrast is that, contrary to Van Til, Schaeffer does not hold that presuppositions are self-authenticating. Instead, he repeatedly advances evidential considerations in support of Christian presuppositions. Thus there are both presuppositional and evidential elements in Schaeffer's case for Christianity. In his essay on Schaeffer's apologetic method (ch. 3), Gordon Lewis offers a more detailed analysis of Schaeffer's apologetic system and shows how Schaeffer's presuppositional and evidential moves can be combined into a single, coherent method of reasoning. However, an indication of the way Schaeffer integrates these diverse elements is evident in sections IV to VI of *The God Who Is There*.

The God Who Is There, Sections IV Through VI

These sections set out Schaeffer's strategy for evangelism, which has both negative and positive aspects.

The essence of the negative side of Schaeffer's evangelistic strategy is the observation that since both the universe and man have been made by God, a man will be at odds with both the universe and himself if he tries to live according to non-Christian presuppositions. But since no man can live completely at odds with the universe, every non-Christian will be inconsistent with his presuppositions at some point. This argument may be summarized in the following eight steps:

1. Every person has a set of presuppositions (GWIT: 121).

2. Each person lives in a reality that consists of two parts: his own nature and the external world.

3. Christian presuppositions fit reality.

4. Non-Christian presuppositions do not fit reality.

5. Since non-Christian presuppositions do not fit reality, the non-Christian lives in a state of tension (GWIT: 122).

6. This tension works in our favor when we speak to him.

7. Therefore, the first step in evangelism is to find the point of tension in the person to whom we are speaking (GWIT: 125).

8. The second step in evangelism is to increase the tension by exposing the consequences that follow logically from his presuppositions (GWIT: 128).

The positive side of Schaeffer's evangelistic strategy is to argue that in a pluralistic world we must engage in pre-evangelism. That is, we must make a case for Christian presuppositions before presenting the gospel when those we are witnessing to do not share our assumptions. Schaeffer's argument for pre-evangelism can be found in section V of *The God Who Is There*. Finally, in section VI Schaeffer argues that we too must be consistent with our presuppositions, and we must do so in practice as well as intellectually (GWIT: 151). The two practical areas in which we must be consistent with our basic presupposition that a personal God exists are our corporate relationships (GWIT: 151) and personality (GWIT: 156).

This completes my survey of Schaeffer's trilogy. I have gone into some detail in my summary of the trilogy since these three books are the foundation of Schaeffer's system. Indeed, as we turn to *How Should We Then Live?* we will see that much of this book is a repackaging of Schaeffer's trilogy placed in a historical context.

HOW SHOULD WE THEN LIVE?

How Should We Then Live? is the name of both a book and a film series based on the book. The book has thirteen chapters; the film series has ten episodes. My exposition will be based mainly on the film series, since I suspect that more people are familiar with it than the book on which it is based. However, the corresponding chapters of the book can be found by consulting appendix 1.

Episode 1 is titled "The Roman Age." In it Schaeffer covers material he has not discussed in any of the books we have surveyed to this point. The basic argument is this: In the Roman age there were two perspectives on life. The Roman view of life was rooted in a finite, relative base of personal but finite gods. The Christian perspective was grounded on an infinite, absolute base of God. Schaeffer argues that the Christian perspective is the better one because the Roman Empire collapsed whereas Christianity continues to this day. Finally, toward the end of the film, Schaeffer draws some parallels between the world of Rome and our own.

Episode 2 is "The Middle Ages." Again, Schaeffer's argument is simple: The pristine purity of the New Testament Church was corrupted in the Middle Ages. In particular, Schaeffer says that there were three areas in which the church struggled with the problem of how to be in the world but not of the world: (1) the attitude toward material possessions, (2) the relationship between church and state, and (3) the relationship between Christian and secular thought. The third issue is central, and here Schaeffer maintains that the Medieval Church was corrupted because Aquinas put reason on the same level as revelation. Furthermore, Aquinas introduced the Aristotelian emphasis on particulars. With the last two points we come to material familiar from *Escape From Reason.*

Episode 3 is "The Renaissance." As in *Escape From Reason,* Schaeffer argues that, following the lead of Aquinas, the secular thinkers of this period made man autonomous. The result is the familiar nature-grace dichotomy with "nature eating up grace." In addition, Schaeffer again claims that the Renaissance thinkers were unable to find universals to give meaning to particulars.

"The Reformation" is episode 4. Schaeffer's basic contention in this segment is that the Reformation corrected the distortions of the early church's teaching that occurred in the Middle Ages. In particular, the Reformation (1) substituted salvation by grace alone for salvation by works, (2) replaced the notion that the church has the same authority as Scripture with the belief that Scripture is the sole authority, and (3) exchanged a mixture of pagan and biblical thinking for just biblical thinking. The parallel between these contentions and chapter 3 of *Escape From Reason* is clear.

Episode 5 is "The Revolutionary Age." Here Schaeffer contends that when countries influenced by the Reformation, such as England and the United States, achieved political freedom, there was no chaos. On the other hand, when countries that lacked the Reformation base, such as France and Russia, achieved freedom, there was chaos. This argument is developed at greater length in Schaeffer's *A Christian Manifesto.*

"The Scientific Age" is the subject of episode 6. Once again, Schaeffer argues that science arose out of a Christian consensus. (Since this argument is familiar from *Escape From Reason*, I will not repeat it.) With the loss of the belief in God, nature is no longer regarded as an open causal system. Instead, it is thought to be a closed system with man as part of the machine. Schaeffer contends that as a result, modern science has produced racism, genetic engineering, determinism, and the use of drugs to control behavior.

In *Escape From Reason* and *The God Who Is There*, the order of the disciplines is philosophy, art, music, general culture, and finally theology. In *How Should We Then Live?* Schaeffer discusses philosophy and theology together in episode 7, "The Age of Non-Reason." Art, music, and general culture are then grouped together and discussed in episode 8, "The Age of Fragmentation." This reordering aside, however, not much else is new.

Episode 9 is titled "The Age of Personal Peace and Affluence." Schaeffer holds that humanism, which he feels has replaced Christianity as the dominant world view, has only two values: personal peace and affluence. He argues that all humanism can justify is sociological law, and this, says Schaeffer, leads to the practice of abortion. These topics are discussed at greater length in *Whatever Happened to the Human Race?* and *A Christian Manifesto*.

The tenth episode is "Final Choices." In this segment of the film series Schaeffer claims that since Christianity no longer provides form for our culture, something must take its place or chaos will result. Schaeffer predicts that what will fill the vacuum is authoritarianism. He concludes by describing the form of authoritarianism he anticipates in the United States. It will (1) be government by an elite rather than a dictatorship, (2) achieve its goals by the use of drugs, genetic engineering, and manipulation of the mass media, and (3) change the laws through the courts rather than through the legislatures.

Schaeffer's analysis of history is discussed by Richard Pierard in his essay on Schaeffer on history (ch. 7).

SCHAEFFER ON ETHICS AND SOCIETY

On the subjects of ethics and society I offer a very brief outline of three books: *Whatever Happened to the Human Race?*, *A Christian Manifesto*, and *The Great Evangelical Disaster*.

Whatever Happened to the Human Race?

This book has two parts. Chapters 1–3 contain discussions of abortion, infanticide, and euthanasia. The second part consists of chapter 4, "The Basis of Human Dignity"; chapter 5, "Truth and History"; and chapter 6, "Our Personal Response and Social Action." At the beginning of chapter 6 Schaeffer connects these two parts by means of three claims that can be expressed as follows: (1) The only thing that will stop the practice of abortion, infanticide, and euthanasia is the knowledge that people have an absolute uniqueness and value; (2) people have an absolute uniqueness and value only if they are made in the image of God; (3) the only way that we can know that people are made in the image of God is through the Bible.

In part II of *Whatever Happened to the Human Race?* Schaeffer claims that people act according to their world view, and he states that the world view which has given rise to the practice of abortion, infanticide, and euthanasia is philosophical materialism—the view that only matter exists. He then says that humanism is usually materialistic in its outlook. However, Schaeffer contends that humanism is inadequate: it cannot explain the "mannishness" of man, since it holds that the universe is basically material.

Then Schaeffer suggests that besides Christianity, the only alternative to the humanism of the West is the pantheism of the East. But pantheism is no more adequate than humanism, in Schaeffer's view, since it too leads to the notion that the universe is impersonal. By contrast, Schaeffer argues that since Christianity maintains that the universe has a personal beginning, it has an adequate explanation of the personality of man. He then concludes the chapter by contending that there are good and sufficient historical reasons for maintaining that Christianity is true.

Dennis Hollinger examines the argument of *Whatever Happened to the Human Race?* and related issues in his essay on Schaeffer on ethics (ch. 8).

A Christian Manifesto

Schaeffer begins this work with his now-familiar contention that there are only two basic world views: the Christian and the humanistic. He asserts that these two world views lead to totally different conclusions in matters of government and law (CM: 24). The Christian world view found its highest expression in the Reformation, which produced a concept of government in which there is a balance between form and freedom (CM: 25). By contrast, the humanist world view stresses freedom at the expense of form, which leads to chaos, which in turn calls forth some kind of authoritarianism to restore order (CM: 29). Schaeffer first argues that the United States was based on the Christian world view. Next he argues that the humanist world view has taken over. Finally, he indicates what he thinks should be done about the situation.

The first of these assertions is developed in chapter 2 of *A Christian Manifesto.* Since it is familiar from both *Escape From Reason* and *How Should We Then Live?* I will not review the details. The second contention is developed in chapter 3. Here Schaeffer claims that the transition from a Christian Society to a secular one occurred around 1848 with the influx of immigrants who did not come from countries that had a Reformation base (CM: 46). The kind of law that operates in secular society is sociological law, in which the majority opinion prevails. Schaeffer claims that the secular humanist society has come to dominate the society of the United States through the courts (CM: 49) and the media (CM: 59).

Chapter 4 addresses the question, What should we do in light of this turn of events? Schaeffer claims that there are two options. The first is to work within the system and try to make it more to our liking. Schaeffer holds that the election of Reagan's conservative administration makes this option a viable one (CM: 73). However, he holds that if this alternative does not produce the desired results, we will have to consider the second option, which is to engage in civil disobedience (CM: 92). In support of this contention Schaeffer claims that it was the course followed by the early Christians and the Christians of the Reformation period (CM: 93-99). The argument is further developed and qualified in subsequent chapters.

This book is examined in detail by Ronald Wells in his essay on Schaeffer on America (ch. 9).

The Great Evangelical Disaster

In his last book, *The Great Evangelical Disaster,* Schaeffer levels several serious charges against his fellow Christians. One complaint is that evangelicals have failed to defend the doctrine of inerrancy. A second charge is that evangelicals have accommodated on the issue of abortion. A third criticism is that Christian colleges and seminaries have been influenced by liberalism. In addition Schaeffer discusses evangelicals' involvement in social action, their attitude toward the World Council of Churches, and their attitude toward the role of women in the church.

James Hurley discusses this book in his essay on Schaeffer on evangelicalism (ch. 10).

The preceding sketch of Schaeffer's system of thought has also introduced the essays that follow. As we turn to these, it may be helpful to note the order in which the essays are arranged.

Part I investigates Schaeffer's conceptual framework by examining both his intellectual roots and his apologetic methodology. Part II examines Schaeffer's analysis of three key disciplines: philosophy, art and music, and modern theology. Finally, part III offers an evaluation of Schaeffer's critique of culture. It first appraises his analysis of the history of Western civilization; next it examines his views about the United States; then it considers his statements about ethics; and it concludes by reviewing Schaeffer's assessment of evangelicalism.

NOTES

[1] Two important works in this regard are David F. Wells and John D. Woodbridge, eds., *The Evangelicals: What They Believe, Who They Are, Where They Are Changing* (Grand Rapids: Baker, 1977), and George M. Marsden, *Fundamentalism and American Culture* (Oxford: Oxford University, 1980).

[2] An example is John Beversluis, *C. S. Lewis and the Search for Rational Religion* (Grand Rapids: Eerdmans, 1985).

[3] For an interesting account of the founding of L'Abri see Edith Schaeffer, *L'Abri* (London: Norfolk, 1969). D. G. Blomberg describes the educational atmosphere at L'Abri in "Apologetic Education: Francis Schaeffer and L'Abri," *Journal of Christian Education Papers* 54 (1975): 5–20.

[4] There is a list of Schaeffer's books in section I of the bibliography.

[5] See section V of the bibliography.

[6] See section IV of the bibliography.

[7] Thomas V. Morris, *Francis Schaeffer's Apologetics: A Critique* (Chicago: Moody Press, 1976).

[8] A table in section I of the bibliography indicates in which volume of *The Complete Works* each book by Schaeffer is located.

[9] References to Schaeffer's books will be given in the text by means of an abbreviation for the title followed by the page number. A list of the

abbreviations can be found at the front of this collection of essays for quick reference.

[10] Although EFR appeared in print first, Schaeffer actually wrote GWIT first (cf. Schaeffer, "Why and How I Write My Books," *Eternity* 24 [March 1973]: 66). Nevertheless, the first two and a half chapters of EFR should be read before GWIT, since they provide material that is presupposed by the argument of the latter. The subsequent chapters of EFR are covered in more detail in GWIT.

[11] The relationship between these books that I have been describing verbally in this paragraph can be seen visually in appendix 1.

[12] Roughly speaking, particulars are individual objects whereas universals are the properties that classes of particulars have in common. Thus "Tom" is a particular, and what all men have in common, "mannishness," is a universal.

Part I

SCHAEFFER'S CONCEPTUAL FRAMEWORK

2

SCHAEFFER'S INTELLECTUAL ROOTS

FORREST BAIRD

To understand the intellectual roots of Francis A. Schaeffer we must first trace the development of the "Princeton Theology" in the nineteenth century and notice its emphasis on the total inerrancy of Scripture and its preference for rationality over religious experience. We must also understand the way in which this theology has led in the present century to separatism from the world and rejection of culture. Finally, we must recognize the influence of presuppositionalism in apologetics. It is the intermixing of these roots that has given flower to the work of Francis Schaeffer.

SCHAEFFER'S EARLY YEARS

Francis A. Schaeffer was born in 1912. Raised under what he later called "liberal preaching in a Presbyterian church,"[1] Schaeffer began to read the Bible carefully as a teenager. By the age of eighteen he had become a born-again Christian. In the summer of 1930 Schaeffer went forward at a tent meeting led by Anthony Zeoli (father of Billy Zeoli, who would later help Franky Schaeffer produce the Schaeffer films). Schaeffer later described this experience:

Forrest Baird is Associate Professor of Philosophy at Whitworth College, Spokane, Washington. He earned the M.Div. from Fuller Theological Seminary and the M.A. and Ph.D. from Claremont Graduate School. He co-edited with Jack Rogers Introduction to Philosophy: A Case Study Approach.

The boy [Schaeffer] walked up the sawdust aisle and when asked, "Boy, what have you come up here for, salvation or re-consecration?" he shrugged his shoulders. This was all new language to him, and all he knew was that he had wanted to step up and take his place with those who believed what he had come to believe. The boy turned to walk down the aisle and out of the tent–resolving before God that he would spend his life making true truth known.[2]

After graduating from Hampden-Sydney College, Schaeffer enrolled at Westminster Theological Seminary in Philadelphia. As a student at Westminster, Schaeffer came under the influence of the Princeton Theology with its emphasis on inerrancy and a rational approach to faith.

THE PRINCETON THEOLOGY

In 1812, exactly one hundred years before Schaeffer's birth, a Presbyterian seminary was established in Princeton, New Jersey. From the very beginning, with the very first professor, Archibald Alexander (1772–1851), the seminary stood for a distinctive understanding of the Scripture. Alexander (who ironically had earlier been president of Hampden-Sydney College) believed that if there were any errors of any kind in the Bible, the trustworthiness of the whole of Scripture would collapse:

If we find a witness mistaken in some particulars, it weakens our confidence in his general testimony. And could it be shown that the evangelists had fallen into palpable mistakes in facts of minor importance, it would be impossible to demonstrate that they wrote anything by inspiration.[3]

Alexander's view of inspiration included not only the ideas, but even the individual words chosen by the authors of Scripture to convey those ideas. As he put it, inspiration was "such a divine influence upon the minds of the sacred writers as rendered them exempt from error, both in regard to the ideas and the words."[4] Whether this understanding of Scripture was a direct continuation of the line from St. Augustine through the Reformers, or whether it was a development of the Scottish Common Sense Realists and Francis Turretin in particular, is a matter of heated debate.[5] But whatever its source, Alexander's understanding of the inspiration of Scripture was to remain the foundation of the Princeton Theology for more than one hundred years and was to deeply influence Westminster Seminary and Francis Schaeffer.

Charles Hodge

Charles Hodge (1797–1878) was a student of Alexander's at Princeton Seminary who later taught at the institution for fifty-eight years. Like his mentor Alexander, Hodge held to a position of full inerrancy for the Bible. Yet Hodge seemed willing to allow that some minor errors of fact in the Bible would not be damaging to the authority of Scripture. In a controversial passage from his *Systematic Theology* Hodge stated,

> The errors in matters of fact which skeptics search out bear no proportion to the whole. No sane man would deny that the Parthenon was built of marble, even if here and there a speck of sandstone should be detected in its structure. Not less reasonable is it to deny the inspiration of such a book as the Bible, because one sacred writer says that on a given occasion twenty-four thousand, and another says that twenty-three thousand, men were slain. Surely a Christian may be allowed to tread such objections under his feet. . . . Admitting that the Scriptures do contain, in a few instances, discrepancies which with our present means of knowledge, we are unable satisfactorily to explain, they furnish no rational ground for denying their infallibility.[6]

Another theme of the Princeton Theology[7] that was to influence Schaeffer was a distrust of personal, mystical religious experience. Alexander had raised some cautions about the use of "internal evidences"—religious experience. Hodge accepted and developed Alexander's concerns. In particular, Hodge was leery of the new emphasis Jonathan Edwards and others were placing on personal experience. Hodge was concerned that faith not be seen as merely an experience. Faith is to be understood as "assent to the truth, or the persuasion of the mind that a thing is true."[8]

In many ways we can see this same concern reflected in Schaeffer. For example, in his attack on Kierkegaard's "leap of faith," Schaeffer speaks of the need for an understanding of faith as a rational commitment to truth. Any "faith" that is not rational, that is merely experience-based, is contentless and incapable of communication.[9] Instead of a "leap of faith," a person should ask sufficient questions about details, about the existence of the universe and man, and then believe based on the truth of the answers given (HIT: 100).

In 1837 a division developed within the Presbyterian church between the "Old School" of those supporting the Princeton Theology and the "New School" of those supporting the personal experience and revivalism of Jonathan Edwards. Hodge was among those who supported the division that resulted in the expulsion of several presbyteries of the New School from the church.[10]

There were other battles for Hodge to fight at this time. In addition to those who were putting too much emphasis on personal experience, Hodge felt the continuing threat of those who put too much emphasis on the use of reason in the form of higher criticism and science. According to Hodge, the problem with much of higher criticism was not in the way it studied words, but in the basic philosophical presuppositions from which it worked. As founder and editor of the *Biblical Repertory and Theological Review* for forty-six years, Hodge published numerous articles attacking the spread of higher criticism.

In his early days Hodge felt that the teachings of science (particularly astronomy) and the teachings of the Bible were perfectly harmonious. "No man now pretends that there is a word in the Bible, from Genesis to Revelation, inconsistent with the highest results of astronomy."[11] However, with the rise of Darwinism it had become clear that secular science and the Bible were clearly at odds. In 1874 Hodge wrote *What Is Darwinism?* in which he claimed that Darwin's theory was "virtually atheistic."[12] When it came to conflicts between science and the Bible, the facts of the Bible on *all* matters—science, geography, etc.—were used to refute the findings of science. Many claim that this position was the foundation for much of the anti-intellectual fundamentalism which was to follow.[13]

A. A. Hodge

As the implications of the attack on the inerrancy of the Bible became clear, Hodge's statement about the "specks of sandstone in the Parthenon" became a problem. Opponents of the Princeton Theology used this image to show that Hodge, at least, was not bothered by minor errors in Scripture. It fell to A. A. Hodge and B. B. Warfield to continue the defense of the inerrancy position of the Princeton Theology. Archibald Alexander Hodge (1823–1886), named after the founding professor of Princeton Seminary, was Charles Hodge's son, born one year after Charles began his long tenure of teaching there. A. A. Hodge believed in a completely inerrant Bible. He stated in a famous article he co-authored with B. B. Warfield,

> . . . The historical faith of the Church has always been that all the affirmations of Scripture of all kinds, whether of spiritual doctrine or duty, or of physical or historical fact, or of psychological or philosophical principle, are without any error. . . .[14]

However, Hodge went on to explain that all the affirmations of Scripture are only without error in the original autographs. In his words, the Bible is without error of any kind ". . . when the *ipsissima verba* of the original autographs are ascertained and interpreted in their natural and intended sense."[15] In other words, all the apparent discrepancies within Scripture are due to problems of transmission or translation. Likewise, the discrepancies between Scripture and science are due to imperfect copies of ancient writings, lost original writings, a lack of understanding of the original writer, lack of "circumstantial knowledge" which would help reconcile apparent differences, or error in the sciences.[16]

Though Hodge was by no means the first to claim that inerrancy applied only to the original autographs, it was his formulation of the doctrine that was accepted by Westminster Seminary and Schaeffer.

B. B. Warfield

Upon A. A. Hodge's untimely death in 1886, Benjamin Breckinridge Warfield (1851–1921) succeeded him at Princeton Seminary. Like those before him, Warfield saw his job as explicating and defending the Princeton Theology. But though his task was the same, the times had changed drastically. Science was leading more and more people to question the biblical account of Creation. Higher criticism was gaining strength in the theological community. Warfield saw the need to defend the faith against these and other threats to orthodoxy. Apologetics became primary in his presentation of Christian theology. As he put it, apologetics ". . . has for its object the laying of the foundations on which the temple of theology is built, and by which the whole structure of theology is determined."[17]

THE REACTION TO THE PRINCETON THEOLOGY

Charles A. Briggs

In the late nineteenth and early twentieth centuries the Princeton Theology began to come under attack. It was these attacks that eventually led to the founding of Westminster Seminary and the movement of separatism with which Schaeffer became associated.

The assault began in 1881 when Charles A. Briggs (1841–1913) and A. A. Hodge were chosen as managing editors of a new journal, the *Presbyterian Review.* The *Review* was charged with presenting opposing viewpoints on the new higher criticism. Almost from the start there were problems between the co-editors. (Briggs, like Hodge a Presbyterian, had not, however, either studied or taught at Princeton.) Beginning cautiously, Briggs eventually mounted a full-scale attack on the Princeton Theology. According to Briggs, the inerrancy position of the Princeton theologians was *not* the view of the Reformers or of the creeds of the Presbyterian church. He stated in an attack on Hodge and Warfield,

> 1. The historic faith of the Church is to be found in the official symbolical books and nowhere else. None of these symbols state that the *"ipsissima verba* of the original autographs are without error."* 2. It is well known that the great Reformers recognized errors in the Scriptures and did not hold to the inerrancy of the original autographs. Are these Princeton divines entitled to pronounce Luther and Calvin heterodox, and to define the faith of the universal Church? 3. The Westminster divines did not teach the inerrancy of the original autographs.[18]

Briggs believed, moreover, that the Princeton theologians' emphasis on inerrancy was dangerous;

> . . . These Princeton divines risk the inspiration and authority of the Bible upon a single proved error. Such a position is a serious and hazardous departure from Protestant orthodoxy. It imperils the faith of all Christians who have been taught this doctrine. They cannot escape the evidence of errors in the Scriptures.[19]

Instead, Briggs claimed that Scripture is the infallible rule of faith and practice, but that there are factual errors and inconsistencies in the Bible. He considered these errors inconsequential. This position, which was later called "limited inerrancy" by its opponents, was held to be unacceptable by the Princeton theologians—and later by Schaeffer, who consistently attacks this position in his writings.

In 1891 Briggs was prevented from taking the newly created chair of Biblical Theology at Union Seminary in New York. Within the year he had been "indicted," exonerated, and finally "indicted" again. In May 1893 the General Assembly suspended Briggs from the ministry of the Presbyterian church on grounds of heresy.

The Tide Turns

The next three decades saw a continuation of the debate within the church. Closely following Briggs's dismissal, Henry Preserved Smith was suspended from the ministry in 1894 for similar reasons. In 1910 the Presbyterian church formally adopted five principles as "essential and necessary doctrines"[20] for ordination, and these included a clear statement of inerrancy. But by the 1920s a strong backlash against the Princeton Theology was gaining a foothold. In 1922 Harry Emerson Fosdick preached a famous sermon entitled "Shall the Fundamentalists Win?" which questioned the prevailing use of the Princeton Theology. Two years later the liberal leadership in the Presbyterian church published a document, known as the "Auburn Affirmation," which objected to the five principles of 1910. In particular, the Auburn Affirmation attacked the inerrancy position of the Princeton Theology.

J. Gresham Machen

The job of once again defending the Princeton Theology fell on the shoulders of J. Gresham Machen (1881–1937). Machen, who had been a student of Warfield's and later taught Schaeffer, joined the Princeton faculty in 1906. Like those before him, he was concerned to defend the inerrant nature of Scripture. Machen graciously allowed that those who hold to a position of "limited inerrancy" (what he called a "mediating view") might still be Christians, but he believed that "It is another question . . . whether the mediating view of the Bible which is thus maintained is logically tenable. . . ."[21] According to Machen, a limited view of inerrancy would almost inevitably lead to a rejection of the authority of Scripture.

Schaeffer later developed this idea and continually pointed out that anything less than a position of full inerrancy would lead to a rejection of the authority of Scripture. Whereas Machen said "limited inerrancy" is not "logically tenable," Schaeffer said it is the "watershed" that divides Christianity (GED: 43–49).

Machen was also, like his predecessors, deeply disturbed by the rise of higher criticism in liberal theologies. As Schaeffer later explained,

> . . . Machen argued that liberalism was really a new religion and not Christianity at all. Since liberalism did not believe in the fact that Christ died in history to atone for the sins of men and women, and that was the only basis for salvation, liberalism was really religious faith in man dressed up in Christian language and symbols. Thus, Machen explained, the only honest thing for the liberal to do would be to leave the churches which were founded on biblical truth (GED: 73).

The problem, according to Machen, was that the liberals were left with no point of authority. Some tried to claim that Jesus was their authority, but without an inerrant Scripture to teach about Jesus such a claim was ridiculous.[22]

Machen was also skeptical about religious experience. In his book *What Is Faith?* Machen explains some of his objections to an experiential approach to faith. In the introduction he states, "Faith, it may be said, cannot be known except by experience. . . . Such [an objection is] only one manifestation of a tendency that is very widespread at the present day, the tendency to disparage the intellectual aspect of the religious life" (Machen: 13). Machen then points out that biblical faith is always faith involving a person.

> But—and here we come to the point which we think ought to be emphasized above all others just at the present day—it is impossible to have faith in a person without having knowledge of the person; far from being contrasted with knowledge, faith is founded upon knowledge (Machen: 46).

There are many ways of coming to faith, the first of which is the

> purely intellectual way. The claims of Christianity, it is said, must be investigated on their merits, by use of a rigidly scientific method; and only if they are established as true may they be allowed to control the emotional and volitional

life. For this method of approach . . . we have the warmest sympathy . . . (Machen: 130).

Theology, according to Machen, is indeed the queen of the sciences—and it is definitely a *science:*

> Theology . . . is just as much a science as is chemistry. . . . The two sciences, it is true, differ widely in their subject matter; they differ widely in the character of the evidence upon which their conclusions are based; in particular they differ widely in the qualifications required of the investigator: but they are both sciences, because they are both concerned with the acquisition and orderly arrangement of a body of truth (Machen: 33).

It is this last point about the truth of theology that was the most important for Machen. Throughout his writings he was concerned to show that doctrine, and in particular doctrine as understood by the Princeton Theology, is not just an opinion, but it is *true.* Schaeffer, making the same point later, would refer to this idea as "true truth."

The Split

In 1925 a special commission was established by the General Assembly to study the controversy within the Presbyterian church. This commission reported back in 1927, stating that the only doctrines necessary for ordination were the doctrines of the church—including the Westminster Confession. In essence this was a repudiation of the five principles established in 1910.

Two years later, the General Assembly approved a reorganization of Princeton Seminary that provided for a more inclusivistic approach. The Princeton Theology that had been taught at the seminary for over a hundred years was no longer the rule. Machen and fellow teachers Robert Dick Wilson, Oswald T. Allis, and Cornelius Van Til and twenty students left the seminary and formed Westminster Seminary in Philadelphia. Here they hoped to continue the Princeton Theology of old and uphold the banner of full inerrancy. (The first class of the seminary included such future leaders as Harold J. Ockenga and Carl McIntire.)

Another point of conflict between Machen and the established Presbyterian church was the treatment given to conservative missionary candidates. In 1933 Machen and other conservative leaders such as McIntire and J. Oliver Buswell, Jr. (then president of Wheaton College) formed the Independent Board for Presbyterian Foreign Missions. Machen became the first president of the board. The General Assembly declared this rival board schismatic and ordered Machen to withdraw from the board. He refused, and in 1935 he was removed from the ministry of the Presbyterian Church. The judgment handed down by the General Assembly sounded much like the judgment in the Briggs case forty-two years earlier, but now the conservatives were on the defensive.[23]

A year later, after much skirmishing, Machen and his followers set up a new denomination, the Presbyterian Church in America. (The name was later changed to the Orthodox Presbyterian Church.) Although the battles with the established Presbyterian church were now over, new conflicts arose within the group which had separated. In 1937 Carl McIntire and J. Oliver Buswell led a group which split from Westminster Seminary over the issues of premillenialism and total abstinence from alcoholic beverages.[24] This group formed a new seminary, Faith Seminary in Philadelphia, and a new denomination, the Bible Presbyterian Church. Francis Schaeffer later recalled these days of "coming out" and the problems that followed:

> The periodicals of those who left [the established Presbyterian church] tended to devote more space to attacking people who differed with them on the issue of leaving than to dealing with the liberals. Things were said that are difficult to forget even now. Those who came out refused at times to pray with those who had not come out. Many who left broke off all forms of fellowship with true brothers in Christ who had not left. Christ's command to love one another was destroyed. What was left was frequently a turning inward, a self-righteousness, a hardness. The impression often was left that coming out had made those who departed so right that anything could then be excused. Having learned such bad habits, they later treated each other badly when resulting new groups had minor differences among themselves (GED: 75).

THE SHAPING OF SCHAEFFER'S THOUGHT

Machen: The Princeton Theology Connection

In 1935 Schaeffer began studying at Westminster Seminary. That he was influenced deeply by Machen's presentation of the

Princeton Theology is quite clear. Schaeffer agreed with Machen that the interpretive method of higher criticism is an evil that must be fought because it leads to a rejection of the authority of Scripture. At one point Schaeffer even implied that it was the method of higher criticism that led to Hitler's rise in Germany![25] Schaeffer also held that a position of "limited inerrancy" was not "logically tenable."[26]

Like Machen, Schaeffer was also skeptical about religious experience in his presentation of the nature of faith. Schaeffer was particularly wary of people like Karl Barth who appeal to an "inward witness" to substantiate their faith. Schaeffer preferred to talk about the objective nature of faith, often repeating Machen's words about the "intellectual way" to faith. Finally, for Schaeffer as for Machen, the key was that theology and doctrine are *true* (Schaeffer's "true truth") in the same way that scientific facts about the world are true.

Van Til: The Presuppositionalist Connection

At Westminster, Schaeffer was also a student of Cornelius Van Til (1895–   ). Van Til had come from a different tradition than the Princeton Theologians, though he came to many of the same conclusions. He held to a position of full inerrancy and was also wary of religious experience. But there were some significant differences. To understand those differences that influenced Schaeffer, we must take at least a cursory glance at the Dutch Reformed tradition, which is best represented by Abraham Kuyper.

Abraham Kuyper

Abraham Kuyper (1837–1920) was a Dutch theologian who sought to apply his Reformed theology to all areas of his life. He founded the Free University of Amsterdam, was a leader in the Reformed Church, and became prime minister of Holland. For Kuyper, Calvinism was a "Life-System" to be lived out in all areas of life. As Bernard Ramm summarizes it, for Kuyper

> Calvinism was not exhausted in our doctrine of salvation. It called forth the entire man and the entire man in his cultural commitments—politics, science, art, education. His entire educational philosophy which he built into the curriculum of the Free University was that Christianity calls us to a total life-perspective, a total way of living, to a Weltanschauung.[27]

In apologetics, Kuyper rejected the use of evidences. Because of the effects of sin, any reasons or evidences for faith will not be recognized by the nonbeliever. Human depravity prevents the use of any "common ground" between the believer and the nonbeliever. The nonbeliever operates on the "natural" principle of unregenerate reason. Through the effects of sin "this natural principle has lost the right of judgment."[28]

This rejection of a common ground led Kuyper to disagree strongly with Warfield's position on apologetics. As already noted, Warfield held that it was the job of apologetics to "lay the foundations" for theology. According to Kuyper, the truth is exactly the opposite: theology is to be the starting point and is to "lay the foundations" for apologetics.[29]

Cornelius Van Til

Van Til agreed totally with Kuyper in rejecting the use of evidences and the primacy of apologetics. Though he taught at the school where the Princeton Theology was being kept alive, he differed strongly with the position on apologetics it had come to represent:

> . . . In Apologetics, Warfield wanted to operate in neutral territory with the non-believer. He thought that this was the only way to show to the unbeliever that theism and Christianity are objectively true. He sought for an objectivity that bridged the gulf between Kuyper's "natural" and special principles. I have chosen the position of Abraham Kuyper.[30]

According to Van Til, if reason is capable of using evidences, then a person's reason has become autonomous—separated from the need for God's guidance. Van Til asks, "Can the difference between the principle of autonomy and that of Christian theism be ignored so that men can together seek to interpret natural revelation in terms of one procedure?"[31] The answer, of course, is no.

Independent of God, reason can do or understand nothing. Not even the law of contradiction can be used apart from God: "Christians should therefore never appeal to the law of contradiction as something which determines what can or cannot be true."[32] Kenneth Kantzer aptly summarizes this point:

> It is impossible . . . to appeal to the unbeliever on the basis of common ground. Epistemologically speaking, the unbe-

liever has no ground on which to stand. No appeal can be made to logic or the laws of human thought, for apart from theism, neither human logic nor its processes of thought have any meaning or validity. No appeal can be made to facts supporting theism, for apart from theism there are no "brute facts." All so-called facts involve interpretation and thus presuppose a viewpoint and the meaningfulness of human thought.[33]

Not only do all facts involve interpretation, but for Van Til there is really only one interpretation that can make a fact a fact: the interpretation given it by God. Indeed, the Christian must deny that "any area or aspect of reality, any fact or any law or nature or history can be correctly interpreted except that it be seen in the light of the main doctrines of Christianity."[34]

Instead of appealing to facts or evidences on common ground, Van Til advocated a position of presuppositionalism. He asserted that there is a basic difference between people who begin with Christian assumptions and those who do not. As a result, any evidences for Christianity will be rejected out of hand by those who have different presuppositions. This being so, the careful development and presentation of Christian evidences is really a waste of time. The role of the Christian apologist, therefore, is one of showing the inadequacy of all other presuppositions. While the Christian can also show the adequacy of the Christian position, the nonbeliever, apart from the working of the Holy Spirit, will not be able to see it.[35]

Schaeffer by and large accepted this presuppositionalism of Van Til. But as Kenneth Harper has pointed out, Schaeffer was not a thoroughgoing presuppositionalist:

> Francis Schaeffer can best be described as an inconsistent presuppositionalist. He readily accepts the distinction Van Til makes between the non-Christian, who begins from a basic atheistic position, and the Christian whose theism permeates every facet of his thought. Therefore, for Schaeffer, as with Van Til, there *are* two humanities. However, Schaeffer believed there is a common ground which both Christians and non-Christians share—something Van Til would deny.[36]

While one might want to quibble a bit with Harper over his understanding of Van Til,[37] it is certainly true that Schaeffer believed it is possible, because of common grace, to have a meaningful dialogue with a nonbeliever. Thus, for Schaeffer a sort of "pre-evangelism" using reason is possible, since the

secular world is not consistent in applying secular presuppositions. The job of the Christian apologist is to find and expose
the logical tension between a person's non-Christian assumptions and the real external world. Schaeffer calls this "taking the
roof off" and states that only after the "roof" has been taken off
is a person ready for the gospel. "The truth that we let in first is
not the dogmatic statement of the truth of the Scriptures but the
truth of the external world and the truth of what man himself
is" (GWIT: 129). Schaeffer adds that we "must never forget the
first part of the Gospel is not 'Accept Christ as Saviour,' but
'God is there'" (GWIT: 132).

McIntire: The Separatist Connection

Despite his respect for Machen, Van Til, and Westminster
Seminary, Schaeffer chose to follow McIntire and moved to
Faith Seminary to finish his schooling. In 1938 Schaeffer
graduated from Faith Seminary and became a pastor in the
Bible Presbyterian Church. While Schaeffer was serving as a
pastor in Grove City, Pennsylvania, and then in St. Louis,
Missouri, McIntire was busy calling together individuals and
denominations that were concerned about the "purity of the
church."

Basing his ideas on the premise that "in all areas of
Christian co-operation the command of Scripture is, 'Touch not
the unclean thing'."[38] McIntire sought to establish a group of
"pure" churches. In 1908 the Federal Council of Churches (later
called the National Council of Churches) had been formed with
most of the larger denominations in America joining. In 1941
McIntire decided it was time to fight the "impure" FCC and
promote a separated church, so he formed the American
Council of Christian Churches (ACCC).

Schaeffer was involved in the ACCC from the beginning.
During his time in St. Louis he was drawn into a controversy
with the Child Evangelism Fellowship. He had become a
powerful force on the local board and, according to one
observer, "was running it as a separatist organization."[39] The
national board of Child Evangelism insisted that its policy of
including all evangelicals be observed on the local level, and it
ordered Schaeffer to include pastors from churches outside the
ACCC on the local board. Rather than submit to this order,
Schaeffer resigned and formed his own organization, Children
for Christ, Inc.

In 1947 Schaeffer was asked to go to Europe by the Independent Board for Presbyterian Foreign Missions, the group begun by Machen. Schaeffer made a survey of thirteen war-torn countries to see if there was "a possible work in Europe." As he recalled the story,

> I came back with a tremendous conviction that we really had a field in which we could be helpful. So, I told the board this. And I waited and the board didn't respond. After some time I wrote and asked why we hadn't heard. They wrote and told me: "We *agree* with you that there is a tremendous field in Europe; but we've concluded that *you* are the only one who would fit in to go and work in that field!"[40]

That same year Schaeffer moved his family to Lausanne, Switzerland. By this time McIntire had decided to expand the ACCC into an international body to fight the newly formed World Council of Churches in much the same way as the ACCC had been formed to fight the Federal Council. The International Council of Christian Churches (ICCC) was formed in 1948 with McIntire as its leader and Schaeffer as its secretary. Schaeffer's relationship with McIntire continued for many years, and Schaeffer was later considered a missionary for the ICCC. During this period, Schaeffer focused much of his attention on neo-orthodoxy and the "soft reasoning" it entailed. Ralph Lord Roy commented on Schaeffer in his 1953 book, *Apostles of Discord,*

> Francis A. Schaeffer, described by McIntire as a "brilliant and consecrated young man" trained at Faith Theological Seminary, declares that neo-orthodox "have evolved the cleverest of counterfeits of true Christianity, yet actually they are further from us than the Roman Catholic Church, and they are even further from us than the Old Modernists." Schaeffer—who has been director of Children for Christ, Inc., secretary of the International Council of Christian Churches and of the Foreign Relations Department of the American Council—charges the neo-orthodox with "mental gymnastics" and "black magic in logic." "Contradictions and change," he says, "are accepted with complacency, and paradoxes with joy."[41]

After moving his family to Lausanne, Schaeffer spent the next year struggling with the depth of his Christian commitment. These struggles formed the basis for his later book, *True Spirituality.* In 1949 he and his family moved to Champery and began to hold services in a local church. In the years to follow, Schaeffer continued to travel throughout Europe presenting what he called his "two-pronged ministry." One part of the ministry dealt with warning the churches against liberalism, while the other part consisted of children's work. As Schaeffer described it,

> The way this worked in practice was I would go into a town—into a place in Finland, for example—and I would have a certain number of talks to give. I would split them about half and half: half on the liberal situation and what was happening in theology and then, in the other half, I would discuss ways to reach and teach the children. So during the first five years, this was the way we worked.[42]

During this time Schaeffer hosted an ICCC meeting in Geneva. Schaeffer read a paper about Karl Barth at that meeting and then sent a copy to Barth. In the fall 1951 issue of the *Journal of the Faith Theological Seminary Alumni Association*, Schaeffer dealt with the answer he received from Barth:

> The simple fact is that I do not think it is possible for Karl Barth, world renowned though he is, to face a Bible-believing Christian if by God's grace he keeps the conversation upon the heart of the weakness of the Transcendental Theology rather than allowing himself to be engulfed in those subtleties of peripheral vagueness which the transcendental theologian loves.[43]

Later in the article Schaeffer claimed that

> . . . In the secular realm existentialism, when judged on commonly accepted grounds, is insanity; and the same must be said for Transcendental Theology in the theological realm.[44]

Schaeffer went on to establish what he considered to be the basic position that a Bible-believing Christian should hold: a reaffirmation of the total inerrancy and objectivism of the Princeton Theology, the presuppositionalism of Van Til, and the premillennialism of Faith Seminary:

> The one who does not rest his authority on the infallible, inerrant Word of God must to some extent be out of touch with the real world. . . . We Bible-believing Christians look at the external world and to us it is an understandable world, for it is the world which God made and of which God informed us in the Revelation He has given. . . . We

understand that [Christ's second] coming will be a *fact* in history just as creation is a *fact* of history and just as Christ's death and resurrection are *facts* of history.[45]

On the basis of this understanding of Scripture, Schaeffer called for a separation from those who do not hold this view of the Bible. Those who do not hold this view of the Bible fit into three categories, all of which must be rejected:

> Brethren, there are today three positions upon which men of our civilization are trying to stand: the first is secularism, and it is exhibited most logically by Existentialism and Modern Art, it says frankly that there is no Authority. It is totally subjective. The second is Rome, and it is subjective in its Authority and therefore its Authority is not sure. The third is the New Modernism with various degrees of the Old Modernism clinging to it and this too is subjective without any real Authority. . . . Let us not compromise an inch with any of these three forms of uncertainty which control the thinking of the world about us in our day.[46]

In 1953 Schaeffer returned to the United States for an eighteen-month visit. During this time he toured churches around the country speaking and raising money. He also received an honorary doctorate from the now-defunct Highland College of Long Beach, California.

Schaeffer was also prominent in a break from the Bible Presbyterian Church that eventually led to the formation of the Reformed Presbyterian Church, Evangelical Synod. This break marked a departure from the ICCC and estrangement from McIntire. McIntire, who managed over the years to alienate just about all his former colleagues, never forgave Schaeffer.[47]

L'ABRI

Upon their return to Europe several problems befell the Schaeffer family. On the voyage across the Atlantic Schaeffer's son was stricken with polio; two months later his daughter contracted rheumatic fever. A few months after that, the Schaeffers' permit to live in Champery was revoked. Schaeffer later recounted,

> In Switzerland each canton has its own Protestant or Roman Catholic religion, and that's been true ever since the Reformation. So you have some Protestant cantons and some Roman Catholic cantons. And we were living in Champery

which was in a Roman Catholic canton. . . . One day I met a man on a train going up to Champery, a little train that goes up from the valley. He sat down next to me and recognized me. He spoke English and asked me if I would talk about what I believe. He explained that he had come from a Roman Catholic background, but he himself was an atheist. So I began to talk. Later he visited our home in Champery. After about a year of his coming to our chalet he became a very strong Christian. But his family was very exercised, even though he had been an atheist and not a strong Roman Catholic. His family stirred up the authorities and then the authorities had our permit removed.[48]

After an amazing series of events,[49] the Schaeffers moved to the tiny town of Huémoz in the southwest corner of Switzerland. On July 1, 1955, the L'Abri Fellowship was started. L'Abri—a French word meaning "the shelter"—is a group of chalets in and around Huémoz. All the visitors at L'Abri lived in homes run by staff couples. Everyone was expected to help with the necessary work in addition to studying. There were lively discussions during meals and at other specially appointed times. But work, study, and prayer took up most of each day. A typical day at L'Abri might begin with some work in the kitchen followed by study in the afternoon and a lecture-discussion in the evening. Or, on a special day of prayer, the schedule might be altered to include a good deal more time for personal and group prayers.

After a *Time* magazine reporter's daughter was converted to Christianity, the magazine brought the mission in the Alps to the attention of Americans. Describing Schaeffer's conception of truth as "uncompromisingly Biblical and fundamentalist," the article quoted Schaeffer as saying,

> If we accept part of the Bible as myth, we might just as well be consistent and accept the whole Bible as a myth. Why, I can have more respect for a Teddy boy who tells me that killing a friend with a bicycle chain is all right. He at least has a philosophy. To people like him we can point out that morality does have a purpose, and can lead them back to the self-consistent system of orthodox, reformative Christendom.[50]

Schaeffer was also quoted in the article about the effectiveness of the L'Abri Fellowship. Although there were few conversions, "those who do become Christians are not likely to be superficial ones." Echoing the words of Machen, Schaeffer described those who become Christians at L'Abri:

They're no fools. When they make a decision, they possess the intellectual framework to make it in. We have had to solve the most unlikely problems, and the Lord has even helped us in preventing certain suicides. But religion isn't a crutch for kids or psychos. Religion is the universal truth. It is irrational to think that watertight doors exist between religion and intellectual thinking. A step of faith is no step in the dark.[51]

However, the atmosphere at L'Abri included more than the rarified air of reason and intellectual pursuit. The L'Abri Fellowship had a strong pietistic, personal, experience-oriented side to its ministry. According to many observers, this experiential, pietistic strain could be traced to Francis Schaeffer's wife, Edith. In her books Edith often talks about how a passage of Scripture "spoke to her"—on some occasions even acknowledging that the passage meant something else entirely before God "used it to speak to her."[52] This pietistic atmosphere, coupled with Schaeffer's strong rationalistic background, provided a blend of study and prayer. The mixture of work, study, prayer, and listening to discussion both in person and on tapes combined to form a warm, homelike atmosphere conducive to spiritual growth.

In the years that were to follow, Schaeffer continued to work with students at L'Abri and to pursue his concerns about the church.

CONCLUSION

In summarizing Schaeffer's relationship to his intellectual roots, there are five strands that interweave to form the fabric of his thought. First and foremost, Schaeffer always stood firmly with the Princeton theologians on the issue of inerrancy. His critics, particularly those who maintain that the Princeton theologians' position is not the continuation of the Reformed tradition, point to his repetition of the themes of Hodge, Warfield, Machen, and the rest as proof of the inadequacy of his thought. His supporters, and even Schaeffer himself in his later writings, point to his continuation of the Princeton Theology as a sign of his courage to stand up for the "watershed" issue of inerrancy.

Second, Schaeffer also always stood with the Princeton theologians on the issue of religious experience. While not denying the experience of faith, Schaeffer emphasized the objective, rational character of belief.

Third, Schaeffer was heavily influenced by Van Til. As already noted, Schaeffer accepted Van Til's presuppositional-ism, though he placed more emphasis on the common ground the believer has with the nonbeliever. Schaeffer's apologetic method is examined closely in the next chapter. Suffice it to say here that he has always seemed uncomfortable when cornered on the question of his apologetical approach. Asked at a large meeting whether he was a presuppositionalist or an evidential-ist, Schaeffer replied,

> I'm neither. I'm not an evidentialist or a presuppositional-ist. You're trying to press me into the category of a theological apologist, which I'm really not. I'm not an academic, scholastic apologist. My interest is evangelism.[53]

Fourth, Schaeffer consistently pursued the separatist ap-proach to dealing with Christians who disagreed with him. Earlier on, he left Westminster to join those who were "more pure" at Faith Seminary. Later he refused to work for Child Evangelism Fellowship with pastors whose denominations did not belong to the ACCC. Even in his last book Schaeffer says that a line must be drawn "when we are asked to work together for the sake of the gospel with others who hold a weakened view of the Bible" (GED: 89).

Schaeffer's appeal in later life to "call out the true evangelicals" was nothing but a continuation of the separatist background from which he came. In some of his writings Schaeffer made it seem as though this call to separate was a new idea—a conclusion to which he came after observing the "devastating effects" of liberalism in Europe. This makes it seem as though it was empirical data that led him to call for separation. In fact, it was a presupposition that he had accepted from at least the time of his leaving Westminster Seminary. Schaeffer consistently tried to show the dire consequences of those who cooperate with Christians who are "not Bible-believing," and he related numerous case studies to back up his claim. But when it comes to the dire consequences of the separatist movement, he had little to say besides acknowledg-ing that there was some "lack of love" on the part of the separatists. Nowhere did Schaeffer acknowledge his own part in the whole separatist movement.

Finally, while many in the separatist movement refused to even consider the secular world, Schaeffer was always con-cerned that Christians understand the secular culture in which they find themselves. Like Kuyper, Schaeffer thought that Reformed theology should apply to all of life. He held that it was a weakness in evangelicalism that led to a refusal to examine culture:

> There has been a great Platonic emphasis that the soul is important but the body, the intellect, and culture are suspect. In other words, by emphasis "salvation" has shut out all else; it's only a matter of getting the soul to heaven. In this situation we have a tremendous emphasis on getting the soul saved but very little emphasis on the Lordship of Christ covering the whole of life. . . . There [are] lots of people who think that if you are interested in cultural or intellectual things, then you must have a deficiency spiritually.[54]

For those people, particularly in the separatist movement, who thought that an interest in the culture was due to "spiritual deficiency," Schaeffer's thought was a breakthrough. Schaeffer became a bridge into an appreciation, albeit a very critical appreciation, of the secular world.

NOTES

[1] Edith Schaeffer, "Family Letter"—a newsletter sent out to members and friends of the L'Abri Fellowship—(July 4, 1975): 14.

[2] Ibid.

[3] Archibald Alexander, *Evidences of the Authenticity, Inspiration, and Canonical Authority of the Holy Scriptures* (Philadelphia: Presbyterian Board of Publication, 1836), 229.

[4] Ibid., 230.

[5] For a clear presentation of this argument, see Jack B. Rogers and Donald K. McKim, *The Authority and Interpretation of the Bible* (San Francisco: Harper & Row, 1979); or Ernest R. Sandeen, *The Roots of Fundamentalism* (Chicago: University of Chicago, 1970), 103–31. For a rebuttal, see Richard Lovelace, "Inerrancy: Some Historical Perspectives," in *Inerrancy and Common Sense*, ed. Roger R. Nicole and J. Ramsey Michaels (Grand Rapids: Baker, 1980), 15–47; or John D. Woodbridge, *Biblical Authority: A Critique of the Rogers/McKim Proposal* (Grand Rapids: Zondervan, 1982).

[6] Charles Hodge, *Systematic Theology*, Vol. I (New York: Scribner's, 1871), 170.

[7] It should be noted that Charles Hodge thought that the Princeton Theology did not name any real movement and so should not be given a distinctive name (cf. A. A. Hodge, *The Life of Charles Hodge D.D., LL.D.*, [New York: Scribner's, 1880], 25). Whether or not the Princeton Theology is the position the church has held since before the Reformation, the way it was formulated is distinctive and warrants a specific name.

[8] Hodge, *Systematic Theology*, III, 42.

[9] For an interesting discussion of this reading of Kierkegaard, see Ronald W. Ruegsegger, "Francis Schaeffer on Philosophy," *Christian Scholar's Review* 10 (1981): 238–54.

[10] See Rogers and McKim, 277.

[11] Charles Hodge, "Inspiration," *Princeton Review* 29 (October 1857): 683.

[12] Charles Hodge, *What Is Darwinism?* (New York: Scribner, Armstrong, and Co., 1874), 173.

[13] For example, see George M. Marsden, *Fundamentalism and American Culture* (New York: Oxford University, 1980), 19–20.

[14] A. A. Hodge and B. B. Warfield, "Inspiration," *Princeton Review* 2 (1881): 225-60; reprinted as *Inspiration* (Grand Rapids: Baker, 1979), 28.

[15] Ibid.

[16] Ibid., 27.

[17] B. B. Warfield, *Studies in Theology* (New York: Oxford University, 1932), 9.

[18] C. A. Briggs, *Whither? A Theological Question for the Times*, 69, as quoted in Rogers and McKim, 354.

[19] Rogers and McKim, 355.

[20] Ibid., 362.

[21] J. Gresham Machen, *What Is Faith?* (Grand Rapids: Eerdmans, 1946), 75.

[22] Ibid., 13. Schaeffer makes the exact same point in GED: 52.

[23] Interestingly, both Schaeffer and at least one of his critics agree on this point (cf. GED: 86 and Rogers and McKim, 368).

[24] Sandeen, 260.

[25] Schaeffer says in GED: 35, "It is interesting to note that there was a span of approximately eighty years from the time when the higher critical methods originated and became widely accepted in Germany to the disintegration of German culture and the rise of totalitarianism under Hitler."

[26] Schaeffer uses the image of a watershed to show how anything less than full inerrancy will lead to the destruction of the church (cf. GED: 43ff.).

[27] Bernard Ramm, *Varieties of Christian Apologetics* (Grand Rapids: Baker, 1962), 180.

[28] Abraham Kuyper, *Encyclopedia der Heilige Godgeleerdheid*, II, 335, as quoted in Cornelius Van Til, *The Defense of the Faith*, rev. ed. (Phillipsburg, N.J.: Presbyterian and Reformed, 1967), 261.

[29] Bernard Ramm, *Types of Apologetic Systems* (Wheaton: Van Kampen, 1953), 185.

[30] Van Til, 265.

[31] Ibid., 260.

[32] Cornelius Van Til, *An Introduction to Theology*, unpublished syllabus, 1949, as quoted in Ramm, *Types of Apologetic Systems*, 188.

[33] Kenneth S. Kantzer, "Unity and Diversity in Evangelical Faith," *The Evangelicals*, ed. by David F. Wells and John D. Woodbridge (Grand Rapids: Baker, 1977), 68.

[34] Van Til, 96.

[35] Cf. Van Til, 104ff.

[36] Kenneth C. Harper, "Francis Schaeffer: An Evaluation," *Bibliotheca Sacra* 133 (1976): 138.

[37] Van Til also believes in a type of common ground, though it is severely limited (cf. Ramm, *Types of Apologetic Systems*, 205–7).

[38] Carl McIntire, "Verily . . . They Have Their Reward," *Christian Beacon* (March 18, 1976): 4.

[39] J. Philip Clark, interview in Glendale, California (February 25, 1976).

[40] "The Lordship of Jesus Christ: An Interview with Dr. Francis A. Schaeffer," *Mission* (February 1974): 11.

[41] Ralph Lord Roy, *Apostles of Discord* (Boston: Beacon, 1953), 216.

[42] "The Lordship of Jesus Christ," *Mission*, 11.

[43] Francis A. Schaeffer, "Modern Man and the Problem of Authority," *Journal of the Faith Theological Seminary Alumni Association* 4, no. 1 (Fall 1951): 3.

[44] Ibid., 7.

[45] Ibid., 8.

[46] Ibid., 10.

[47] See McIntire, "Verily," *Christian Beacon*, 2–7.

[48] "The Lordship of Jesus Christ," *Mission*, 12.

[49] For a summary of the events that led to the founding of L'Abri, see Edith Schaeffer, *L'Abri* (Wheaton: Tyndale House, 1969).

[50] "Mission to the Intellectuals," *Time* (January 11, 1960): 48.

[51] Ibid.

[52] For example, in the book *L'Abri* (p. 76), Edith Schaeffer talks about how God used a passage in Isaiah to give her assurance that things were going to work out. She writes, ". . . I had the tremendous surge of assurance that *although this* [the passage from Isaiah] *had another basic meaning,* it was being used by God to tell me something" (my italics).

[53] Quoted in Jack Rogers, "Francis Schaeffer: The Promise and the Problem," *Reformed Journal* (May 1977): 12–13.

[54] "The Lordship of Jesus Christ," *Mission*, 17.

3

SCHAEFFER'S APOLOGETIC METHOD

GORDON R. LEWIS

For anyone interested in Francis Schaeffer's approach to defending the Christian faith, 1976 was a baffling year. In that year three books came out with three mutually exclusive interpretations of Schaeffer's apologetic method. In *Francis Schaeffer's Apologetic: A Critique*, Thomas V. Morris identified Schaeffer as a presuppositionalist. In *The Justification of Knowledge*, Robert L. Reymond regarded Schaeffer as a representative of the empirical apologetic tradition. And finally, in *Testing Christianity's Truth Claims: Approaches to Apologetics*, the present writer found Schaeffer's method to be neither deductive nor inductive, but verificational.

Why these differences of opinion? Unfortunately, Schaeffer did not help his interpreters by publishing his own method of reasoning or by comparing it with the methods of other apologists.[1] Nevertheless, Schaeffer's writings disclose an underlying strategy for justifying his conclusions. "We approach an area methodically when we study it according to a plan."[2] Undoubtedly Schaeffer had in mind a plan. Like detectives we must seek to uncover it by means of a critical investigation.

Gordon R. Lewis is Professor of Systematic Theology and Philosophy of Religion at Denver Conservative Baptist Seminary in Denver, Colorado. He holds the M.Div. from Faith Theological Seminary and the M.A. and Ph.D. from Syracuse University. His published works include Testing Christianity's Truth Claims *and* Integrative Theology *(with Bruce A. Demarest).*

PREREQUISITES FOR CRITICAL INTERPRETATION

The place to begin, however, is not with Schaeffer but with some acceptable ground rules for launching an investigation.

Interpretive differences are frequently faced by people familiar with the history of biblical hermeneutics. Since alternative and even contradictory interpretations can be attributed to a passage, any proposed interpretation needs to be supported by critical considerations. By critical interpretations I mean those that are justified by interaction with influential alternative interpretations as to their consistency, comprehensiveness, and viability in accounting for the lines of relevant data (such as the author's date, sources, purpose, historical and cultural context, and explicit and implied assertions documented from the author's relevant writings in their contexts).[3]

I suggest that critically responsible interpretations of Francis Schaeffer's apologetic method interact with influential alternatives, achieve some measure of objectivity by appeals to sound criteria of truth, and test the coherence of the proposed interpretation's account of such relevant lines of data as the dates of his primary works, his sources, his purpose, the historical and cultural context, and his documented assertions.

In addition, we must see what the options are in regard to the apologetical method. Reymond and many others hold that there are only two methods of justifying truth claims—presuppositional and evidential. We need to consider whether those are our only two options in defending our religious beliefs philosophically.

Three Methods of Reasoning in General

Three methods of reasoning to justify the truth of a conclusion are listed in a recent treatment of methodology: inductive, deductive, and abductive (variously called retroductive, hypothetical, verificational, or critical).[4] Although there are other methods of reasoning, for purposes of this essay we consider only these three.[5] Figure 3.1 offers a means of comparing these in visual form.

1. The *inductive* method starts with an "objective" mind observing specific phenomena and infers general conclusions with degrees of probability.[6]

2. The *deductive* method starts with assumed premises

(presuppositions), and reasons to conclusions with the possibility of syllogistic certainty *if* the premises are true.

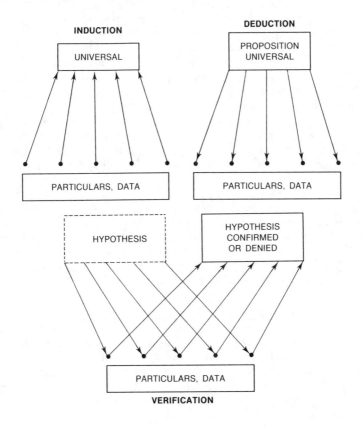

Figure 3.1. Three Methods of Justifying Beliefs

3. The *verificational*, or scientific, method addresses a problem by starting with tentative hypotheses from any type of experience (presupposition, observation, creative intuitions, imagination, etc.). Then the verificational method subjects these hypotheses to testing and confirmation or dis-confirmation by the coherence of their account with the relevant lines of data.

The verificational method is sometimes considered a type

of inductive reasoning because it tests hypotheses by their conformity to empirical data. But it could also be considered a type of deductive method because it starts with hypotheses, which are sometimes confused with presuppositions. However, verificational reasoning is a third method, having a distinctly different logical starting point. As C. S. Pierce distinguished abduction from induction and deduction, it is a mode of probable inference "whereby hypotheses are generated, moving from a particular case to a possible explanation of the case."[7] N. R. Hanson spoke of retroduction as "the process of starting from anomalous facts and ending with explanatory hypotheses."[8] John Warwick Montgomery finds that "scientific theories are conceptual Gestalts, built up retroductively through imaginative attempts to render phenomena intelligible."[9]

The order of the steps in the verificational method also distinguishes it from the other methods. Copi suggests these steps in order: sharpening the problem, proposing preliminary hypotheses, collecting additional facts, formulating a hypothesis that should explain all the facts encountered, deducing further consequences, testing the consequences and applying the confirmed hypothesis for practical purposes.[10]

Three Methods of Apologetic Argument

Defenders of Christian truth claims may use all three types of inference (inductive, deductive, abductive), but one becomes distinctive of each apologetic method. Furthermore, each distinct apologetic method can be further delineated by reference to some common elements. The major elements in an apologetic method include:

(1) The Logical Starting Point
(2) Common Ground
(3) Criteria of Truth
(4) The Role of Reason
(5) The Basis of Faith

Using these five points for comparison and contrast, we can more clearly present and differentiate the three primary options in Christian apologetics. A brief overview of these three approaches to justifying Christian beliefs will aid critical interpretation and evaluation of Francis Schaeffer's writings.

First, there is the method of an *evidentialist*, or *inductivist*, using the traditional theistic arguments and Christian evidences. Consider in brief outline the perspective of one of the more consistent inductive apologists, J. Oliver Buswell, Jr.

(1) An inductivist thinks that all knowledge begins with sense perception and that the logical starting point in any justification of truth claims is sense data.

(2) Both Christians and non-Christians have common ground in the same or similar sense data and ability to approach it with an open mind (*tabula rasa*) or objectivity.

(3) The final criterion by which all truth claims are tested is their correspondence with relevant observations.

(4) Human reason is not only capable of interpreting presuppositions and making deductions from them, but is also responsible for critically testing truth claims by the observable evidence and causal inference.

(5) Belief requires, not total confirmation, but high probability.[11]

Second, compare the method of a *presuppositionalist* as expressed in the apologetic of Cornelius Van Til.

(1) The logical starting point is not sense data, but the ultimate assumption that gives meaning to all else, the God revealed in inspired Scripture as understood in the unrevised Westminster Confession.

(2) There is no common ground in principle between non-Christians and Christians, although in fact both may share the same sensory data and linguistic and logical tools.

(3) No criteria of truth may function either to confirm or disconfirm the presupposition that the God of the Bible exists.

(4) The appropriate role of reason is interpretive of Scripture and deductive from Scripture. Any attempts critically to test claims for the truth of theism or the Bible place apostate human reason above God's revelation.

(5) The basis of faith is not in any amount of sensory evidence nor in coherent accounts of it, but the self-authentication of the assumption.[12]

Finally, compare and contrast a third proposal for justifying knowledge of Christianity's truth, the *verificational* method of Edward John Carnell.

(1) The logical starting point for a verificationalist is not the data of sensory experience, nor an assumption beyond investigation, but a hypothesis (the existence of the God of the Bible) to be tested and confirmed or disconfirmed.

(2) Although non-Christians may have contradictory metaphysical presuppositions, they have both sensory and personal (internal, existential) experiences in common. These elements of common ground can be used to derive agreement on criteria of truth.

(3) The criteria by which all proposals for knowledge and belief are examined include logical non-contradiction, factual adequacy (conformity to external or sensory data of human experience), and existential viability (conformity to the internal data of human experience).

(4) Reason, though affected by the Fall, is aided at least by common grace: and non-Christians as well as Christians are responsible critically to distinguish true from false prophets claiming to speak for God. Reason also has important interpretive and applicational functions.

(5) Although the object of faith is unseen (God, who is spirit), the basis of faith is observable and confirmable. The confirmed hypothesis leads away from idols to the living God.[13]

The preceding methodological comparison may seem theoretical, but had Schaeffer outlined his method like this, he would have spared his readers much misunderstanding. Since he did not, Schaeffer's writings have been interpreted as representing each of these three apologetic methods. Unless all three are considered, a conclusion concerning his method is critically insufficient.

Historical, Cultural, and Literary Givens

A critical interpretation must also take account of the relevant background. To determine which of the three methods best fits the thought of Francis Schaeffer, a critical interpretation gathers the givens in the situation: his most relevant writings, their dates, their purposes, the audience he targeted, his sources, and the content he taught.

Which of Schaeffer's writings provide the primary data concerning his apologetic method? Schaeffer himself identifies them. Although published second, he says, "*The God Who Is There* was written first and lays the groundwork, establishes the terminology, and sets out the basic thesis." *Escape From Reason* "works out this principle particularly in the philosophical area of Nature and Grace." *He Is There and He Is Not Silent* "deals with one of the most fundamental of all questions: how we know and how we know we know" (HIT: ix). In Schaeffer's mind the teaching of the three books makes "a unified base" (HIT: ix). He says these three books "constitute a conscious unity" from which "all the other books have come" and "on which they depend" (HIT: x).

In what cultural milieu were these three books written? The first two were published in 1968 and the last in 1972. All three were worked out of dialogues with questioning people during the turbulence of the controversial Vietnam War and the countercultural movement. The impact of anti-establishment attitudes and a popular existentialism upon the youth were of primary concern to Schaeffer. Other contributing influences on those he sought to help in Europe came from Marxism, philosophical analysis, eastern mysticism, neo-orthodoxy, dead orthodoxy, inauthentic fundamentalism, and anti-intellectual evangelicalism.

What were Schaeffer's primary purposes? He sought to communicate a strong, clear, and honest Christian message and to demonstrate its cultural and personal relevance and reality.[14] He sought to confirm the truth of the Christian message and to demonstrate its relevance for life lived to its fullest.

Whom did he intend to reach? To whom did he direct his writings? The target for Schaeffer's ministry was not professional scholars, logicians, or philosophers, but laypeople in general and young people in particular. This popular purpose is important for understanding the meanings of certain key terms.

Did Schaeffer expect his apologetics only to strengthen Christians? He sought to communicate Christianity's truth and relevance to both Christians and non-Christians. He wasted no time on whether apologetics is only for believers; both the doubting Christian and the non-Christian need honest answers to honest questions about the truth of the faith. The Holy Spirit could use His sword, the truth of the Word of God, with pre-Christians as well as Christians.

Schaeffer's purpose, then, was *both* evangelistic (to non-Christians) *and* pastoral (to Christian questioners). Critical interpretations will take into account Schaeffer's vocation. He was not a specialist in logic, writing for scholarly journals, but a general practitioner in pre-evangelism, evangelism, and rehabilitation of people in the Christian church.

An interviewer asked him, "You have been described in many ways. How do you view yourself, as a theologian, a philosopher, or a cultural historian?" Schaeffer replied,

My interest is evangelism. To evangelize in the twentieth century, one has to operate across the whole spectrum of disciplines and have answers for the questions. I think we often sell Christianity short, not putting forth the richness we have in Christ for the total culture and the total intellectual life. Evangelism, then, is two things: first of all, giving honest answers to honest questions to get the blocks out of the way so that people will listen to the Gospel as a viable alternative and then secondly, showing them what Christianity means across the whole spectrum of life.[15]

However, Schaeffer's pre-evangelistic and evangelistic ministry in its most popular form affirmed that the gospel *is true*. Was a method of justifying that claim unimportant to this busy pastor-evangelist? Far from it. In 1968 he wrote that the change to a nonrational view of "the way we come to knowledge and truth is the most crucial problem, as I understand it, facing Christianity today" (GWIT: 13). The choice for Christians who speak the truth popularly is not between *a* method and *no* method. Some kind of plan is generally present. The only real choice is between using *sound* and *unsound ways* of reasoning on behalf of their faith.

In discussions of methods for testing the very foundations of our Christian faith, it is not *God* who is on trial. Nor is it Schaeffer who is in court in this chapter. In the dock is Schaeffer's apologetic method and that of his interpreters. Not only to help others, but to maintain our own inner integrity in life-shaking crises, we need to have cogent reasons for turning in repentance from all other gurus and being disciples of the Lord Jesus Christ alone.

From which sources did Francis Schaeffer draw? We have little evidence. Unfortunately, his addresses that became books did not document his sources with footnotes. Yet we may infer that he knew of Van Til's presuppositionalism from student days at Westminster (see ch. 2). From student days at Faith Theological Seminary he was aware of Allan A. MacRae's emphasis on testing critical theories by the biblical and historical evidence. Presumably he read such writers as C. S. Lewis, Elton Trueblood, Edward John Carnell, and others. As to which sources may have been most influential, we can better infer when his method has been more thoroughly researched and presented.

With some of the historical and cultural data to be explained before us, we return to the critical question: "Which hypothesis without contradiction accounts for the content of his relevant writings in their purposes and cultural milieux with the fewest difficulties?"

SCHAEFFER'S METHOD CRITICALLY INTERPRETED

Schaeffer's Own Description of His Method

The first step toward resolving this question is to notice that Schaeffer explicitly uses the term "verification" for his approach. People who have despaired of a unified philosophy of life, Schaeffer says, can regain rationality "on the basis of what is open to *verification* and discussion" (EFR: 82). "Verification," as Schaeffer defines it in his glossary, is "The procedure required for the establishment of the truth or falsity of a statement" (GWIT: 180).

Are basic presuppositions too ultimate for verification? For Van Til presuppositions are by definition excluded from the verificational process; for Schaeffer they are not. Schaeffer's "presupposition," like Van Til's, is "A belief or theory which is assumed before the next step in logic is developed. Such a prior postulate often consciously or unconsciously affects the way a person subsequently reasons" (GWIT: 179). But influential as presuppositions are, Schaeffer invites people to act only after giving an adequate base of knowledge, or sufficient evidence (GWIT: 141). Schaeffer does not ask people to trust themselves to a God they do not have reason to believe exists.

Anyone who takes a verificational approach to apologetics faces the possibility of his assumptions being falsified. It is clear that Schaeffer faced it himself. First, in his late teens he concluded that the liberal teaching in his Presbyterian church answered nothing: "Finally, I could go on with this no longer, and I became an agnostic."[17] Second, speaking to other evangelists, he says, "Men must know that with integrity we have faced the reality of the dark path they are treading" (GWIT: 131–32). Finally, Schaeffer's advice to prospective apologists is to struggle with the questions of Christianity's truth themselves. "We must have faced the question, 'Is Christianity true?' for ourselves" (GWIT: 128). (It is questionable whether, if he held Van Tilian presuppositions, Schaeffer could have seriously addressed that question—the fundamental question of apologetics—whether Christianity is true or false.)

Commenting on Luke's prologue (1:1-4), Schaeffer says, "What is open to *verification* can also be communicated verbally in writing" (GWIT: 141). The teaching of Scripture touches, not only on "religious truth," but also on "the cosmos and history which are open to verification" (GWIT: 108). Schaeffer says, "I want to suggest that scientific proof, philosophical proof and religious proof follow the same rules." Then he mentions criteria of truth by which to test proposed answers, that is, hypotheses (GWIT: 109).

Schaeffer's frequent use of explicitly verificational terminology seems rather conclusive in itself. However, it may be objected that perhaps Schaeffer used verificational terminology loosely for popular purposes without genuinely using its method. That possibility must be taken seriously, for in nontechnical writing, terminology may not give the same signals as it would in technical writing. So we need to consider more substantive matters. Did he hold a verificational stance on the five elements of an apologetic method we have distinguished: starting point, common ground, criteria of truth, role of reason, and basis of faith?

What Is Schaeffer's Logical Starting Point?

Although we must start with ourselves, Schaeffer explains that "when the Bible says that man is created in the image of a personal God, it gives us a starting point." More precisely, "it tells him the adequate reference point, the infinite personal God" (EFR: 87).

Schaeffer's most characteristic logical starting point is the existence of the "infinite and personal" God of the Bible. His emphasis distinguishes his "presupposition" from alternative assumptions in the East and the West. "The gods of the East are infinite by definition—the definition being 'god is all that is'. This is the pan-everything-ism god. The gods of the West, on the other hand, have tended to be personal but limited: such were the gods of the Greeks, Romans and Germans. But the God of the Bible, Old and New Testaments alike, is the infinite-personal God" (GWIT: 94).

Schaeffer's most complete logical starting point, when the entire Christian system is in question, includes trinitarianism with loving communication among the three persons. "If one begins to consider the Christian system as a total system, one must being with the infinite-personal *triune* God who is there, and who was communicating and loving before anything else was" (GWIT: 104).

If the questions at issue are more limited, his logical starting point may be more limited. "If one begins to consider how sinful man can return to fellowship with God, one must begin with Christ, His person and work" (GWIT: 104). On another occasion the starting point is the space-time fall of humanity from its original moral state. "But if one begins to consider the differences between Christianity and rationalistic philosophy's answers, one must begin with understanding that man and history are now abnormal" (GWIT: 104). Again, Schaeffer may sum it all up as "the propositional communication from the personal God before us" (GWIT: 109).

So the content of Schaeffer's logical starting point may be the infinite God, the personal God, the triune God, the propositional revelation in Scripture, the fallenness of humanity, or Jesus Christ the God-man, Savior and risen Lord.

Schaeffer is not the only person to start with presuppositions, for everyone has basic ways of looking at life or grids through which to see the world (HSWTL: 19). One of Schaeffer's "general principles to guide communication with twentieth-century man" observes that "every person we speak to, whether shop girl or university student, has a set of presuppositions, whether they have analyzed them or not" (GWIT: 121). He adds, "It does not seem to me that presuppositional apologetics should be seen as ending conversation with the men about us" (GWIT: 126).

"Presuppositions" are people's "answers" that "should be chosen after a careful consideration of what world view is true" (HSWTL: 20). So Schaeffer can ask, "Does the Bible's answer or does John Cage's chance music speak of what exists?" (GWIT: 109). Naturalists accept "with an implicit faith the presupposition of the uniformity of natural causes in a closed system" (GWIT: 111).

However, volitional commitment to a presupposition does not make it true. Because in his view presuppositions can be verified and shown to be true or false, Schaeffer would communicate better if he called presuppositions "hypotheses." He helpfully uses "presupposition" primarily to detect the most basic tenets of belief systems and to address those ultimate issues. But he does not use the term in the way Van Til does as meaning beliefs *too ultimate to be verified*. Van Til would not ask, as Schaeffer does, "Is the biblical position intellectually possible? Is it possible to have intellectual integrity while holding to the position of verbalized, propositional revelation?" (HIT: 62).

When Schaeffer says, "More than ever before, a presuppositional apologetic is imperative," (GWIT: 15) he does not imply that presuppositions are beyond examination. He means that it is imperative to detect presuppositions, especially epistemological assumptions that make any truth about reality impossible, and by appealing to common ground help people see that truth is possible with intellectual integrity.

What Is Schaeffer's View of Common Ground With Non-Christians?

In respect to God's infinity we are separated from his being, but with respect to God's personality "we are made in the image of God" (EFR: 83). Hence, "our basic relationship is upward" (EFR: 86), and we can begin with ourselves, not as infinite, but as "personal" (EFR: 88). The Fall does not mean that we cease to bear humanness or God's image. In our fallen state we have in common with non-Christian human beings the qualities of love, beauty, humanness or mannishness, rationality, longing for significance, fear of nonbeing, and scientific data (EFR: 88–90).

Humanness, as Schaeffer analyzes it, includes rationality (inductive and deductive), the sense data of empiricists, and internal, existential data such as the overwhelming importance of love (GWIT: 97). In his glossary Schaeffer defines the "mannishness of man" as "Those aspects of man, such as significance, love, rationality and fear of non-being, which mark him off from animals and machines and give evidence of his being created in the image of a personal God" (GWIT: 178). Because a fallen person remains in the image of God, "whatever he may say about himself, . . . he cannot go on living in meaninglessness" (GWIT: 58). He can feel the tension between the real world and his assumptions; he can feel dead. For man in revolt is purposeless and morally dead (GWIT: 130).

These data are not "neutral," Schaeffer explains, because "regardless of a man's system, he has to live in God's world" (GWIT: 126). Metaphysically all non-Christians also depend on God, as Van Til emphasizes. But Schaeffer does not assume that the epistemological order is the same as the metaphysical order.

Non-Christians share with Christians not only some moral

absolutes but also, in universal fallenness, both unbased guilt feelings and real guilt in a moral framework under the divine Judge (GWIT: 102). But merely quantitative or psychological considerations cannot explain the distinctions humans draw between right and wrong, justice and injustice. Moral problems occur among all people universally and constitute data to which to appeal in showing the adequacy of the Christian hypothesis of the Fall (GWIT: 102, 104, 124). Moral standards are absolute (universal and necessary) because they rest in God's character; that is why breaking them makes man culpable (GWIT: 105).

Non-Christians also share some cognitive absolutes in the divine image. Humans as such are rational, that is, have the "power to reason consistently" (GWIT: 179). The law of non-contradiction is not from Aristotle, but part of our being created in the image of God (If you have A, it is not non-A).*

Because God created us in His image, God is not in an absolutely different order. We are finite while God is infinite, but we can understand revelation from God, though only in part. Similarly, in human conversations with people of different backgrounds, we have true communication, but it is never exhaustive (GWIT: 97). Schaeffer considers the content of the image of God to have provided what modern theology lacks—a basis for verifiable facts and knowing not only the phenomenal world, but also the content of words with referents above the line of despair, the noumenal world (GWIT: 98–99).

Schaeffer's common ground personally, ethically, factually, and logically is shared by unbelievers even though they deny the adequate explanatory hypothesis. "In my earlier books and in the previous chapters of this book [*He Is There and He Is Not Silent*] we have considered whether this presupposition is in fact acceptable, or even reasonable, not upon the basis of the Christian faith, but upon the basis of what we know concerning man and the universe as it is" (HIT: 65).

Schaeffer's understanding and use of elements of common ground as a point of contact with unbelievers fits most coherently with a verificational method. Unlike the inductive approach, he majors on inner, existential values as well as outer empirical data. And unlike the presuppositional approach,

---

*Schaeffer would have done well to define the law of non-contradiction more carefully. His popular purposes actually led him to inaccuracy, since not every "opposite" is a contradictory (GWIT: 14).

Schaeffer's method discovers and appeals to factual and personal data in confirmation of his hypothesis.

What Are Schaeffer's Criteria of Truth?

We may begin this point of discussion by observing that Schaeffer holds that "both a clear comprehension of the importance of truth, and a clear practice of it, even when it is costly to do so, is imperative if our witness and our evangelism are to be significant in our own generation and in the flow of history" (GWIT: 169). For a theory to be considered true, Schaeffer says, it must (1) "be non-contradictory" and (2) "give an answer to the phenomenon in question." Furthermore, (3) "We must be able to live consistently with our theory" (GWIT: 109).

Although Schaeffer spoke of the first two as one step in "proof" and suggested they serve best together, he said they are as distinct as logical relations and factual relations.

Illustrating his application of these criteria from the nature of man, Schaeffer tests other possible answers and finds these hypotheses inconsistent or inadequate to account for all types of data. Christianity, in contrast, "constitutes a non-self-contradictory answer that does explain the phenomena and which can be lived with, both in life and in scholarly pursuits" (GWIT: 111). Again, "The Christian system is consistent as no other system that has ever been. It is beautiful beyond words, because it has that quality that no other system has—you begin at the beginning and you can go to the end. . . . And every part and portion of the system can be related back to the beginning" (GWIT: 156).

Schaeffer challenges all comers to show whose presuppositions fit the facts of what is (HIT: 65). Making it even more explicit, he asks, "Which of these two sets of presuppositions really and empirically meets the facts as we look about us in the world?" (HIT: 66). In other terms, "Christianity is not only true to the dogmas or to what God has said in the Bible, but it is also true to what is there" (HIT: 17).

In regard to living consistently with a view, Schaeffer asks whether people believe in the objective value of personal existence. Love comes face to face with the decision to push or not to push the button that destroys a person or the race. If there is no lasting meaning to the race, then why not push the button? There is no reason to keep it alive, struggling in pain.

However, if there is real meaning of personality, it is reasonable to have love and compassion, a real reason to keep humanity alive (GWIT: 90).

Schaeffer's emphasis on viability has been taken to be "a pragmatic element in evangelical apologetics."[18] Norman Geisler's only reference to Schaeffer in his *Christian Apologetics* might leave his readers with the idea that even with the positive contributions of pragmatism listed, Schaeffer's apologetic is subject to the serious criticisms also listed against the pragmatic theory of truth. However, not one of Geisler's excellent criticisms of the pragmatic criterion of truth has any force against Schaeffer's coherence criterion, which incorporates factual and existential data in a coherent whole.

Schaeffer's apologetic is far from pragmatic. It begins with more than methodological hypothesis; it begins with a content-full, Christian hypothesis, the God of the Bible. It is no undefined, whatever-works element in evangelical apologetics. Schaeffer's viability criterion is inseparable from the logical and factual criteria. It includes existential data, but that does not make it pragmatic.

Geisler's criticisms of Carnell's "combinationalism" also try to reduce the threefold test of truth to pragmatism, to the question of which system "works."[19] However, analogies prove nothing, and so Geisler's "leaky bucket" analogy proves nothing against "combinationalism." Furthermore, as an illustration the analogy lacks relevance. No apologetic method requires the omniscience of the apologist. Geisler admits that truth is non-contradictory, that empirical data are necessary, and that the truth makes a difference in life.

The necessary but insufficient contributions of logic, fact, and viability as criteria of truth can be better illustrated. A more relevant analogy likens them to checks and balances among the legislative, executive, and administrative branches of government. In our finite, fallen world of Watergates, political spokesmen need as many checks and balances on them as possible. Just as surely in a fallen world (with Jim Jones–type cult leaders speaking for God), our method for discovering the truth needs as many check and balances as possible.

The evidence cited above from Schaeffer's writings indicates that his test of truth is more probably the test of a verificational method than an inductive, deductive, or pragmatic method.

What Is the Role of Reason for Schaeffer?

Rationalism is dismissed as involving autonomous man at the center of the universe seeking to be independent of anything else, "to build a cantilever bridge out from himself across an infinite gorge" (EFR: 88). Is that not a popular description of the role of reason in the inductive reasoning of traditional apologetics and evidences? Schaeffer's approach also dismisses "blind authority" (EFR: 84). Is that not a popular description of the initial acceptance of the basic presupposition of presuppositionalists?

Reason defines terms to avoid exploitation of their ambiguities in a semantic mysticism (GWIT: 179; "Semantics," 80). Words need to be defined before they can be used in communication (GWIT: 146).

Reason precedes faith, defining what, how, and why we are expected to believe. "You cannot have a personal relationship with something unknown. That something must be understood and defined" (GWIT: 144). "Then having understood who it is with whom I am to have a personal relationship and how I may have it, comes the actual step of entering into that relationship" (GWIT: 144). "The invitation to act comes only after an adequate base of knowledge has been given" (GWIT: 141).

The biblical signs were evidences in space and time to the truth of the prophets and apostles' claims to have transcendent knowledge. The evidence they gave was "good and sufficient" that Jesus was the Messiah prophesied in the Old Testament (GWIT: 141). "We are not asked to believe until we have faced the question as to whether this is true on the basis of the space-time evidence" (GWIT: 141). "Rationality is needed to open the door to a vital relationship to God" (GWIT: 112). Rationality involves recognizing that an affirmation and its denial cannot both be true. The way out of the irrationality of the times is to reinstate the law of antithesis, by which Schaeffer means non-contradiction.[20]

So for Schaeffer, reason has a critical responsibility in testing, examining, proving, seeing whether what is claimed is true. It also has interpretive and defining functions, once the cognitive revelation has been confirmed.

The "necessity" that Schaeffer claims characterizes his case for Christianity is not one of technical, logical necessity, but a descriptive necessity and certainty that arises in the absence of any other coherent, viable options. Having tested the live options of which he is aware, he has found the one that coherently fits the facts and "There is no other way" (HIT: 71). Schaeffer may be faulted for not testing more alternatives, but in the total context of his thought it is more probable that he speaks of a descriptive "necessity" rather than a technical, deductive conclusiveness.

Reason, for Schaeffer, also contributes to spirituality. "As the Christian grows spiritually he should be a man who consciously, more and more brings his thought world as well as his outward world under the norms of the Bible" (HIT: 82) In spiritual growth there develops an increasing integration of the inward and outward man under the same norms, values, and knowing (HIT: 84).

What Does Schaeffer Mean by Faith?

Clearly the object of faith is the invisible, infinite, personal God who has spoken in Scripture. Yet God is not an ineffably infinite Being, but one who communicates and acts, providing a visible basis of faith. The basis of faith is the coherent and viable biblical account supported by visible, verifiable evidences.

As a person is faced with God's promises, Christian faith means bowing twice: First, he needs to bow in the realm of being (metaphysically)—that is, to acknowledge that he is a creature before the infinite-personal Creator who is there. Second, he needs to bow in the realm of morals—that is, to acknowledge he has sinned and therefore that he has true moral guilt before the God who is there. Third, a person must hear and receive as true and relevant the message that Jesus Christ died in space-time-history on the cross, and that when He died His substitutionary work of bearing God's punishment against sin was fully accomplished and complete. Fourth, believing the cognitive truths of the gospel attested by adequate evidence, a person commits himself to the living Christ of which the gospel affirmations speak. "On the basis of God's promises in His written communication to us, the Bible, do you (or have you) cast yourself on this Christ as your personal Savior—not trusting in anything you yourself have ever done or ever will do?" (HIT: 135)

In more traditional words, faith involves knowledge (*notitia*) and assent (*assensus*) to the truth of theism, human dependence and guilt before the Creator, the provision of the crucified and risen Savior, and the commitment (*fiducia*) or trust in the living Christ as Savior and Lord. Because faith begins with knowledge it requires a reliable cognitive basis.

In view of the converging lines of evidence from Schaeffer's view of the logical starting point, common ground, criteria of truth, the role of reason and the basis of faith, I conclude with strong probability that Schaeffer's apologetic method was a nontechnical version of a verificational method. (Figure 3.2 compares the three methods of apologetics as we have summarized them.) Before that conclusion can stand, however, we need to consider the alternative interpretations of Schaeffer's method and their objections to the verificational interpretation.

ALTERNATIVE INTERPRETATIONS OF SCHAEFFER'S METHOD

Was Schaeffer a Presuppositionalist as Morris Claims?

According to the interpretive hypothesis of Thomas V. Morris in *Francis Schaeffer's Apologetics*, Schaeffer's method was presuppositionalist.[21] In the name of critical analysis, Morris does not stop to justify that classification, but proceeds "to explicate" and "analyze" Schaeffer's "presuppositional approach to theistic argumentation" (Morris: 12–13). Morris' criticism that Schaeffer has not adequately defined some of his key terms (Morris: 43) does have warrant, and no doubt contributed to Morris' classification. Knowing that Schaeffer studied under Cornelius Van Til, the father of recent presuppositionalists, and that Schaeffer called himself a presuppositionalist may have seemed sufficient to Morris, who was a graduate student in philosophy when he wrote his book on Schaeffer. However, interpreters of philosophy must not assume, but rather determine whether a former student (Aristotle, for example) uses key terms in the same way as his mentor (Plato). Were Schaeffer a technical logician majoring in methods of justifying truth claims, his calling himself a presuppositionalist might settle the question. In the case of an evangelist who calls himself a presuppositionalist, it is indispensable for a critical interpreter to determine what he means by that and how it works out in his actual practice.

Morris may also have derived comfort for his presuppositional interpretation because Schaeffer claimed "necessity" for his arguments (Morris: 31). However, Morris reads into Schaef-

3 METHODS OF APOLOGETICS / 5 POINTS OF COMPARISON	1. EVIDENTIAL (Buswell)	2. PRESUPPOSITIONAL (Van Til)	3. VERIFICATIONAL	(Carnell & Schaeffer)
1. LOGICAL STARTING POINT	Sense Data	Presupposition of the God of the Bible	Hypothesis of the God of the Bible	Hypothesis of the God of the Bible
2. COMMON GROUND	Observable Evidence	None (in Principle) Logic Sense Data Moral Law (in Practice)	Law of Noncontradiction External Sensory Data Internal Data of Justice and Love	Logic Observable Evidence Personal, Human
3. CRITERIA OF TRUTH	Correspondence of Ideas to Observations	None; Scripture Self-Authenticating	Logical Noncontradiction Factual Adequacy Existential Viability	Not Contradictory Fits the Facts Can Live by It Without Hypocrisy
4. ROLE OF REASON	Induction Interpretation Application	Deduction Interpretation Application	Verification Interpretation Application	Verification Interpretation Application
5. BASIS OF FAITH	Intellectual Probability	Assumed Biblical Authority	Intellectual Probability Psychological Certitude Moral Responsibility	The View Confirmed to Be True

Figure 3.2. Comparison of Three Methods of Apologetics

fer's popular language "ultimate philosophical necessity" (Morris: 81), but does not read out of Schaeffer a necessity "universally compelling toward the same conclusion" (Morris: 82). Schaeffer's "necessity" can be better accounted for in terms of his popular purpose as a descriptive "necessity," for lack of other hypotheses to test (as far as he was then aware).

It is not that Morris is unaware of the hypothetical method. Twice he quotes Schaeffer to the effect that he is testing presuppositions (obviously as hypotheses rather than untestable presuppositions) by whether or not they "fit the facts" (Morris: 19, 56). Furthermore, Morris cites Colin Brown's interpretation of Schaeffer in which "Schaeffer's use of 'presupposition' is understood to mean 'hypothesis.'"

> Schaeffer's approach may be compared with a set of hypotheses in science. In the first instance, a hypothesis presents an unproved theory designed to account for something hitherto not understood. A good hypothesis is one which makes sense of the observed facts and takes into account the maximum number of other observed facts.[22]

Colin Brown in turn called attention to Howard Root's suggestion of "a new type of natural theology" in which the Christian faith could be presented as a "hypothesis."

> It suggests explanations for phenomena which are otherwise inexplicable. It makes sense of what at first seemed senseless. It gives wholeness to life which is missing in other views. This is so whether we look at the universe in general or at personal experience of life. . . . it [the Bible] does provide a key which gives coherence and meaning to life as a whole.[23]

Finally, in summarizing Schaeffer's epistemological argument (or better data), Morris admits that "it seems as though he is applying a principle recognized in scientific confirmation theory for the orthodox Christian presuppositional system" (Morris: 63). Had Morris himself supplied definitions of "presupposition" and "definition" from Schaeffer's *usus loquendi*, he might have concluded that Schaeffer employed confirmation principles in relation to his theistic hypothesis.

Morris outlines a skeletal case for the truth of Christian claims, starting with rival hypotheses to be tested by relevant observations, leading to a cumulative confirmation of the one more probable and therefore true (Morris: 95–96). It is unfortunate that he did not see that Schaeffer was doing much the same thing with less technical terminology.

As a result, Morris' criticisms of Schaeffer may apply to presuppositional methods, but do not apply to the verificational or confirmational interpretation of Schaeffer presented above. A presuppositionalist may "misunderstand the process involved in hypothesis selection" (Morris: 78), but not Schaeffer. Presuppositionalists may "fail to recognize predispositions as well as presuppositions" (Morris: 83), but not the "chaplain" to the countercultural youth of the sixties. Morris admits that Schaeffer's "ministry as a whole is very nonmechanical" (Morris: 80).

Morris would have done well to have taken more time for critical interpretation before engaging in critical evaluation. Had he researched more completely what Schaeffer teaches on logical starting point, common ground, criteria of truth, role of reason, and basis of faith, his criticisms would not have missed the mark. Then he would have seen that Schaeffer had in mind an apologetic system very similar to the one he outlines. It starts with claims considered as hypotheses (Morris: 98) and then leads to cumulative confirmation and degrees of probability (Morris: 96–97).

As it is, in his entire book Morris makes no serious attempt to expound Schaeffer's views with any degree of objectivity. There was place for this in his short first chapter, entitled "The Pre-evangelistic, Presuppositional Argument." While there is some discussion of Schaeffer's starting point and rational necessity, no explication of Schaeffer's views on common ground and criteria of truth can be found, and these are serious omissions.

Schaeffer's verificational apologetic conforms to Morris' "three general conditions" to be met by an apologetic method. Morris says presuppositions must allow for the possibility of a proposed belief, there must be reason for believing it rather than a contradictory belief, and it must fit consistently with other confirmed beliefs (Morris: 110–11). Has not Schaeffer worked with the criteria of the possible in connection with the factual and the non-contradictory? Has not Schaeffer sought to show that "the Christian faith is not an isolated activity divorced from the rest of life"? Has not Schaeffer proclaimed and described the relevance of biblical truth for every realm of life (Morris: 112)? Has not Schaeffer also challenged all "the major beliefs that a man holds which are inconsistent with Christian claims" (Morris: 113)? Does Morris seriously think he has challenged "all" (Morris: 113)? I disagree with Morris' claim that he has formulated a more complete method of effectively presenting the truth of Christianity to our contemporaries in the thirteen pages of his chapter 9 (Morris: 115).

In short, the only major book on Schaeffer's apologetics has not increased the probability of the interpretive hypothesis that Schaeffer was a presuppositionalist.

Was Schaeffer an Inconsistent Presuppositionalist as Harper Claims?

Kenneth Harper faced difficulties in understanding Schaeffer's "presuppositional" position, but did not give up that interpretation. In light of Schaeffer's study under Van Til and his emphasis on "presuppositions," Schaeffer would appear to be a presuppositionalist. "However," Harper hastens to add, "it would be far too simplistic to stereotype Schaeffer as a presuppositionalist without further describing his relationship to that school."[24]

Harper then says, "Francis Schaeffer can best be described as an *inconsistent presuppositionalist*" (Harper: 138). Schaeffer "believes in common ground between Christian and non-Christian," something Van Til would deny in principle (Harper: 138), and seems to see some intellectual validity in the inductive theistic proofs (Harper: 139). Even so, Schaeffer seems "very cautious in his application of the traditional proofs for Christianity" (Harper: 139).

Schaeffer's parable of mountain climbers in the Alps destined to freeze to death, to which Harper calls attention, differentiates his faith from that of presuppositionalists. The option of dropping into the fog from the icy ledge without any knowledge of a ledge ten feet below is not what he means by faith. Rather, he hears a voice of an experienced climber from another ridge claiming to know that there is a ledge ten feet below and if they hang and drop they will be able to survive till morning. Schaeffer says, "I would not hang and drop at once, but would ask questions to try to ascertain if the man knew what he was talking about and if he was not my enemy." If the name he gave was a common one in the Swiss Alps and I was convinced by his answers to sufficient questions, I would drop (HIT: 99–100). Clearly Schaeffer requires knowledge through the fog of whom he is expected to believe and why he should believe him. Yet Kenneth Harper says, "The solution the parable offers is *not* that in which Schaeffer normally engages" (Harper: 139).

To hold that Schaeffer was an inconsistent presupposition-alist flies in the face of his insistence that the *The God Who Is There, Escape From Reason,* and *He Is There and He Is Not Silent* "represent a unified concept which was developed over a long time of experiential knowledge . . . and is now being worked out in various disciplines" (HIT: xi). As with any responsible writer, we ought to exhaust every possibility of understanding Schaeffer consistently before concluding that a person who consciously defended non-contradiction as a test of truth flatly contradicted himself.

Was Schaeffer an Inconsistent Empiricist as Reymond Claims?

Robert L. Reymond states that "because of his imprecision in definition and inarticulation of concepts, I have found his [Schaeffer's] books to be difficult to understand."[25] Already agreeing that Schaeffer could have defined terms more carefully and developed his method more systematically, I would suggest that Robert Reymond's difficulties are in even larger part due to his own failure to consider more than two ways of justifying truth claims. That failure to consider other methods of justification seems inexplicable in a book like *Justification of Knowledge,* devoted as it is to methodologies.

So in spite of the difficulties, Reymond places Schaeffer and Carnell in the traditional, evidential category along with such diverse writers as Aquinas, Warfield, Buswell, Montgomery, Pinnock, and McDowell. The section of his book similarly classifying Carnell shows a lack of critical interaction with Carnell's sustained rejection of an inductive or empirical approach.

"But my main criticism," writes Reymond,

> is the (uncritical?) dialectic in Schaeffer which calls for both what occasionally really does appear to be a presuppositional methodology (GWIT: 93) and also a test for truth devised by and acceptable to apostate man (GWIT: 109) rather than a self-authenticating test for truth which Scripture claims itself to be (Ps. 119:142, 151; Dan. 10:21; John 16:13; 17:17; II Tim. 2:15) and which the Westminster Standards confess. I detect real tension in Schaeffer's thought at this point (Reymond: 147).

Yes, the Scriptures assert their own truth, but the passages listed do not address the issue of how Paul, for example, would assure Athenian pagans that what *he* taught is true. The focus of this chapter is apologetic methods for supporting claims about God and Scripture. Apologists for the Bible are on trial, not the Bible per se. The Westminster Confession has been affirmed and adhered to by apologists of all three methods (Buswell, Van Til, and Carnell).

To regard Schaeffer as an inconsistent empiricist fits no better than the classification of Schaeffer as an inconsistent presuppositionalist with the fact that he put his account together coherently. No contradiction arises on a verificational interpretation of Schaeffer's thinking. His criteria of truth come, not from apostate man, but from the God who is there, who is consistent, and who created the existential givens of human experience. So both "apostates" and Christians have something in common—they remain human and remain in God's image in God's world. And the Scriptures continue to challenge humans (of both types) to examine, try, test, prove, and hold fast only what is true and good. Although people are metaphysically dependent on God for everything, it does not follow that knowledge of any truth is impossible until they affirm the existence of God.

Like Van Til, Reymond repeatedly charges that the methodology of all these people makes concessions to "apostate man." "Furthermore, it implies that men, apart from Christ, have by their own autonomous *pou sto* justified their claimed privilege to judge any and all other truth claims" (Reymond: 117). Does Schaeffer, by inviting people who have despaired of meaning to evaluate his claims for Christ, encourage the pre-Christian to operate from an apostate *pou sto*? (Reymond: 141).

Reymond's charge that Schaeffer does encourage this fails to consider that, in Schaeffer's thought, although the non-Christian is fallen he remains in the divine image of his Creator and sustainer. Nor has Reymond taken adequate account of common grace and the fact that Scripture uses the law of non-contradiction. Until the claim that the laws of logic come from the Creator and not apostate man is answered, the repetition of the charge of "apostasy" will fall on deaf ears. The Scripture also appeals to visible "signs" and existential fruit to support the truth of revelation claims of both prophets and apostles.[26]

The verificational method in apologetics has existed explicitly at least since Elton Trueblood's *The Knowledge of God* (1939), his later *Philosophy of Religion* (1957), E. J. Carnell's *Introduction to Apologetics* (1948), and my *Testing Christianity's Truth Claims* (1976). It may also be found in Colin Chapman's *Christianity on Trial*, Os Guinness' *The Dust of Death*, and Colin Brown's brief proposals in *Philosophy and Christianity*. Unfortunately, Francis Schaeffer has not documented his sources, but it is inconceivable that he was unaware of some of the earlier writings of these verificationalists.

The alternative interpretations of Schaeffer's apologetic method are inconsistent and less adequate than the verificational interpretation. We turn then from interpretation of Schaeffer's method to evaluation of his verificational method.

SCHAEFFER'S METHOD CRITICALLY EVALUATED

Geehan's Assessment of Schaeffer's Method

E. R. Geehan, a presuppositionalist, has more objectively interpreted Schaeffer's apologetic method, calling it "presuppositional" (in quotes only), and showing how his verificational principle challenges both rationalism (humanism) and Christianity to account for the external world and the mannishness (personalness) of man.

Rationalism, in assuming the uniformity of nature, fails to account for nature's order and reduces humans to machines. In contrast, Geehan says that Schaeffer shows how the Christian hypothesis of the infinite God can explain the origin of the cosmos, and starting with a personal God can explain the existence of persons.[27] Geehan clearly recognizes that Schaeffer's case for the infinite, personal God is not another inductive "theistic proof" (Geehan: 14).

Clearly E. R. Geehan's ability as a Van Tilian presuppositionalist to discover Schaeffer's verificational approach shows that the interpretive problems of others (Reymond and Harper) were not all the fault of Schaeffer's lack of technical definitions and popular language. Since Geehan's objective criticisms are directed to the apologetic method Schaeffer used, they merit more careful attention. After summarizing Schaeffer's argument, Geehan asks, "Is this argument sound?" Then he raises a number of issues. Here I respond only to those most directly related to apologetic method.

Geehan's first questions is

> Dr. Schaeffer, if a non-Christian agreed with your argument as it develops in *a-d*, *would it be logically necessary* for him to agree with your assessment of Christianity as found in *e*?

No, Schaeffer's conclusion is not justified by a technically necessary logical implication, but by a highly probable practical necessity, given the alleged lack of other hypotheses to test and the improbabilities of the non-Christian options. Evangelist Schaeffer presents his conclusion as necessary descriptively or existentially. A more precisely worded verificationalist like Trueblood or Carnell would state the point in terms of probabilities. Had Schaeffer spoken of the degrees of probability or defined "necessity," he would have communicated the nature of his reasoning more clearly.

Second,

> Dr. Schaeffer, . . . you adopt certain criteria of proof for truth. Do you understand these criteria to be infallible guides to what is, with absolute certainty? (Geehan: 17)

The inspired Bible alone provides certainly true assertions. The best that apologists for the Bible by the scientific (or any other) method can achieve, when applied to entire world views, is corroboration or plausibility "beyond reasonable doubt." Evidence may have been destroyed or have limited availability; researchers have finite amounts of time and limited abilities and may be unaware of all the possible hypotheses or presuppositions to test. But a highly probable case for the safety of a bridge may lead to complete psychological confidence in driving over it. Psychological certitude and moral conviction may result from conclusions based on high probability from converging lines of evidence.

Geehan rightly thinks that adherents of other revelation-dependent religions (e.g., Islam) could use the same criteria and find their claims consistent and adequate to the facts. Indeed they do. Justifying our religious truth claims in a pluralistic world calls for more than getting agreement on the criteria. Testing live options by them may demand long hours of research and dialogue. But if the Christian hypothesis is true to what is there, contradictory assumptions will fail at one or the other of these points. Not all proposals are equally informed, consistent, and relevant. The givens of logic, fact, and value are not wax noses of infinite pliability. Bring on the hypotheses from any source: alleged revelation, creative imagination, etc. Then the challenge begins.

The verificational approach is not advocated as easy. Because Schaeffer has worked through these issues for years, his brief reports make it sound simple. Usually pre-evangelists will not find it quick and easy to show that their explanatory hypothesis provides a more coherent and viable account with fewer difficulties than contradictory hypotheses.

Third,

> Dr. Schaeffer, you use biblical doctrines to answer your apologetic questions, yet you nowhere mention that these doctrines (creation, the sovereignty of God, the Fall and responsibility of man, the Trinity, the deity and humanity of Christ, the "personality" and "rationality" of God) are conceptually elusive, having long histories as recalcitrant puzzles within Christian theology. I hope this situation will be remedied in the future. (Geehan: 17)

Geehan also asks how "mystery" fits in with rationally and scientifically sound explanations.

Although fallen people cannot create knowledge of the infinite God, Schaeffer has argued for the possibility that fallen man who remains in some respects in the image of God can receive cognitive truth in part. "So God can speak and tell us about Himself–not exhaustively, but truly" (EFR: 83). Repeatedly Schaeffer has emphasized that no one can fully comprehend God or God's revealed truth. For him the mysterious is the incomprehensible, but not the illogical, the unreal, or the irrelevant.

If Geehan wants a concept of "mystery" that uses only analogies to render the God of revelation unknowable, then I would join Schaeffer in differing on that point. So would Robert Reymond, who follows Van Til in large part, but effectively answers passages considered to deny some univocal understanding and answers Van Til's analogical knowledge to the exclusion of a single point of univocal truth held by God and man. Even an analogy has a univocal point (Reymond: 98–104).

Again, if Geehan wants "mystery" to allow for paradoxes and contradictions, I would join Schaeffer in questioning his basis for that hypothesis. And we would concur with Reymond's further criticism of Van Til's acceptance of paradoxes or contradictions in divine revelation. Of course, mistaken interpretations of two passages may contradict, but proper interpretations will not.

To affirm otherwise, that is, to affirm that two scriptural statements that relate to the same theological question, when *properly* interpreted, can be paradoxical, that is, contradictory to the human existent, and true for human reason is to make Christianity and the Bible upon which it is based irrational and strikes at the nature of the eternal Logos who speaks through its content (Reymond: 104).

Neither the Father nor Christ nor the Holy Spirit can lie or contradict themselves. Furthermore, if truth may *appear* irresolvably contradictory, the detection of *real* falsehood is impossible. I have yet to hear what criterion can distinguish a profoundly contradictory mystery from a superficially contradictory muddle.

Geehan's request that Schaeffer inform his people that the doctrines he uses have "conceptually elusive" histories and are "recalcitrant puzzles" within Christian theology, seems inappropriate in view of Schaeffer's popular purpose, for one thing. What evangelist may be expected to lose his audience with intellectual puzzles? For another thing, the question may reflect more upon Geehan's lack of a method for decision making in theology, than upon Schaeffer. All sorts of views that someone has called Christian have been held in the history of thought. One of the values of the verificational method is that as history provides multiple hypotheses, we have criteria by which to evaluate and decide on complex and involved doctrinal issues. Difficult and time-consuming as that may be, we find some to be non-contradictory, adequate, and viable, and others to be incoherent, less adequate explanatory hypotheses, or not as viable.[28]

Geehan's fourth question is

Dr. Schaeffer, after reading all your works I am still very much in the dark about your own personal synthesis of theology and apologetics. I do not understand how you view the relationship between the two. Where does the regenerating work of the Holy Spirit fit into your apologetic method? In what sense is this divine work *necessary?* Of what importance to apologetics is the doctrine of the Fall? How is fallen man different from *finite* man, noetically speaking? How does the doctrine of election fit into a *thoroughly rational apologetic* for the Christian faith? (Geehan: 17).

Again Schaeffer might respond that these are important questions for those involved with methodology as a science, but he is concerned to present a method in evangelistic ministry. Nevertheless, verificationalists have answers to suggest. The "most thoroughly rational" verificational apologetic will confirm hypotheses concerning the God disclosed in the Jesus of history and the teaching of Scripture on the basis of many converging lines of data as beyond reasonable doubt. Convincing as the confirmation may be, the unregenerate may regard it a stumbling block or call it foolishness. But in disbelieving the gospel they add to themselves further judgment, because it is in fact wisdom from above. Whenever the message gains credibility with a non-Christian, it is because the Holy Spirit has been opening the depraved mind and heart through common grace and preliminary illumination and witness to the truth of special revelation.

What is the difference between the saved and the lost noetically? The unregenerate may not be unintelligent. They may read Hebrew and Greek and write scholarly commentaries on the Bible. By common grace they may also follow the reasoning of a standard research method. They may be predisposed to find flaws in the argument because of their critical method or pride. They may not want to admit dependence on God, accountability to God, or guilt before God. By nature the unregenerate "do not accept the things that come from the Spirit of God" (1 Cor. 2:14).

The great difference of the regenerate is a Spirit-enabled *receptivity* to these Spirit-revealed truths. Truth—non-contradictory, factual, and viable truth, not wishful thinking—is the content to which the Holy Spirit witnesses. The Holy Spirit alone can regenerate, but he has chosen not to regenerate alone. He has sovereignly chosen to use human instruments presenting truth. He uses apologists as well as preachers, pre-evangelists as well as teachers. Yet the best of methods available by common grace are only a means the Spirit may or may not be pleased to use to help a person along the way to new life in Christ.

But as necessary as argument for truth about the real world may be, it is not sufficient in itself to change human nature. Since the Holy Spirit has chosen to work through human means, apologetic method (like exegetical or homiletical method) is necessary; but since the Holy Spirit must be pleased to work through it, no apologetic method is sufficient in itself.

Wolfe's Assessment of the Critical Method

Some strengths and weakness of Schaeffer's critical method, as well as comparisons with Trueblood and Carnell, are brought out in David L. Wolfe's *Epistemology: The Justification of Belief.*[29] Wolfe distinguishes his "critical method" of obtaining justified beliefs from pure rationalism or naïve empiricism. Inductive inference, despite its usefulness in limited areas, is not capable of taking us from the known to the unknown. It calls on us to operate without making any assumptions in advance about the outcome of our investigation. To gain knowledge, reason must grow bold and propose conclusions that go well beyond the data at hand. It is unlikely that we experience anything independent of some set of assumptions.

Recognizing the omnipresence of assumptions, Wolfe finds the logic of the critical method needed. Three steps are involved in a critical method: (1) proposing an interpretation of experience, (2) testing it by some criteria, and (3) drawing conclusions concerning the adequacy or inadequacy of the interpretation (Wolfe: 33). On this showing, Schaeffer's proposed answers, criteria for testing them, and conclusions, though less technically expressed, are in line with critical method.

Wolfe's criteria for making sense out of total interpretations or metaphysical theories contribute greater precision to Schaeffer's "answering the phenomena" or "fitting the facts." Wolfe finds four criteria: (1) internal consistency, (2) the coherence of the statements with one another, (3) comprehensiveness or adequacy for all possible experience, and (4) congruency, fitting something and fitting it all. Unfortunately, Wolfe seems unable to justify the universality and necessity of his criteria by appeals to those "interested in a project." To that extent he defends a critical method uncritically (Wolfe: 52–55).

Hypotheses are true for Wolfe provided that they withstand the criticism to which they continually stand open. But a criticism is of concern only when it indicates violation of one of the criteria. Confirmed hypotheses may be called corroborated, plausible, or even probable (in a nonmathematical sense) (Wolfe: 65).

Wolfe says,

> As nearly as I can tell, the most sustained, explicit attempt to apply critical interpretation to religious belief occurs in D. E. Trueblood's book *Philosophy of Religion.* In this book Trueblood sets forth belief in God as a theistic hypothesis.

This hypothesis is supported by cumulative evidence that renders the hypothesis highly probable. . . . His procedure is to take various types of human experience (scientific, moral, aesthetic, historical, and religious) and ask with reference to each kind of experience, "If theism is true, what would we expect to be the case in this area of experience?" The designated area of experience is then examined to see if the hypothesis is confirmed or not. . . . Trueblood argues that in each case we do, in fact, find a confirmation (or verification or probability) (Wolfe: 34–35).

Wolfe adds, "In a similar approach Carnell, who adds to the hypothesis of theism the truth of Scripture, tests his hypothesis by systematic fitting of the fact and a consistency with other beliefs known to be true" (Wolfe: 35). His conclusion becomes more probable as "progressively verified" (Wolfe: 36).

Wolfe raises two problems with the critical approach that apply to Schaeffer as much as Trueblood and Carnell. First, the form of argument is alleged to be fallacious—affirming the consequent. If p, then q; q; therefore p. This difficulty faced in the scientific method generally can be overcome by many repeated, converging lines of evidence. I have discussed this further elsewhere.[30]

The second problem for Wolfe reflects a weakness in his own presentation of a critical approach. He speaks of an "arbitrariness to criteria" (Wolfe: 55). However, to those committed to a project they are not arbitrary, nor necessarily circular. Instead they stand in judgment on all interpretive schemes from a quite different logical level; they are criteria for, and not contents of, belief (Wolfe: 55–56). Schaeffer has insisted that the criteria are found in the image of the Creator in human existence. But Schaeffer has not spelled out the way in which these absolutes (for people committed to any project) come to explicitness or consciousness. Carnell's proposal deserves more consideration than it has received.

In his *Christian Commitment*, Carnell derives the criteria of truth from the *imago dei* via a kind of existential *analysis*.[31] Analysis is not inductive inference from experience to something outside of experience. Neither is analysis a mere phenomenological description of experience. Analysis is a reflective discrimination of the various elements already present in experience. And we are simply to ask what, if anything, makes it meaningful.

For meaningful thought and communication, Carnell

found the law of non-contradiction to be indispensable. For meaningful experience, relating to reality cannot be optional. For meaningful life, higher values, such as living out of love for God and others, make life worth living. To the value of love may be added ethical absolutes such as human dignity and rights and the demand for justice. True hypotheses about life will thus be non-contradictory and adequate to the data of external and internal experience.[32]

These absolutes do not make people autonomous. They come from the Creator and make people responsible. They mean that we can approach non-Christians with confidence in their worth as persons, with respect for their rights, justly and lovingly, factually and logically. Granting that some consciousness of these norms can be attained, we need not push every pre-Christian to the point of nihilistic despair (with Schaeffer). Neither will we present Christianity as the mere fulfillment (rather than the negation) of the non-Christian's longings (with Pinnock). Christians call non-Christians to join them in repenting for failing to live up to these standards, and to believe the gospel and trust in Jesus Christ. Until they do, these absolutes are the basis of the non-Christian's responsibility and accountability before God.

If the God who created us with these standards has any once-for-all plans, and if he purposes to act uniquely in history at particular times and places, we will only know by special revelation. And if a claim to divine revelation is to be accepted as true, it should cohere with all these invariables. No person's *claim* that the Book of Mormon or the Koran contains divine revelation is self-authenticating. The same is also true of claims made for the Bible.

Conclusion

What are the *weaknesses* of Schaeffer's apologetic method? First, his use of key terms ("presupposition," "necessity") has not been technically consistent with his method. Some of these terms were undefined or not well-defined, leading interpreters astray. Second, even with his practical purposes, some recognition of influential sources in a brief select bibliography would have helped. Third, Schaeffer often thinks he has examined all possible hypotheses when he has examined few. Finally, suffering from an all-too-common occupational hazard of popular speakers, Schaeffer tended to overstate the conclusiveness of his case for Christianity.

What are the *strengths* of Schaeffer's apologetic method? Schaeffer has faced the basic question of justifying beliefs, even ultimate presuppositions. Presuppositionalists never actually address the issue. Inductivists imagine an objectivity and freedom from personal involvement in interpretation that is unrealistic.

Schaeffer takes the most realistic logical starting point of the three methods. The admission of pre-understandings is more candid than the inductivist's claim to objectivity. No knowers start with purely objective data; all knowers have assumptions. Schaeffer's logical starting point also avoids reasoning in a circle as in presuppositionalism. The content of Schaeffer's starting point is not apostate man's logic, or a closed system of natural law, but the infinite-personal God of the Bible. As I have previously argued elsewhere,[33] Reymond's repetition of Van Til's false charge of an apostate starting point must again be called irresponsible misrepresentation. The content of the logical starting point is identical in Schaeffer and Reymond. Although the content is the same as Van Til's, its status is not that of a privileged assumption beyond challenge, but of a hypothesis that may or may not be confirmed.

Schaeffer's view of common ground takes into account the whole person with an analysis of meaningful humanness disclosing logical principles giving meaning to thought, empirical data providing for meaningful contact with nature, and existential types of data providing for values, ethics and health of the inner person. It includes empirical data, but is not limited to that as in inductivism. It includes the law of non-contradiction as in Reymond, but is not limited to that. It includes existential data from the uniqueness of personal existence, but is not limited to that. Although the metaphysical explanatory hypotheses are not shared with non-Christians (with Van Til and Reymond), the logical, empirical, and existential data are the same. Theologically this is consistent with the image of God not being destroyed by the Fall, and with common grace and providence.

The criteria of truth for Schaeffer are superior to the inductivist's sheer correspondence with empirical data, and to the presuppositionalist's alleged self-authentication. Schaeffer demands in a non-technical way logical non-contradiction, empirical fit, and existential authenticity. Because Schaeffer's criteria provide the greatest number and kinds of checks and balances, it provides the best way of discounting erroneous hypotheses and justifying true hypotheses.

Schaeffer's view of the role of reason is not limited to empirical observation and induction or to mere interpretation. Reason has the responsibility of creatively proposing hypotheses and critically testing their explanatory power by all the relevant data. Because of the extensiveness and number of the hypotheses and the lines of data, as well as the finiteness and fallenness of researchers, etc., confirmation cannot rise above probability. When the credentials of biblical revelation have been found warranting belief, then it is in order for reason to exegete that revelation and proclaim it (with Van Til). However, as we have seen, responsible interpretation also involves critical assessment of alternative hypotheses.

The basis of faith for Schaeffer does not rest on induction from empirical data alone, nor on presupposition alone. Belief in the God of the Bible is supported by a high degree of probability because of the many lines of converging evidence *intellectually*. Faced with such conclusiveness in other areas, we are morally responsible for acting and have a *psychological certitude* in doing so. Presuppositionalists' claims to certainty confuse the intellectual and psychological categories. Their certitude is based on the validity of their deductions from their presuppositions. But they have not seriously tested other presuppositions, and their own is too ultimate for confirmation.

A critical or verificational approach, whether presented in more technical philosophical terms by Carnell and Wolfe or in more popular terms by Schaeffer, provides the most realistic, cogent, and practically applicable way to engage in pre-evangelistic dialogue with people holding conflicting truth claims.

NOTES

My thanks are expressed to Jonathan Smith on the faculty of Colorado Christian College in Denver for collecting relevant literature and contributing some helpful initial insights in a research paper on "Schaeffer's Apologetic Method," and to Charles Moore of Denver Seminary's adjunct faculty for his valuable suggestions after reading a draft of this essay.

[1]For a helpful discussion of the branch of logic known as "Methodology," see the article by that name in J. Grooten and G. Jo Steenbergen, *New Encyclopedia of Philosophy* (New York: Philosophical Library, 1972), 271.

[2]Johannes B. Lotz, "Method," in *Philosophical Dictionary*, ed. Walter Brugger and Kenneth Baker (Spokane: Gonzaga, 1972), 249.

[3]See Bernard Ramm, *Protestant Biblical Interpretation* (Grand Rapids: Baker, 1979), and other standard volumes on hermeneutics.

[4] See "Methodology" in William L. Reese, *Dictionary of Philosophy and Religion: Eastern and Western Thought* (New Jersey: Humanities, 1980), 355.

[5] *Testing Christianity's Truth Claims* (Chicago: Moody, 1976). For other methods see an older work, William Pepperell Montague, *The Ways of Knowing, or the Methods of Philosophy* (New York: Macmillan, 1925).

[6] Reese, "Induction," in *Dictionary of Philosophy and Religion,* 251–52.

[7] Ibid., "Abduction," 1.

[8] Ibid., "Retroduction," 491.

[9] *The Suicide of Christian Theology* (Minneapolis: Bethany Fellowship, 1970), 276. Montgomery's enthusiastic endorsement of retroduction as a *theological* method raises the question of why he does not use it more for *apologetic* purposes.

[10] Irving M. Copi, *Introduction to Logic,* 6th ed. (New York: Macmillan, 1982), 475–84.

[11] These points are more thoroughly developed and documented in my *Testing Christianity's Truth Claims,* 45–71.

[12] Ibid., 125–48.

[13] Ibid., 176–284.

[14] Francis Schaeffer, "Why and How I Write My Books," *Eternity* 24 (March 1973): 76.

[15] *Christianity Today* (8 October 1976): 20 [18].

[16] Lewis, *Testing Christianity's Truth Claims,* 296–300.

[17] Schaeffer, "Why and How I Write My Books," 64.

[18] Norman Geisler, *Christian Apologetics* (Grand Rapids: Baker, 1976), 110–11.

[19] Ibid., 131.

[20] Schaeffer has not adequately defined antithesis in his glossary as "Direct opposition or contrast between two things" (GWIT: 177).

[21] Thomas V. Morris, *Francis Schaeffer's Apologetics: A Critique* (Chicago: Moody, 1976), 17, 36. Hereafter this work is cited in the text as Morris.

[22] Colin Brown, *Philosophy and the Christian Faith* (London: Tyndale, 1969), 265.

[23] Ibid., 273–74.

[24] K. C. Harper, "Francis A. Schaeffer: An Evaluation," *Bibliotheca Sacra* 133 (April 1976): 138. Hereafter cited in the text as Harper.

[25] Robert L. Reymond, *The Justification of Knowledge* (Nutley, N.J.: Presbyterian and Reformed, 1976), 147. Hereafter cited in the text as Reymond.

[26] Another example of this illicit either/or classification, entitled *Van Til and the Use of Evidence* (Phillipsburg, N.J.: Presbyterian and Reformed, 1980), lists well-known presuppositionalists and evidentialists. Then author Thom Notaro names as "siding more or less with one or the other position: E. J. Carnell, Gordon Lewis, Bernard Ramm, John Gerstner, Francis Schaeffer and Norman Geisler." Notaro then writes, "Though some of these figures are difficult to categorize, their contributions generally lend support to *either* a presuppositionalist *or* an evidentialist persuasion" (13).

Neither Carnell nor Schaeffer nor I can be accurately interpreted in this uncritical manner. Again, until "critical evaluations" are preceded by "critical interpretation," their intended contributions will continue to miss their mark.

[27] E. R. Geehan, "The 'Presuppositional' Apologetic of Francis Schaeffer," *Themelios* 9, no. 1 (1972): 10–15. Hereafter cited in the text as Geehan.

[28] Applications of the verificational method in theological research may be seen in my *Decide for Yourself: A Theological Workbook* (1970) and *Integrative Theology,* Vol. 1 (Grand Rapids: Zondervan, 1986).

[29] David L. Wolfe, *Epistemology: The Justification of Belief* (Downers Grove, Ill.: InterVarsity, 1982). Hereafter cited in the text as Wolfe.

[30] Lewis, *Testing Christianity's Truth Claims*, 205–6.

[31] E. J. Carnell, *Christian Commitment* (New York: Macmillan, 1958), 34.

[32] Ibid., 40, 42, 45.

[33] Gordon R. Lewis, "Van Til and Carnell," in *Jerusalem and Athens*, ed. E. R. Geehan (Nutley, N.J.: Presbyterian and Reformed, 1971), 349–62.

Part II

SCHAEFFER'S ANALYSIS
OF THE DISCIPLINES

4

FRANCIS SCHAEFFER ON PHILOSOPHY

RONALD W. RUEGSEGGER

It is clear from the first chapter that philosophy plays a central role in Schaeffer's thought. In his account of the history of Western civilization Schaeffer makes frequent references to both philosophers and philosophical concepts. Furthermore, Schaeffer's analysis of the disciplines of art, music, and theology is patterned after his interpretation of philosophy, which holds that Hegel initiated a shift from absolute to relative truth and Kierkegaard brought about a shift from reason to a leap of faith. Schaeffer also discusses metaphysics and epistemology to show that the presupposition that God exists solves more problems in these areas than does the presupposition that God does not exist. Finally, in his discussion of morality, Schaeffer argues that the rise of philosophical materialism has led to an abandonment of the belief in the dignity of man and hence to the practice of abortion, infanticide, and euthanasia.

We also saw in the first chapter, however, that Schaeffer's writings are very repetitive. Accordingly, instead of examining Schaeffer's books individually, I will develop a systematic exposition of Schaeffer's views about philosophy. We should begin by considering his general conception of philosophy.[1]

Portions of this essay appeared under the same title in Christian Scholar's Review *10 (1981): 238–54. I am grateful to the editor of that journal for permission to incorporate parts of the article into this essay. For a reply to that article see Gordon H. Clark, "A Semi-defense of Francis Schaeffer," CSR 11 (1982): 148–49. I respond on pages 150–52.*

SCHAEFFER'S GENERAL CONCEPTION
OF PHILOSOPHY

Toward the beginning of *The God Who is There*, Schaeffer offers an analysis of the history of secular philosophy. He refers to the thinkers in this tradition as "rationalistic optimists," and he notices the following shift in their thinking. Originally, he says,

> they believed they could begin with themselves and draw a circle which would encompass all thoughts of life, and life itself. . . . The only real argument between these rationalistic optimists was over the circle that should be drawn. One man would draw a circle and say, "You can live within this circle." The next man would cross it out and draw a different circle. The next man would come along and, crossing out the previous circle, draw his own–*ad infinitum*.

However, in the end these "philosophers came to the realization that they could not find this rationalistic circle and so . . . they shifted the concept of truth and modern man was born" (GWIT: 17–18).

The shift Schaeffer is describing here is, of course, the crossing of the line of relativism discussed in chapter 1. Because Schaeffer holds that all modern philosophy is under the line of relativism, he sees a uniformity in modern philosophy.

> . . . though there appear to be many forms of philosophy today, in reality there are very few. They have a uniform cast about them. You might listen, on the one hand, to the defining philosophy as taught in Cambridge, and then turn, on the other hand, to the existentialism of, say, Karl Jaspers, and think there was no unity between them. But this is not so. There is one basic agreement in almost all of the Chairs of Philosophy today, and that is a radical denial of the possibility of putting forth a circle which will encompass all. In this sense the philosophies of today can be called in all seriousness anti-philosophies (GWIT: 22).

Let us take a closer look at the sketch Schaeffer offers of the different systems of modern philosophy. The first one he discusses is Existentialism. This movement has its roots in the thought of the nineteenth-century Danish thinker, Søren Kierkegaard (1813–1855).

Although there are both religious and secular versions of Existentialism, several themes are common to all thinkers in this tradition. First, whereas many philosophers had held that what man does (his existence) is governed by who he is (his essence), Existentialists argue that existence has priority over essence. Second, Existentialists stress man's freedom: for Kierkegaard it is freedom to choose to be the self that God has ordained man to be; for the secular Existentialists it is absolute freedom to choose one's own essence. Third, Existentialists have often emphasized the individual over against the system. Finally, many Existentialists, particularly Kierkegaard, have stressed the importance of subjectivity or passion over against objectivity. It is the latter emphasis in Kierkegaard's writings that particularly disturbed Schaeffer. However, since Schaeffer's treatment of Kierkegaard will be examined in detail below, we will not pursue it further at this point.

Besides Existentialism, which has its roots in the Continent, Schaeffer mentions two forms of Anglo-Saxon philosophy, Logical Positivism and Defining Philosophy (GWIT: 24). The latter movement is more commonly known today as Ordinary Language Philosophy, or Analytic Philosophy. Interestingly, both Logical Positivism and Ordinary Language Philosophy owe much to the writings of the twentieth-century philosopher, Ludwig Wittgenstein (1889–1951).

Wittgenstein's main interest was the relation of language to the world. In his *Tractatus* he assumed that the sole function of language is to describe the world. In particular he held that elementary propositions picture the atomic facts which make up the world, and more complicated propositions are built up from these elementary propositions by the use of logical connectives such as "and," "if," and "or." The *Tractatus* was very influential among a group of thinkers known as the Vienna Circle. Their thought came to be known as Logical Positivism, and was popularized in the Anglo-Saxon world by A. J. Ayer in *Language, Truth and Logic*. Two doctrines are particularly associated with this movement. The first one is the claim that all knowledge is grounded on objects of which we are directly aware—namely, sense data such as noises or patches of color. The second doctrine is the claim that statements which cannot be tested against immediate experience are either analytic—such as "triangles have three angles"—or they are meaningless in reference to the factual world. The Logical Positivists held that religious, ethical, and aesthetic statements belong to the latter category.

Schaeffer offers a short critique of Logical Positivism in *The

God Who Is There and longer treatment of it in chapters 3 and 4 of *He Is There and He Is Not Silent*. One criticism Schaeffer makes in the latter is that Logical Positivism is inadequate because it overlooks the role of the knower in its explanation of how knowledge is possible (HIT: 49). This is a valid objection. However, it is curious that Schaeffer faults Logical Positivism for not giving due recognition to the subjective and yet, as we shall see, rejects Kierkegaard's analysis of the knowing process, which stresses the subjective.

The second criticism of Logical Positivism focuses on the claim that the immediate objects of perceptual knowledge are sense data. If this is the case, Schaeffer writes, then "you have no reason within the system to know . . . that what is reaching you is data" (HIT: 50). In this, Schaeffer seems to be saying that if what we are directly aware of is restricted to sense data in our own minds, then we have no way of knowing that there are objects which lie outside the mind to cause the sense data.

Schaeffer's own view is that we know that what reaches us is data because "we know that the thing is there because God made it to be there" (HIT: 71). There is an interesting parallel here between Schaeffer and Descartes, since both appealed to God's veracity to show that our senses are trustworthy. However, whereas Descartes grounded his belief in God on the ontological argument, Schaeffer appeals to empirical considerations. As a result, Schaeffer's reasoning is circular here: he appeals to God to justify his belief in the external world, but he believes in God because of the existence and nature of the external world.

Schaeffer is right, however, that the theory of knowledge put forward by Logical Positivism is unsatisfactory. First, it became clear that if knowledge must be derived from what we are directly aware of, not only religious and moral but also scientific knowledge is ruled out. But this was unacceptable to the Positivists since they regarded science as the paradigm of knowledge. Second, the verification theory of meaning proved untenable. It cannot be the case that we have to test a proposition to see if it is meaningful, because if the proposition were not meaningful it could not even be tested.

Several years after Wittgenstein wrote the *Tractatus,* he came to realize that language has many other functions besides describing the world. Hence, instead of equating the meaning of a word with the object it refers to, he came to identify the meaning of a word with whatever its use might be. Wittgen-

stein developed these views in his *Philosophical Investigations,*
and from this book a movement arose known as Ordinary
Language Philosophy. Schaeffer calls this movement "Defining
Philosophy" and he offers the following description of it: "The
starting-point with those who subscribe to this philosophy is,
as the title suggests, definition. They say they will on no
account take any first step without rationally and logically
defining the terms they use. And they will go no further than
can be accurately defined" (GWIT: 25).

Although Schaeffer holds that "this is good, in so far as
they have demonstrated that some problems cease to exist
when they have carefully defined the terms involved," he
claims that "this defining philosophy deals with the details
only. It would not claim to be a system. In this sense, as a
contrast to classical philosophy, it is anti-philosophy" (GWIT:
26).

Once again we see Schaeffer claiming that modern philosophy is actually anti-philosophical in nature. In this case he
bases this claim on his belief that Defining Philosophy is only
interested in details. However, in saying this, he is evidently
unaware of recent developments in what he refers to as
"Defining Philosophy." Stephen Davis has a pertinent remark
in his review of *How Should We Then Live?*

> Perhaps it could once be said that analytic philosophers
> concerned themselves only with linguistic analyses and
> ignored what Dr. Schaeffer calls "the big questions," but this
> is certainly no longer true and has not been true for years. I
> think it would be difficult to think of *any* major philosophical
> question (including the "big" ones) that has not been dealt
> with carefully and thoroughly by analytic philosophers in the
> last 30 years.[2]

With this background in mind, let us now look at
Schaeffer's treatment of specific philosophers and philosophical
problems.

SCHAEFFER ON THE HISTORY OF PHILOSOPHY

Schaeffer mentions numerous philosophers in his books:
Plato, Aristotle, Aquinas, Kant, Hegel, Kierkegaard, and Heidegger, to name a few. However, because of the sheer number
of the individuals he mentions he often devotes less than a
paragraph to each one. The results are usually unsatisfactory.

To avoid falling into this same trap, I have decided to direct my remarks to Schaeffer's account of three central figures: Aquinas, Hegel, and Kierkegaard.

Aquinas is important because Schaeffer holds that during the Middle Ages the pristine purity of New Testament Christianity was tarnished, and Aquinas' thought dominated this period. With regard to Hegel and Kierkegaard, we saw in my discussion of *The God Who Is There* in chapter 1 that Schaeffer maintains that two major shifts have occurred in the way modern non-Christians think. The first is a shift from the belief that truth is absolute to the belief that truth is relative. Schaeffer holds that Hegel is responsible for this shift. The second shift is from the belief that reason can arrive at truth to the belief that truth can only be arrived at by a leap of faith. Schaeffer blames Kierkegaard for this change. Moreover, Schaeffer maintains that these two shifts in philosophy have been mirrored by similar shifts in art, music, and theology. Thus an in-depth look at Schaeffer's treatment of these three figures should shed some useful light on Schaeffer's entire apologetic enterprise.

Thomas Aquinas

Schaeffer's account of Aquinas' influence on subsequent thought is governed by two assumptions. The first is the claim that "Aquinas brought [the] Aristotelian emphasis on individual things—the particulars—into the philosophy of the late Middle Ages, and this set the stage for the humanistic elements of the Renaissance and the basic problems they created" (HSWTL: 52).

The second assumption is the claim that Aquinas held that "the will of man is fallen, but the intellect was not" (EFR: 11). According to Schaeffer, this is equivalent to making the intellect autonomous, or independent, which in turn produced three bad results. First, Aquinas thought that one could develop natural theology independently from the Bible. Second, Aquinas made philosophy independent from Scripture. Third, Aquinas made it possible for the arts to develop apart from Scripture.

I will proceed as follows in my evaluation of Schaeffer's contentions. First, I will sketch Aquinas' epistemology. This will shed light not only on Aquinas' conception of the intellect and the will, but also on his views about particulars and universals. Then I will sketch Aquinas' position on the relation between natural theology and philosophy. His impact on the development of the arts will not be mentioned, since that topic is outside the scope of this essay.

Schaeffer is right that Aquinas' epistemology and metaphysics is basically Aristotelian. With regard to epistemology, Aquinas distinguishes three faculties in man: the vegetative (which comprises the powers of nutrition, growth, and reproduction), the sensitive (which includes the exterior and interior senses), and the rational (which consists of the active and passive intellects and the will).[3] Our concern is with the sensitive and rational faculties.

According to Aquinas, although the senses naturally apprehend particulars, the object of cognition is the concept, or universal. The heart of Aquinas' epistemology is his account of the transition from sensation to cognition. In sensation a particular image, or phantasm, arises in the imagination. The first step in the process of transforming this image into a concept occurs when the active intellect illumines the phantasm and abstracts from it the universal, or *intelligible species*. (Some contemporary Thomists compare this process to the way an x-ray shows the bones in a body.) The active intellect then produces in the passive intellect the *species impressa*. Finally, the response of the passive intellect to this implantation is the *species expressa*—the universal concept. Aquinas refers to these as universals *post rem*, that is, universals as abstracted from objects.

In addition to universals *post rem*, Aquinas holds that there are universals *ante rem* (prior to things) and universals *in re* (in things). As for universals *ante rem*, Aquinas maintains that universals are prior to things on the ground that when God created the world, his universals ideas served as the exemplary patterns as he created the particulars that make up our world. Finally, universals *in re* are universals in particular objects serving as their essences.

This sketch of Aquinas' epistemology necessarily has left out many details, but it shows that universals play an important role in Thomistic philosophy. First, universals are central in Aquinas' epistemology because knowledge is of the universal. Second, universals are important in Aquinas' metaphysics since they play significant roles in his account of creation and his conception of substance. It is true that in following Aristotle, Aquinas placed more importance on particulars than Plato did. However, Plato had a difficult time finding *any* role for particulars in his system. By contrast, Aquinas' incorporation of particulars as well as universals seems to be a step in the right direction, rather than a mistake as Schaeffer sees it.

The second assumption that governs Schaeffer's account of Aquinas' influence on subsequent thought is that Aquinas holds that the will is fallen but the intellect is not. To Schaeffer, the claim that the intellect is not fallen makes the intellect autonomous. He supports this charge by saying that Aquinas makes both natural theology and philosophy independent of Scripture.

As to the first contention, the following passage from Aquinas' *Summa Theologiae* shows that Aquinas does not hold that natural theology is totally independent from Scripture.

> Even as regards those truths about God which human reason can investigate, it was necessary that man be taught by a divine revelation. For the truth about God, such as reason can know it, would only be known by a few, and that after a long time, and with the admixture of many errors; whereas man's whole salvation, which is in God, depends upon the knowledge of this truth. Therefore, in order that the salvation of men might be brought about more fitly and more surely, it was necessary that they be taught divine truths by divine revelation. It was therefore necessary that, besides the philosophical disciplines investigated by reason, there should be a sacred doctrine by way of revelation.[4]

It is more difficult to deal with the assumption that Aquinas has made philosophy independent of Scripture. It is true that, unlike Augustine, Aquinas draws a *distinction* between theology and philosophy. To be specific, Aquinas holds that some truths are proper to theology since they can only be known by revelation, some truths are proper to philosophy since they have not been revealed, and some truths are proper to both theology and philosophy since although they have been revealed they can also be known by reason.

On the other hand, it is not quite accurate to say that Schaeffer makes philosophy *independent* from Scripture. Bonaventure had excluded Aristotle from the ranks of metaphysicians on the ground that he lacked the light of faith. Aquinas replied that unless we wish to condemn reason as such we must say that it is at least *theoretically* possible for a secular philosopher to develop a satisfactory metaphysics. Nevertheless, Aquinas acknowledged that it is not *practically* possible for a secular philosopher to do so, because on the one hand God is the first principle of true philosophy, and on the other hand the intellect is weak.

Although much more could be said on all these topics,[5] it does seem that Schaeffer overstates his case when he asserts that Aquinas made man's reason–and thereby products of man's reason such as natural theology and philosophy—independent from revelation. However, it is true that subsequent thinkers who lacked Aquinas' Christian commitment were able to develop Aquinas' thought in the direction that Schaeffer suggests.

Another philosopher who is central in Schaeffer's account of the history of philosophy is Hegel.

G. W. F. Hegel

Schaeffer discusses Hegel in several of his books.[6] The following account from *Escape From Reason* is typical:

> What [Hegel] said was this. Let us no longer think in terms
> of antithesis. Let us think rather in terms of thesis–-
> antithesis, with the answer always being synthesis (EFR: 41)

In the next paragraph, Schaeffer traces out the implication of this understanding of the nature of thought for one's conception of truth: "Truth as truth is gone, and synthesis (the both-and), with its relativism, reigns."

There are two contentions here that need to be distinguished if we are to properly evaluate Schaeffer's views. The first is the claim that Hegel held that thought is synthetical rather than antithetical. The second is the claim that when thought is understood to be synthetical, relativism results.

There is no question but that Schaeffer is right about the former contention. Hegel was an absolute idealist who believed that "thought in its very nature is dialectical."[7] Perhaps the best way to understand what Hegel means by this statement is to contrast dialectical thought with understanding, which precedes it.

Hegel defines understanding as thought which maintains the fixity and distinctness of characters and treats such limited abstractions as having a subsistence and being of their own (*Logic*: 143). Although he holds that understanding has the indispensable function of making precise distinctions, he nevertheless maintains that it is inadequate in two respects. First, it is abstract: "It maintains half-truths in their isolation, whereas the idealism of speculative philosophy carries out the principle of totality and shows that it can reach beyond the inadequate formularies of abstract thought" (*Logic:* 67). Second, it is static: It is unable to reconstruct the Absolute's unfolding in history because its concepts are fixed, whereas reality is dynamic.

However, in the dialectical stage of thought, finite, fixed distinctions supersede themselves and pass into their opposites (*Logic:* 147). This happens when we become aware that categories normally thought to be opposed and distinct are really only one-sided abstractions that are mutually dependent. Copleston cautions us that we should not make the common mistake of regarding these opposite as contradictions—despite the fact that Hegel occasionally calls them such:

> Hegel's so-called contradictions are much more often contraries than contradictions. And the idea that one contrary demands the other, an idea which, whether true or false, does not amount to a denial of the principle of non-contradiction. Again, the so-called contradictory or opposed concepts may be simply complementary concepts. A one-sided abstraction evokes another one-sided abstraction. And the one-sidedness of each is overcome in the synthesis. Further, the statement that everything is contradictory sometimes bears the meaning that a thing in a state of complete isolation, apart from its essential relations, would be impossible and 'contradictory.' . . . Here again there is no question of denying the principle of non-contradiction.[8]

Since there is this transition of thought from one-sided abstractions to another, one of the essential features of dialectical thought is movement. Thus Schaeffer is right when he claims that Hegel made thought synthetical.

However, Schaeffer's second claim, that relativism has its origin in Hegel's notion that thought is synthetical, is open to question. It is the case that Hegel's doctrine that thought is dialectical entails that there are degrees of truth. Since only the final phase of the dialectic gives the complete picture of reality, or the Absolute, only the proposition expressing the synthesis of the last triad is unqualifiedly true: the thesis, antithesis, and synthesis of all prior triads are only partially true. But to say that all statements which fall short of a full description of the Absolute are only partially true is not to say that all truth is relative to the observer. In other words, there *is* absolute truth for Hegel, even if there is only one instance of it. By contrast, the relativism whose origin Schaeffer is trying to locate holds that there is no absolute truth whatsoever.

Rather than looking for the roots of contemporary relativism in Hegelian idealism, I suggest that we would have more success if we consider the changes in thought brought about by Hegel's predecessor, Kant. One of Kant's aims in the *Critique of Pure Reason* was to explain how it is possible to have knowledge that is both a priori (not dependent on the senses) and synthetic (informative about reality). Since he had been persuaded by Hume that the senses do not yield a priori knowledge, Kant instituted what he calls a "Copernican Revolution" in the theory of knowledge.

Copernicus had proposed that the motion of the planets could be better explained by holding that the earth rotates around the sun, rather than the sun rotating around the earth as previously taught. In a similar fashion, Kant proposed that if we cannot explain our possession of synthetic a priori knowledge on the supposition that the mind conforms to objects, we should consider the possibility that objects conform to the mind. Specifically, Kant argued that after objects act on our senses, our minds organize and structure this sensory data by imposing mentally created notions on them. These mind-produced ways of making sense experience intelligible include such ideas as space, time, cause and effect, and substance and attribute.

Since what we experience, according to Kant, depends in part on what we contribute to the act of knowing, what we know is relative to the knower. But Kant's version of relativism is moderate compared with later versions. Kant thought that all knowers impose the same interpretative concepts on experience. The resulting relativism only creates a gap between knowers and the known. However, subsequent thinkers have developed Kant's relativism further by maintaining that not all knowers bring the same concepts to experience.[9] The result is a more radical relativism in which there is a gap among knowers as well as a gap between knowers and the known.

Another reason it is more plausible to say that contemporary relativism has its origin in Kant rather than Hegel is that Hegel's thought is in some respects just a modified form of Kantianism. Moreover, the modification Hegel introduced has not been as influential on contemporary epistemology as Kant's original insight was. Roughly speaking, the modification Hegel made was to reject Kant's claim that there are objects which are independent of the knower and which cause sensations in him. As a result, he held that reality itself is a product of thought. This is absolute idealism. This movement has been out of vogue ever since Moore and Russell redirected philosophy in a realist direction at the beginning of the present century. However, Kant's claim that knowledge is relative to the perceiver is compatible with realism.

Hegel, however, is not the chief villain for Schaeffer. That honor goes to Søren Kierkegaard. According to Schaeffer, Hegel was merely the doorway to the line of despair; it was Kierkegaard who was the first man under the line.[10] We must see, therefore, whether Schaeffer is right when he claims that Kierkegaard brought about a change in our conception of how we know truth.

Søren Kierkegaard

According to Schaeffer, after Hegel showed that reason is synthetical rather than antithetical, "Kierkegaard came to the conclusion that you could not arrive at synthesis by reason. Instead, you achieve everything of real importance by a leap of faith" (GWIT: 21). Schaeffer frequently equates Existentialism with irrationalism.[11] In fairness to Schaeffer it must be said that this interpretation of Kierkegaard has been a common one. However, in recent years a different reading of Kierkegaard has been advanced, its most prominent spokesperson being C. Stephen Evans. In what follows I will summarize this alternate interpretation of Kierkegaard as it is set out by Evans in his recent book, *Kierkegaard's "Fragments" and "Postscript": The Religious Philosophy of Johannes Climacus.*[12]

"Climacus" is a pseudonym for Kierkegaard, and it is important to identify Climacus' perspective at the outset. Evans informs us that Climacus "represents an intellectual outsider's point of view" on Christianity (Evans: 207–8). However, drawing from several entries in Kierkegaard's journal, Evans shows that the Danish philosopher "personally shares Climacus' view. The only difference is that at least in his later years Kierkegaard is personally committed to Christianity" (Evans: 239).

Since Climacus embodies the outsider's perspective on Christianity, he employs abstract, philosophical categories such as "paradox" and "the absurd" in his portrayal of Christianity. The tenet of Christianity that Climacus finds most paradoxical and absurd is the Christian doctrine that God became incarnate in the person of Jesus. He says, "What is the Absurd? The absurd is, that the eternal truth has come into being in time, that God has come into being . . . exactly like any other individual human being. . . ."[13]

Besides referring to this event as a paradox that is absurd, Climacus speaks of it as a contradiction. It is doubtless this consideration that has led Schaeffer repeatedly to level the charge of irrationalism against Kierkegaard in particular and Existentialism in general. Evans, however, argues that the contradiction involved in the Incarnation is not a logical or formal one. We have already seen that when Hegel speaks of contradiction in connection with dialectical thought, the opposites are more often complementary concepts than contradictories. Evans notes that Kierkegaard's use of contradiction should be understood against this background:

> The Hegelians were familiar with the concept of a contradiction as positing a task for thought. For Hegel all such contradictions are relative and can and must be "mediated" or resolved. On this view no boundaries can be set to reason, and rational thought can penetrate reality completely. Climacus wishes to explain a contrasting view that posits boundaries or limits to rational understanding. In Hegelian language this is simply the concept of a contradiction that cannot be mediated or resolved by thought. Such a contradiction would be "absolute" in comparison to the relative oppositions that thought is capable of resolving. But the opposition that resists mediation is not necessarily a formal contradiction in the contemporary sense (Evans: 214).[14]

Rather than seeing the Incarnation as a formal or real contradiction, Evans argues that it is merely an apparent one, where an apparent contradiction is a state of affairs that "appears counterintuitive or even impossible because attempts to describe the situation require the use of logically contradictory expressions" (Evans: 219). It seems, therefore, that what Kierkegaard is maintaining is that faith is *above* reason rather than *against* reason, and hence he is not espousing the irrationalist line that Schaeffer ascribes to him.

This conclusion is reinforced when we examine what Kierkegaard means by the term "leap of faith." Once again Evans clears the air:

The actual decision to become a believer Climacus calls "the leap." This expression, taken from Lessing, has been much misunderstood. In popular presentations the Kierkegaardian leap is presented as a "blind leap" or a "leap in the dark," which are expressions that Climacus never uses. The leap is neither blind nor arbitrary, since Climacus insists that the individual must have a clear idea of what he is leaping to (Christianity precisely defined by means of God's transcendent entrance into history) and why he might choose to leap (the consciousness of sin).

The leap is simply Climacus' metaphorical way of emphasizing that the decision to become a Christian is a choice, a free personal decision. Every choice is for Climacus a "leap," a decisive resolution of the self made possible by passion (Evans: 274–75).

Thus, whatever one considers Kierkegaard means by contradiction or his views about the leap of faith, Schaeffer seems to have misunderstood the Danish thinker's contentions.

More generally, I think that we must conclude our review of Schaeffer's discussion of the history of philosophy by saying that several of his main contentions are questionable. First, although Aquinas does emphasize particulars, he does not do so at the expense of universals. Nor does Aquinas seem to have made reason as autonomous as Schaeffer claims. Second, if the shift from an absolute to a relative conception of truth must be attributed to any single historical figure, our study suggests that Kant is a more likely candidate than Hegel. Finally, a fuller understanding of Kierkegaard's thought suggests that he did not advocate an irrationalistic view of faith.

SCHAEFFER ON THE PROBLEMS OF PHILOSOPHY

Just as Schaeffer discusses a wide range of individuals in his analysis of the history of philosophy, so he treats a a variety of issues that we may refer to as the problems of philosophy. Once again I offer an in-depth discussion of only a representative sample of these. The main branches of philosophy are epistemology, metaphysics, and ethics. The epistemological topic I have chosen is Schaeffer's discussion of the problem of universals. The metaphysical issue is his discussion of philosophy of mind. I will not say anything about ethics since Schaeffer's treatment of ethical issues are dealt with in chapter 9.

The Problem of Universals

As Schaeffer recognizes,[15] one way of introducing what is known as "the problem of universals" is to consider the basis for our application of common names. The basis for our application of a proper name like "John" is the individual to whom the name refers. What is the basis for our application of a common name like "chair" or "tree"? Traditionally there have been several answers to this question. At one extreme is the position known as nominalism, which holds that there is no basis in the things referred to for our application of common names. A centralist view, known as the resemblance theory, holds that the basis of our application of common names is the similarity between objects. Finally, at the opposite end of the spectrum from nominalism there is the view known as realism, which holds that the basis of our application of common terms is an objective essence shared by all objects of the same kind. Two versions of realism have developed: one, known as Medieval Realism, holds that the objective essence is a common element in objects; the other, known as Platonic Realism, holds that the objective essence is a separate Form that particular objects copy or exemplify.

The problem with nominalism is that it fails to explain why we apply a common name to one class of objects rather than another. This leaves us with a choice between the resemblance theory on the one hand and some version of realism on the other. What is at issue in this choice is whether resemblance is primitive or derivative. In other words, when two objects resemble each other, do they do so by virtue of having some attribute or relation in common? If they must share a common property to resemble each other, then some version of realism will be true. If two objects can resemble each other without sharing a property, then the resemblance theory is the more plausible view.[16]

Schaeffer is a realist on the issue of universals. The fact that he sides with the realists on this question is not necessarily an objection to this aspect of his epistemology. What *is* noteworthy is that the version of realism which he seems to favor is the Platonic variety,[17] and very few realists find this version of realism defensible any longer. Moreover, Schaeffer also says some things about universals that are decidedly odd. For example, when discussing Leonardo da Vinci, Schaeffer says that "mathematics only deals with particulars, not universals"

(EFR: 18). However, most philosophers would argue that if there are any universals at all, mathematical relationships are among the best candidates.

The last consideration suggests that although Schaeffer introduces his discussion in the traditional philosophical contexts, he may be working with a somewhat different concept of universals. In particular, it is interesting to note that Schaeffer equates universals with absolutes. A closer look at his definitions of "absolutes" will show, however, that although there are some important links between the two notions, there are some even more important differences.

On page 145 of *How Should We then Live?* Schaeffer defines an absolute as that which (1) "always applies," and (2) "provides a final or ultimate standard." Now, if this is the sense in which Schaeffer is using the work "absolute," then his assimilation of the notion to that of a universal is unobjectionable. First, since a universal is true of every member of a class, it may be said to be that which always applies. Second, since Schaeffer thinks of a universal as a Platonic Form, it may also be said to be that which provides the ultimate standard.

In the glossary of *The God Who Is There*, however, Schaeffer also says that "absolute" is "used as an antithesis of relativism." If this is Schaeffer's sense of the word, then it is radically different from the notion of a universal. This can be seen by considering the fact that whereas the polar concept of the absolute is the relative, the polar concept of the universal is the particular. In short, the absolute-relative contrast is an epistemological contrast, whereas the universal-particular contrast is a metaphysical one. Because Schaeffer runs these two categories together, he seems to hold that we must have universals in metaphysics if there are to be absolutes in epistemology. However, if it is recognized that universals and absolutes are distinct, this need not be the case.

Schaeffer's Philosophy of Mind

Schaeffer's main discussions of philosophy of mind occur in chapters 1 and 5 of section III of *The God Who Is There* and chapter 1 of *He Is There and He Is Not Silent*. Since these separate discussions have been nicely integrated into one coherent argument by Thomas Morris,[18] I will follow his outline in my exposition of Schaeffer's views.

As I showed in the first chapter to this book, Schaeffer's

procedure is to identify a key question to be answered on a given topic and then argue that the Christian presupposition answers this question much better than the non-Christian presupposition does. The question to be answered in this case is, "Why is there something rather than nothing?" The non-Christian presupposition is that the universe has an impersonal beginning, and the Christian presupposition is that the universe has a personal beginning.

Schaeffer contends that if we accept the non-Christian answer to the question "Why is there something rather than nothing?" we are faced with this choice: either personality is not real, or it is real. Against the view that personality is not real he advances three objections. First, if personality is not real, then human aspirations for meaning, significance, purpose, love, beauty, and order become enigmatic. Second, "to deny that man is different from all that is non-man is to contradict the testimony that man has borne concerning himself for thousands of years" (Morris: 27). Finally, "no man who denies the reality of personality can live consistently with this view."

If we accept these objections, then we must hold that personality is real despite the fact that the universe had an impersonal beginning. This is perhaps the alternative favored by most non-Christian thinkers. Schaeffer also has three objections to this alternative. First, "if men do indeed have . . . real aspirations for personal fulfillment in a universe that is finally impersonal, then those aspirations are ultimately unfulfillable and finally meaningless" (Morris: 27–28). Second, Schaeffer claims that no one has ever explained how personality could have arisen from the impersonal. Third, a universe which has an impersonal beginning would give rise to a conflict between unity and diversity.

Let us focus on the second of these objections since it occurs frequently in Schaeffer's writings. Schaeffer's own statement of this objection is worth citing since it is particularly strong. He says, "No one has presented an idea, let alone demonstrated it to be feasible, to explain how the impersonal beginning, plus time, plus chance, can give personality" (GWIT: 8).

Now, although I agree with Schaeffer that the personal cannot be derived from the impersonal, it is not correct to say that "no one has presented an idea" as to how this could come about. The scientific literature on the psychology of cognition and the philosophical literature on philosophy of mind are full of attempts to do precisely what Schaeffer claims no one has even proposed. More significantly, this kind of assertion misleads Christians who are not cognizant of recent developments in these fields into thinking that all is well. Because this matter is important, I will show in some detail how the development of science has raised a serious problem for anyone who wishes to hold that man is different from the rest of nature.

One of the claims Schaeffer makes throughout his books is that science had its origin in the Christian world view. This claim has recently been supported by Stanley Jaki.[19] However, in addition to the cultural matrix provided by Christianity, another factor contributing to the birth of science during the Middle Ages was the influence of Neoplatonic, Pythagorean mathematics. The role of mathematics in the birth and development of science has been thoroughly documented by E. A. Burtt.[20] I will briefly summarize his account and then point out the relevance it has for Schaeffer's views about philosophy of mind.

Once it was recognized that the earth is a globe, it was natural to take the earth as a point of reference in charting the motions of the planets. The result was the theory that the planets travel in concentric paths around the earth. It was soon realized, however, that the turning of concentric spheres could not account for all the observed motions of the planets. In the second century A.D. Ptolemy proposed that the irregularities could be explained by the hypothesis that a planet's path is an epicycle (a circle on a circle). About a millennium later, Copernicus realized that the motion of the planets could be equally well explained by conceiving of the sun rather than the earth as the center of the universe and maintaining that the planets revolve around it.

The advantage of Copernicus' hypothesis was that it simplified Ptolemy's highly complex geometry of the paths of the planets (Burtt: 36). Nevertheless, accepting his proposal required one to abandon the report of the senses that the earth is unmoving. One reason Copernicus was willing to set aside the report of the senses was that he had come under the influence of the Pythagorean element in Neoplatonism, and the Pythagoreans held that reality could be described mathematically (Burtt: 40–45). In short, Copernicus was willing to abandon the report of the senses that the earth is unmoving in order to achieve the simplicity which the mathematical approach produced.

Kepler was also influenced by the Neopythagorean element in Neoplatonism, but he went further than Copernicus and claimed that there must be other mathematical relationships in the heavens than Copernicus realized (Burtt: 49). He discovered three important mathematical relationships, one of which is known as the law of elliptical paths, which says that the planets describe orbits that are ellipses, with the sun as one focus. Kepler's discovery of these mathematical relationships led him to adopt the distinction between primary and secondary qualities of physical objects. Primary qualities are those that can be described mathematically, such as size, shape, and weight. Secondary qualities are those that cannot be described mathematically, like color and taste.

Galileo also adopted the Copernican system of astronomy. Since a consequence of the Copernican system is that the earth is in motion, it was natural for him to extend the mathematical study of mechanical motions to the earth and objects on it (Burtt: 62). One consequence of Galileo's mathematical study of mechanics was that he followed Kepler in making a distinction between primary and secondary qualities. But Galileo went further and maintained that secondary qualities are subjective (Burtt: 74). Thus, for Galileo the world of primary qualities consisted of that which is absolute, objective, immutable, and mathematical, whereas the world of secondary qualities consists of that which is relative, subjective, fluctuating, and sensible.

The implication of the series of events I have just described for one's conception of man are profound. Burtt has beautifully described them, and I will quote him at length.

> Till the time of Galileo it had always been taken for granted that man and nature were both integral parts of a larger whole, in which man's place was the more fundamental. . . . Now, in the course of translating this distinction of primary and secondary qualities into terms suited to the new mathematical interpretation of nature, we have the first stage in the reading of man quite out of the real and primary realm. Obviously man was not a subject suited to mathematical study. His performances could not be treated by the quantitative method, except in the most meager fashion. His was a life of colors and sounds, of pleasures, or griefs, or passionate loves, of ambitions, and strivings. Hence the real

world must be the world outside of man: the world of astronomy and the world of resting and moving terrestrial objects. . . . Quite naturally enough, along with this exaltation of the external world as more primary and more real, went an attribution to it of greater dignity and value. . . . Man began to appear for the first time in the history of thought as an irrelevant spectator and insignificant effect of the great mathematical system which is the substance of reality (Burtt: 78–80).

The preceding suggests that Schaeffer has missed the real source of the difficult problems in philosophy of mind. As I pointed out in chapter 1, Schaeffer claims that as scientists gave up the belief in God they also gave up the belief that the universe is open to God's intervention and replaced it with the belief that the universe is a closed system of cause and effect. According to Schaeffer, the result of this new conception of the universe is that man is now part of the machine that is nature and therefore is no longer free.

While I agree with Schaeffer that man is now seen to be part of nature, it seems to me that this is not due to the fact that the world view of scientists has changed from a Christian one to a non-Christian one. Instead, if the account Burtt has given of the origin and development of science is correct, the problem lies in the very nature of science itself. The problem, in short, is to find a way to reconcile the first-person perspective of everyday experience with the third-person perspective of science.[21] Merely working from a Christian as opposed to a secular world view does not resolve this problem.

CONCLUSION

In the preceding pages I have examined Schaeffer's account of the history and problems of philosophy. With regard to the history of philosophy, I have argued for a somewhat different interpretation of the thought and role of Aquinas, Hegel, and Kierkegaard. As for the problems of philosophy, it seems to me both that Schaeffer is not completely clear about what is at issue in the problem of universals and also that Schaeffer has overlooked the difficulty that the development of science has posed for philosophy of mind.

When I point out weaknesses in Schaeffer's account of the history and problems of philosophy to students, I typically receive one or more of the following responses from some members of the class. One objection is that Schaeffer cannot really be mistaken since what he has said has been a help to so many people. Of course, no one wants to overlook the help that Schaeffer has been to many inquiring Christians. However, it is also true that some have been turned away from Christianity by the weaknesses noted above. Furthermore, if one has been helped by a weak argument, there is always the potential for the weakness in the argument to be pointed out with the result that the individual will once again be perplexed. Only truth can ultimately help a person.

Another response to my critique is to ask me whether I have something better to put in the place of Schaeffer's system. However, what these questioners want is often just a better version of a simple, all-embracing system that shows that Christianity is true. Unfortunately, there just isn't any viable system that is all-encompassing and problem free. The best we can hope for is a series of detailed analyses of the particular topics and disciplines with which Schaeffer deals.

A final response I sometimes hear is that Schaeffer is not a scholar but merely an evangelist. Although this description of Schaeffer is incompatible with his advertisement to the public as one of the most profound thinkers of our times,[22] I think it is indeed important to recognize that Schaeffer is a popularizer rather than a scholar. As such it is not fair to expect him to understand the details of philosophy as well as someone who is trained in the discipline. Accordingly, to the extent that my criticisms of Schaeffer are correct, they should be taken as attempts to bring Schaeffer's readers to a fuller understanding of the subjects he treats.

Nevertheless, I think there are several lessons to be learned from this situation. The first, which I have already mentioned, is that it is a mistake to promote Schaeffer as an authority in philosophical matters. He was not, and saying so only sets up false expectations. Second, and more importantly, the fact that Schaeffer is enormously popular among evangelicals, despite his not being an authority, suggests that all too often we are satisfied with simple answers to complex questions. Specifically, while one agrees with the conclusion that Schaeffer is arguing for—namely, that Christianity is true–the reasons he advances for his conclusion are often inconclusive. However, because Christians naturally agree with Schaeffer's conclusion that Christianity is true, there is the subtle danger of also assuming that his arguments for Christianity are sound.

The preceding observations are important because they can be generalized. Schaeffer is not the only popularizer among evangelicals, and many of the preceding points apply as well to popular figures in other fields. There are several factors that may explain our tendency as evangelicals to follow popularizers. One of these is a lack of knowledge. For example, if one is not informed about geology, the notion that the earth is only a few thousand years old may seem obviously true in light of the Genesis accounts. But perhaps an even greater factor than our lack of education is our belief that Christianity is true–indeed, completely true. It is very easy for us to allow the unequivocalness which belongs to the revealed Gospel to spread to our own man-made systems of theology, philosophy, or science. The remedy is to recognize that no matter how carefully we try to integrate our faith and our learning, our attempts to think "Christianly" about the various disciplines should be clearly distinguished from the Gospel that informs them.

NOTES

[1] Those who are not familiar with philosophy will find Mark B. Woodhouse, *A Preface to Philosophy*, 3rd ed. (Belmont, Calif.: Wadsworth, 1984), a helpful introduction to the discipline.

[2] Stephen T. Davis, Review of HSWTL, *The Evangelical Quarterly* 50 (1978): 111.

[3] My sketch of Aquinas' thought is largely drawn from Frederick Copleston, *A History of Philosophy*, vol. 2 (New York: Newman, 1950), chs. 32, 37, and 38.

[4] Thomas Aquinas, *Summa Theologiae*, in *Basic Writings of Saint Thomas Aquinas*, ed. by Anton C. Pegis, rev. of the English Dominican Fathers' translation (New York: Random House, 1945), I, q. 1, a. 1.

[5] For a fuller treatment of these issues see John F. Wippel, 'The Possibility of a Christian Philosophy: A Thomistic Perspective,' *Faith and Philosophy* 1, no. 3 (July 1984): 272–90.

[6] See GWIT: 20, EFR: 40–42; HIT: 45–46; and HSWTL: 162–63.

[7] William Wallace, trans., *The Logic of Hegel*, 2nd ed. (London: Oxford University, 1892), 18. Hereafter cited in the text as *Logic*.

[8] Frederick Copleston, *A History of Philosophy*, vol. 7 (New York: Random House, 1950), 177.

[9] There are a variety of versions of radical relativism, but one of the most influential ones has been put forward by Thomas Kuhn in his book *The Structure of Scientific Revolutions*, 2nd ed. enlarged (Chicago: University of Chicago, 1970). One reason Kuhn's account has been so influential is that he has argued for relativism in science, the one discipline that most people think has the greatest objectivity. Specifically, Kuhn maintains that initially all facts relevant to a

certain phenomenon seem equally important (p. 15). As a result there are a variety of interpretations of the phenomenon. The diversity disappears when one particular construction of the facts, which he calls a *paradigm*, attracts an enduring group of supporters. Kuhn defines a paradigm as "universally recognized scientific achievements that for a time provide model problems and solutions to a community of practitioners" (p. viii).

The connection between Kuhn's account of the development of scientific theories and relativism lies in his claim that "the choice between competing paradigms proves to be a choice between incompatible modes of community life" (p. 94). The reason paradigms are relative to different communities is that "since a paradigm determines what counts as a solution to a problem, no member of one school will be able to win over a member of the other school by appealing to his own paradigm" (p. 109). Hence science does not proceed by accumulating facts; it proceeds by revolutions.

[10] Cf. EFR: 42–43; HIT: 46; and HSWTL: 163.

[11] For an instance where Schaeffer equates Existentialism with irrationalism see WHHR: 143.

[12] C. Stephen Evans, *Kierkegaard's "Fragments" and "Postscript": The Religious Philosophy of Johannes Climacus* (Atlantic Highlands, N.J.: Humanities, 1983). Hereafter cited in the text as Evans. For another work by Evans that focuses on the notion of subjectivity and discusses other thinkers as well as Kierkegaard, see *Subjectivity and Religious Belief* (Washington: Christian University, 1978).

[13] Søren Kierkegaard, *Concluding Unscientific Postscript*, trans. by David F. Swenson and Walter Lawrie (Princeton: Princeton University, 1941), 188.

[14] Evans provides additional reasons why Kierkegaard does not use "contradiction" in a formal sense on pp. 214–19.

[15] See HSWTL: 144–45 and HIT: 38.

[16] For a good discussion of the problem of universals see A. D. Woozley, *Theory of Knowledge* (London: Hutchison University Library, 1949), 68–98.

[17] For indications that Schaeffer favors Platonic Realism see HIT: 38–40 and HSWTL: 144. To be sure, Schaeffer does not agree with the particular separate objective essences that he thinks Plato posits. Nevertheless, he has praise and no criticism for Plato's view that there must be separate objective essences. To be specific, in HSWTL he says that "Plato did understand something crucial," namely "that if there are no absolutes, then the individual things (the particulars, the details) have no meaning." And if one turns to p. 39 of HIT, the view he attributes to Plato clearly involves a separate objective essence, and there is no suggestion that Schaeffer balks at this. He writes, "Plato . . . put forward the concept of ideals which would provide the needed universal. For example, let us think of chairs: let us say that there is somewhere an ideal chair, and that this ideal chair would cover all the particulars of all the chairs that ever were. . . . So when we use the word 'chair' there is a meaning *that is beyond* our mere gathering up of the particulars about chairs" (my emphasis).

[18] Thomas V. Morris, *Francis Schaeffer's Apologetics: A Critique* (Chicago: Moody, 1976), esp. 25–30. Although I will sometimes be quoting Morris, the statements he makes are easily traceable back to Schaeffer.

[19] Stanley Jaki, *The Road of Science and the Ways to God* (Chicago: University of Chicago, 1978), 14–34.

[20] E. A. Burtt, *The Metaphysical Foundations of Modern Physical Science* (London: Routledge and Kegan Paul, 1924). Hereafter cited in the text as Burtt.

21 For fuller discussion of this problem see William Hasker, *Metaphysics* (Downers Grove, Ill.: InterVarsity, 1983), 81–100. C. Stephen Evans addresses the larger problem of the relation between the biblical and scientific conceptions of man in his *Preserving the Person* (Downers Grove, Ill.: InterVarsity, 1977), especially chs. 8–10.

22 For example, the following description occurs on the dust jacket of HSWTL: "Francis Schaeffer, theologian and philosopher, foremost evangelical thinker of our day, whose brilliant analysis of Western man's development and future direction is the result of forty years of intensive study of humanism and Christian truths." And in the introduction to the various episodes of the film series based on WHHR, Schaeffer is described as "one of the world's most respected thinkers."

5

SCHAEFFER ON ART AND MUSIC

HAROLD M. BEST

INTRODUCTION

Until quite recently, decisions about artistic practice among evangelicals have been left to one of two forums: the church with its concepts of appropriateness, and secular culture with its popular, academic, and classical institutions. Appropriateness within the church has been decided by local congregations, pastors, and music committees—less commonly by artistic practitioners. The fit of the art has been based largely on associative pragmatism: if the desired result is achieved, the art is deemed acceptable. This practice has allowed for the intermingling of both good and bad art. The layperson may be ignorant of the distinction, the artistic often frustrated by the mixture.

The remainder of art is described one of three ways: (1) though traditionally sacred and appropriate for other churches, it does not fit this particular one; (2) though new, secularly popular, and appealing to this or that sector of the citizenry, including the younger people of the church in

Harold M. Best is the Dean of the Conservatory of Music at Wheaton College, Wheaton, Illinois. He holds degrees from Nyack College, Claremont Graduate School (M.A.), and Union Theological Seminary (D.S.M.). Among his publications are "God's Creation and Human Creativity" in The Nature of Christian Learning *and "Heritage, Culture and Curricular Policy" in* Design for Arts in Education *(March–April 1985).*

question, it is inappropriate, at least for the present; (3) though its general flavor is reputed to be of high quality, it is of sufficient complexity and unfamiliarity to render it inaccessible. While its quality and suitability are lauded by the few, its incapability to minister is alleged by the many. It is suited to the concert hall and academe. Stated another way, the issue of appropriateness has turned more on the distinctions between function and worth, familiarity and newness, results and quality, rather than on a carefully constructed view of the place of all of music and art in the life of the Christian.

In the last twenty years, primarily in evangelical higher education, attempts have been made to restate the case along more basic, integrative lines. Human creativity and culture have been relocated within the framework of God's Creator-hood and his handiwork. Excellence has been described as the norm of stewardship. The concept has been challenged that popular and elitist forms of expression are justified simply by the difference between pragmatism and idealism. Instead, each is seen to possess legitimate identities, intrinsic and varietal worth, and the ability to intermingle and influence each other.

Through the growth of the discipline of ethnomusicology and the study of world creativity, musical and artistic categories are no longer pitted against each other, but are analyzed internally and contextually. Aesthetic theories are not just limited to the artifacts of high culture, but open to those of anonymous, primitive, functional and commercial artworks. Finally, the older classical divisions between sacred and secular have been questioned, if not dissolved. In their place biblical concepts are being articulated that insist that all of life is sacred, not by virtue of what its cultural labels are, but by what motivates us to undertake our tasks and to exercise discernment in doing them. Sacred and secular have moved from categories of "other-worldly" and "this-worldly" to faithfulness and faithlessness. In this sense, a Beethoven sonata or a tribal artifact may be as much a sacrifice of praise as a Gregorian chant or a metrical psalm.

Francis Schaeffer has participated in this shift of thinking. For example, in *Art and the Bible* he reminds his audiences that to be Christian is not to be discultural, that the arts are not peripheral to the Christian life, but are in fact doxologies in themselves (AB: 10). He is not hesitant to speak out against artistic mediocrity, which evangelicals seem so prone to take for granted (AB: 9). He brings Scripture to bear on the rightness of bringing beauty to the worship and praise of God (AB: 11–18). Quite literally, Francis Schaeffer puts God on the side of quality. For this alone, he deserves the thanks of countless, artistically caring evangelicals.

Schaeffer's thought about art and music is grouped two ways. In *Escape From Reason*, *The God Who Is There*, and *How Should We Then Live?* the relationship of artistic and musical content to the history of thought, especially in what transpired in relation to the so-called line of despair, is foremost. Besides the concept of the relationship of world view to artistic content, there is virtually no other material in these writings that might be considered a working theory for artists and musicians. In short, there is more example than principle.

Art and the Bible proceeds differently. It is divided into two essays and devotes far more time, especially in the second, to principles of artistic activity. The first essay, "Art in the Bible," attempts to establish the biblical legitimization of art exclusively through the use of scriptural narrative: the creation of man; the building of the tabernacle, temple, and Solomon's throne; Jesus' reference to the brazen serpent; the use of music and dance; and finally, a curious reference to the art of heaven (Revelation 15:2–3), connected to which, for the only time in that essay, there is mention of a Western artist, Paul Robert (AB: 30).

The second essay, "Some Perspectives on Art," is devoted to the outlining and discussion of eleven principles intended to develop a Christian perspective on art in general. Here biblical references give way to specific artistic works drawn primarily from Western culture. The essay concludes with a brief postscript on the Christian life as a work of art—a winsome thought, but because of what is stated, it belongs more to the annals of piety.

ANALYSIS OF *THE GOD WHO IS THERE* AND *HOW SHOULD WE THEN LIVE?*

These two volumes, virtually repeating each other, contain the essence of Schaeffer's concept of the role of art and music in the exegesis of philosophical thought up to and beyond the line of despair, as well as his grasp of artistic and musical process in the large flow of history. Since extended analyses of Schaeffer's philosophical approach are undertaken in chapter 4, comments will be limited here to his decision to put art and music where he did in the "staircase," and to the equation that he seemingly strikes between truth and beauty. For purpose of reference, the staircase is shown below.

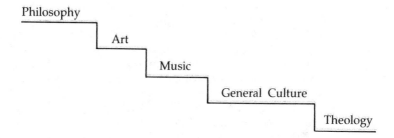

Figure 5.1. Steps in the Line of Despair

This is a chronological model. It assumes that the philosophical thought culminating in Kierkegaard crossed the line of despair in the Impressionists and Debussy, who in turn opened the door to modern art and music. This discloses Schaeffer's chief thesis, upon which virtually all of his remaining artistic commentaries are based: *What one believes shows in what one makes.*

In the case of the Impressionists and Debussy, Schaeffer says that the substantive procedural changes found in their art are, in and of themselves, expositions of the shifts in thought systems from truth-as-absolute to truth-as-relative. Carried out to the full extent of artistic creativity, this assumes that every artistic style, national and individual, in whatever historical framework, every artistic and artifactual medium, whatever the cultural location, will disclose the world view of its maker. That Schaeffer makes no systematic attempt to show how this takes place, and that he fails to deal with the phenomenon of world creativity with its plethora of belief systems, is unfortunate.

There is no quarrel with the idea that artists have world views, nor with the idea that they might well attempt to speak them into their artifacts. There is a serious question, however, as to whether the nature of art is such that it is able to show these with the force and accuracy that Schaeffer alleges. The following shows how closely he actually links things believed to things made.

The various steps on the line—philosophy, art, music, theatre and so on—differ in details, and these details are interesting and important, but in a way they are only incidental. The distinctive mark of the twentieth century intellectual and cultural climate does not lie in the differences but in the unifying concept. This unifying concept is the concept of a divided field of knowledge.

Whether the symbols to express this are those of painting, poetry or theology, is incidental. The vital question is not the symbols used to express these ideas (for example, the words of the existential philosophers or the sounds of musique concrete), but the concept of truth and the method of attaining truth involved. *The watershed is the new way of talking about and arriving at truth, and not the terms the individual disciplines used to express these ideas* (GWIT: 44).

There are times in Schaeffer's writing when he wishes to disavow this kind of Platonic thinking, this union of truth and beauty, but there are other equally obvious instances, such as the above, when he seems just as prone to fall victim to it. Ronald Ruegsegger provides insight into this tendency by noting that when Schaeffer equates universals and absolutes he also equates their polar concepts, particulars and relativities.[1] In other words, if an absolute, truth, is equal to a universal, beauty, this must mean that their opposites, relativity and particulars, are likewise equal. If relativity equals particular, then a particular is not an aspect of the universal, but its antithesis. If this is so, and if Schaeffer's frame of reference is used, then showing a belief artistically can only be done relativistically.

This means that the philosophical model that Schaeffer has adopted contradicts his idea that belief systems can be directly shown in art works. Instead, artists can only end up with relativized portrayals of their world views, the exact opposite of what Schaeffer expects. There are further reasons, discussed in the final section, as to why a simplified connection of world view and artifact is less than useful. The purpose here is only to show the way Schaeffer's philosophical thought contradicts his artistic thesis.

The remainder of this section will be given over to Schaeffer's interpretation of artistic content, change, and context. Because of the unevenness of treatment, chronological gaps, and sudden compressions of thought, it seems prudent, even at the risk of a certain amount of repetition, to comment on several representative art works.

THE VISUAL ARTS

Impressionism and Schaeffer's "Fragmentation"

Schaeffer calls Van Gogh, Gauguin, and Cézanne the three pillars of modern art (GWIT: 30ff.; HSWTL: 183ff.). He connects their failed quest for an artistic universal with crossing the line of despair. But how does he know that they personally passed this line? If it was simply the chronological follow-through of philosophical thought, this overlooks the complex stylistic evolution from years back which just as easily explains why these artists did what they did. If passing the line of despair is shown by the presence of deep personal psychological problems, as Schaeffer alleges in the case of Van Gogh, then one can assume a plethora of lines of despair all through art history, based simply on the emotional conditions of any number of creative people.

If seeking a universal brings one to despair, then all great artists despair—if *universal* means an all-embracing absolute realized in an essentialized art piece. However, if universal means *universalizing*, then all artists, especially the great ones, whether they personally despair or not, do succeed. Universalizing in this sense is another word for integration, synthesis, and interrelationship. Great art means, alludes to, and suggests many things at once, and this is part of its glory. And Schaeffer makes far too little provision for this phenomenon. Indeed, he almost completely overlooks it.

Schaeffer comments about other Impressionists. He mentions the "curious twist in the way naturalists were painting" (HSWTL: 183), and describes the hypothetical viewer seeing what the artist pictures but asking himself if there is any meaning. Schaeffer concludes by saying that such art had become sterile and alleges that artists such as Monet, Renoir, Pissarro, Sissley, and Degas,

> . . . painted *only* what their eyes brought them, leaving the question as to whether there was a reality behind the light waves reaching the eyes. They called it "following nature" (HSWTL: 183).

This is a confusing sequence of thought. First, if the painter is a naturalist, he can only paint naturally and not distortedly. If he does not, he is not a naturalist. Second, viewers through the ages have always been asking for meaning in art. This is both one of the glories of art and one of the tasks of art education. Great art always goes beyond its precedent, not subtractively but metamorphically. It is part of the privilege of the artist to say something yet another way: to bring paraphrase, newness, even disturbance both to himself and to the observer.

If an artist chooses to paint earth, tree trunks, and branches in silvery greens and blues, as Van Gogh did in *Souvenir de Mauve,* it does not mean that he has forgotten or is denying the true color of these created objects. Instead, he is making something that is above all else internally consistent and propositionally true—not in the ethical sense, but in the procedural sense. The new and heightened insight into a relationship among color, object, and context provides the viewer with yet another look into the creation and into the mystery of human creativity.

Just because God decided to use greens and browns instead of silvery tones does not mean that he could not have done it another way. Since Van Gogh was, above all, created in God's image, and since being created this way carries with it the unusual privilege of imagining things, it makes both artistic and theological sense to say that a highly gifted human imaginer can paraphrase the creation—not outdo it—without giving the Creator the slightest offense.

When a person views *Souvenir de Mauve,* he is struck with the incredible inner consistency of this masterpiece. It is not a world unto itself; it is not a distortion of reality; it is not the replacement of reality with a dream, as Schaeffer accuses the Impressionists, any more than the surreal composite of the Son of God in the Book of Revelation (1:12–16) is a replacement for the bodily resurrected and ascended Christ. Instead, it is a new way of seeing based on stunning insight. The creation is the reference point for both the artist and the viewer, and each is free to return to the creation and rejoice in it at will. It is obvious that the Van Goghs, Monets, and Cézannes rejoiced to the point of intoxication.

Further along, Schaeffer states that with Monet's series of poplar tree paintings, especially *Poplars at Giverney, Sunrise,* and *Poplars at Epte,* their dreamlike quality—to Schaeffer a replacement for reality—signals the demise of Impressionism and the door to modern art. This would be quite a useful statement about how art leads to artistic change it if did not so negatively imply that the next steps toward fragmentation and distortion were the hallmarks of modern art. It would be just as enlightening to say that these paintings are quite realistic in the same way one sees objects impressionalized by heat waves on a hot sunny day. Somehow this does not fit Schaeffer's model, because his presuppositions will not allow it.

Referring to Cézanne, Schaeffer links his preference for geometrical form to a frustrated search for a universal:

> As philosophy had moved from unity to a fragmentation, this fragmentation was also carried into the field of painting. The fragmentation shown in post-Impressionist paintings was parallel to the loss of hope for a unity of knowledge and philosophy. It was not just a new technique in painting. It expressed a world view. Cézanne reduced nature to what he considered its basic geometric forms. In this he was searching for a universal which would tie all kinds of particulars and nature together. Nonetheless, this gave nature a fragmented broken appearance (HSWTL: 184).

This confuses the issue. Even if it could be aesthetically shown that Cézanne's paintings at this particular time used only basic geometric forms, it would be necessary for Schaeffer to go further in proving how this particular activity is a comment on brokenness and fragmentation.

All artists seek structural and procedural mechanisms by which they attempt to make their works cohere and, on occasion, allow them to show more than usual. This is not a search for a universal, but a part of the universal quality of man to seek out ways to bind things together systematically—quite simply, a search for grammar. Grammar is to poetry what music theory is to composition and engineering is to architecture. Hence, the grammar of the geometrical forms is for Cézanne a constructional means to an end and need not be seen as distortion or the incipient fragmentation of reality. Since the creation itself proceeds grammatically and since geometry is an aspect of natural law, one can just as easily credit Cézanne for thinking creationally in the same way that Seurat, with his Pointillism, could be credited for thinking molecularly, or for that matter, improving stylistically on the dot-by-dot method of color printing: a clear instance of an artistic paraphrase of technology.

We must differentiate between fragmentation as means and fragmentation as end. For example, if we were philosophically to describe fragmentation, we would not write fragmentedly to accomplish this. If we did, the final message would be nonexistent. If one of the definitions of art is wholeness and internal unity, then a fragmented work of art would no more be a work of art than fragmented writing would be understandable, even if it were attempting a description of fragmentation.

Fragmentation is a legitimate compositional technique. Composers may break thematic material up into smaller pieces as a way of developing their ideas. This is done quite often to show the implosive power of the material and the manifold transformations of which it is capable. In other words, if fragmentation is the primary process, there will be something else, some other syntactical event, which holds the work together. Such is the case with Cézanne.

Schaeffer uses Duchamp's famous painting *Nude Descending a Staircase* as an example of fragmentation gone awry. But he seems to miss the point of the painting. It is not fragmentation as an end result—a world view—but fragmentation as a compositional process. The result is an amazing semi-abstract stylization of stop-action photography. Again, as in the case of Seurat, a relationship between art and technology is seen.

Michelangelo and Schaeffer's Eisegesis

As one continues with Schaeffer's thought, it becomes increasingly apparent that he depends heavily on eisegesis. With his comments on Michelangelo's *The Captives* and *David* and the work of Duchamp, this approach is shown in the extreme (HSWTL: 71ff.; GWIT: 35).

The Captives is a group of four unfinished sculptures entitled *Youthful Captive, Atlas, Bearded Captive,* and *Awakening.* Each is still largely embedded in the stone, giving an initial impression of a struggle to break out. Schaeffer says this:

> They make a real humanistic statement: Man will make himself great. Man as man is tearing himself out of the rock. Man by himself will tear himself out of nature and free himself from it (HSWTL: 71).

This is eisegesis nearly rampant. First, by all accounts these are unfinished works. One can only conjecture as to how much of the stone Michelangelo would have allowed to remain had he finished them. But more crucial is the inference drawn by Schaeffer that the struggling figures represent man breaking away from nature and making himself great. How can one know from this art piece that Michelangelo is making man great? And what is wrong with breaking away from nature, especially when taken in light of two concepts: one from Schaeffer, the other from Scripture? In Schaeffer's model of nature eating up grace (HSWTL: 55), he criticizes man for so bowing to the natural that grace is put aside; yet with *The Captives,* he criticizes the work for breaking away from nature. Perhaps the figures are struggling for grace—who can know? The artifact simply cannot speak that way. (Moreover, if Schaeffer means something else by "breaking away from nature," he is obligated to say so with far more precision.)

The example from Scripture is simply that which is found in Genesis when God tells Adam to maintain a sovereignty and a control over nature. In a scriptural sense, breaking away from nature may well be realizing the importance of the Creator over the creature and the stewardship man is to exercise over both the creation and his creativity.

Schaeffer comments on the humanism of *David,*

> . . . let us notice that the *David* was not the Jewish David of the Bible. *David* was simply a title. Michelangelo knew his Judaism, and in the statue the figure is not circumcised. We are not to think of this as the biblical David but as the humanistic ideal. Man is great! (HSWTL: 70–71).

Further on, Schaeffer says,

> The David was the statement of what the humanistic man saw himself as being tomorrow! . . . Even the disproportionate size of the hands says that man is powerful. The statue is idealistic and romantic (HSWTL: 72).

First of all, as to leaving David uncircumcised, Michelangelo also showed him as facially non-Semitic. There is no alarming precedent here. All through history, artists have recontextualized people, places, and things. Medieval and Renaissance art depicting biblical subjects shows contemporaneous clothing, buildings, and local environments. Ethnic religious art shows biblical figures as oriental or negroid, with clothing and architecture to fit the adjusted context. Schaeffer provides his own correction in *Art and the Bible:* "Christian art should differ from country to country. . . . If a Christian artist is Japanese, his painting should be Japanese, if Indian, Indian" (AB: 51)—and by extension, if Italian, Italian. Thus the validity of *David.* This need not be humanism, but human creativity working contextually and cross culturally.

The question of David's disproportionate hands is defensible three ways. First, Michelangelo spares himself from clichéd realism in order to seek a stylization of strength and vigor. It must be remembered that David killed an animal barehanded (1 Sam. 17:34–36). Second, Michelangelo certainly had formal and aesthetic reasons. The larger hands are part of an overall aesthetic strategy in which tension and release are sought out and found. Third, Michelangelo knew as well as anyone that realism is not literalism. In *Pietà*, for instance, the Virgin Mary is larger than Christ. It is quite easy to figure out that if she were standing she would be seven feet tall, with Christ much shorter, yet her head is the same size as His. Using Schaeffer's thought pattern, is this an example of Mary overshadowing Jesus with all of the doctrinal implications attached thereto, or is it simply an attempt at achieving aesthetic balance and grace? Surely the artistic eye of Michelangelo, not his world view, is the gift to admire and to take account of.

In the comments about Duchamp, whom Schaeffer calls "the high priest of destruction," there is a description of the painting *Le passage de la vierge à la mariée* that includes these words:

> Naturally every man or woman who goes to look at the picture tries to find . . . something which relates to its title. But no matter how long one looks one finds no picture of a virgin, nor a virgin becoming a married woman. Thus he causes the viewer to make himself dirty (GWIT: 35).

How can Schaeffer conclude dirtiness out of this painting, which by his own admission does not show any such thing, unless (1) sex is implicitly dirty; (2) proceeding from virginity to marriage is only sexual; (3) becoming one in marriage has no mystery to it? (4) people look for what they wish to find?

Schaeffer seems to overlook the biblical viewpoint that behavior issues from the heart. If we go to a painting which has no literal picture of sexual behavior or, for that matter, if we go to the Song of Songs, which does, and become dirty, is the art or the heart to blame? Schaeffer seems to feel that it is the art; Scripture plainly says that it is the heart.

Along this line, Schaeffer takes his readers all too quickly from Duchamp to the *happenings* of the sixties, then to the later environmental art movement. In his description of the Environment art show (Amsterdam, 1965) he comments,

. . . you felt permeated by a total context which was almost subliminal. Almost against your wish you got drawn into the mood of the room. I watched young couples going through these rooms in Amsterdam. I knew that most of them did not understand what they saw. But I was certain that by the time they came out, the atmosphere would have had its effect and then moral defenses would have been weakened. . . . Though the girl could not perhaps analyze what she saw, yet surely she would be more ready to say "yes" by the time she came out (GWIT: 35–36).

Schaeffer has just said that artists have gotten to the point where they don't communicate (GWIT: 35). Now he is describing a kind of communication that is so powerful that it can take place even though the content is not known by the observer. If by "not known" he means "not literal," then at least we can assume that to him communication is based on literalism. If he is talking about transmitting a message that comes about irrespective of knowing content, then he lands squarely in the lap of a different definition of art than he has continually offered.

Then, his reference to some sort of acquiescence on the part of the female observer seems to contain the sexual slant found in his remarks earlier about Duchamp's painting. We are again reminded that people bring their world views to art more often and with far greater conviction than they take them away. Schaeffer seems to forget that those ready to say "yes" are already morally predisposed to do this.

Finally, Schaeffer's treatment of Paul Klee and Jackson Pollock deserve comment. He quotes a statement from Klee concerning the way in which intellect "dies away miserably" in the face of the final mystery of art. Schaeffer interprets this to mean that Klee places himself in a dichotomy, hoping that somehow art will find meaning, ". . . not because there is a spirit to guide the hand, but that through it the universe will speak though it is impersonal in its basic structure" (GWIT: 66).

It is difficult to know how Schaeffer inferred this from Klee. When we read Klee's writings about his creative process, we discover a humility coupled with refreshing insight into the artistic process seemingly nurtured directly or indirectly by a Judeo-Christian world view. His concept of artistic creativity as "Genesis eternal"[2] is outrightly and rampantly joyful, even childlike. His intellectual capabilities and consistency are such that his critic would do well to be schooled by him.

In dealing with Jackson Pollock, Schaeffer employs both verbal and photographic illustrations to demonstrate how Pollock made his drip paintings (HSWTL: 190, 195). Here we find an example of outright error, whether by intent or a lapse in scholarship—one only hopes it is the latter. Whether Pollock experimented with swinging paint cans as alleged and illustrated in the Schaeffer photograph is quite beside the point. It is well known that Pollock personally and painstakingly manipulated these works. By placing the canvas on the floor he could stand over it and around all four sides to accomplish the task he had in mind. These paintings, whether one likes them or not, are to be taken in the fuller context of Pollock's work. He was a gifted artist who worked in many styles, of which the drip paintings are but one. In addition, he was out to accomplish a specific procedural task, that of breaking away from the object-centered and perspectively bound compositional processes of much of pre-twentieth-century art. He came to this task as a serious and gifted technician.

More importantly, when we compare the photograph of Pollock's painting with that of the mechanism Schaeffer set up in the photograph, we must be concerned over the superficiality of the exercise. First, there are only five paint cans, hung at such widely spaced intervals that no linear or chromatic polyphony of the kind realized by Pollock could be achieved. Second, the very swinging of the cans produces a grouping of sterile, patterned shapes, which any schoolboy knows will result when compound pendulum motions are initiated.

The Schaeffer result is exactly the opposite of Pollock's and contradicts his own criticism: Pollock turns out to be the individual who exercised control; the Schaeffer "painting" turns out to be robotic, predictable—the kind of pseudo-twentieth-century art one can find at any walk-on weekend sidewalk art show. Whether we like these drip paintings or not, we must admit that it is obvious that a human being made the one and a contraption the other.

Finally, who is to say whether some cross section of the creation, galactic or microscopic, does not actually appear the way Pollock demonstrated in his drip paintings? There is a profound difference between seeing the creation superficially and seeing into it.

MUSIC

Schaeffer's coverage of this subject is thinner than that of art, partly, one suspects, because of the generally more abstract quality of music. Even so, Schaeffer depends on exactly the same general thesis of world-view-in-artifact.

An initial comment is necessary on Schaeffer's use of sources. He uses Grout's *A History of Western Music,* a standard, respected, essentially undergraduate-level book on Western high art music.[3] In *The God Who Is There,* he quotes extensively from a *New Yorker* profile article on John Cage and a review by Leonard Marcis in *High Fidelity* magazine about Leonard Bernstein's Third Symphony, the *Kaddish* Symphony (GWIT: 70–74). He also quotes from Joseph Machlis' *Introduction to Contemporary Music*[4] and from Leonard Bernstein's *Norton Lectures* given at Harvard in 1973 (HSWTL: 190-193).

With the possible exception of Grout and Bernstein, the books and articles are of questionable substance for the kind of basic thinking Schaeffer should be trying to do. In particular, the Machlis is a very popularized, music appreciation-type textbook and carries with it little weight of insight and scholarly substance. Beyond the technical and scholarly quality of these works, they bear no evidence of anything except typical secular thinking about the arts. Nonetheless, Schaeffer leans on both their data and their interpretations to support his own, seemingly without asking the question as to whether music criticism, along with music compositions, can also be said to contain a world view.

Generally speaking, Schaeffer makes more mention of music prior to the twentieth century in *How Should We Then Live?* than in *The God Who Is There.* Even so, coverage is generally sparse until the period of the Reformation and its outflow into the music of the Baroque period, particularly that of Bach and Handel. Schaeffer quite rightly underscores the emphasis on congregational involvement brought about by the influences of Luther. However, the emphasis is less on the process than on the names of composers who participated in it.

Moreover, the references are loose and somewhat misleading. Composers such as Hassler and Praetorius are identified only as hymnwriters—a far too limiting descriptive—who "later brought forth more complicated forms" (HSWTL: 90). There is no mention of what these complicated forms were, nor of the diversity of musical process and style characteristics shown by each of these great composers. Then, two extremely important figures, Schütz and Buxtehude, are identified only peripherally. Schütz is said to be influenced by Gabrieli, and Buxtehude is identified mainly by reference to a historically true but irrelevant anecdote about Buxtehude's tying the naming of his successor at Lübeck to the marrying of his daughter.

In all this it is quite easy to note the difference in treatment between music and art. So far there is virtually no connecting musical activity to world view in the way it was done with art. Instead, there are names, dates, anecdotes, and loose references to output. It is as if the Reformation is to Schaeffer a generic protective for all practitioners found within its historical and environmental boundaries.

But this is not sufficient. There is a more complex weave of influence and counterinfluence than is implied. For instance, in treating Handel, whom Schaeffer places squarely in the Christian camp, no note is taken nor explanation given of the strong italianate, extra-Reformational and secularized influences that came to bear on his musical style, and no explanation of why several of the choruses in *Messiah*, parts I and II, are virtually direct borrowings from some of his earlier secularly texted Italian chamber duets.[5] The text was changed to that of the *Messiah* libretto.

Schaeffer and the "Demise of Tonality"

Schaeffer essentially skips over musical activity from early Classicism to late Beethoven, and has virtually nothing to say about any of the music of France, Italy, or Spain, from the Baroque Era to the twentieth century. With the line of despair, both *The God Who Is There* and *How Should We Then Live?* unite in virtually repeating each other. Even then, curious leaps and fusions take place. In *How Should We Then Live?* Schaeffer refers to Schoenberg's and Stravinsky's respect for Beethoven's late quartets and implies that they were the German door to modern music (HSWTL: 190, 193). In so doing he makes no mention of the musical substances and processes that link these composers together, nor does he take account of the distinctly Russian and French influence on which Stravinsky's music so much depends. Likewise, in France he links Debussy, whose music he speaks of as being "fragmented," to Pierre Shafer and *musique concrète* (GWIT: 37).

A few comments are necessary about the Beethoven-

Schoenberg link. Much of Schaeffer's concern over twentieth-century music appears to be related to the demise, if it can be called that, of tonality. He connects Schoenberg's system of twelve-tone composition to modern thought by describing it as a nonresolving system, in contrast to that of Bach, whose music contained resolution ". . . because as a Christian he believed that there will be resolution both for each individual life and for history" (HSWTL: 193).

This statement is misleading. First, it overlooks the fact that resolution in music is more than what one does with pitches. Second, it fails to recognize that resolution itself is relative to its context. If any music, Schoenberg's or Bach's included, proceeded in a constant state of tension—which is another word for irresolution—this state would become its own redundancy; it would simply lose its effect. More importantly, Schoenberg saw into relativity exactly the way he should. Just as in the creation everything is relative to everything else, and is in motion with regard to everything else, so with pitch relationships. The comparing of tonality to moral absolutes is simply another example of the confusion of truth and beauty, of things believed and things done.

Third, one could argue hypothetically that a state of constant variation (Schaeffer's description of Schoenberg's style) is at least as biblical as tonality, in that the nonrepeating, ever-developing, ever-evolving force of Judeo-Christian eschatology—for which there is no internal resolution and whose only hope lies in a final apocalypse from the outside—is more analogous to continuous variation. By contrast, tonality and the classical recapitulatory forms connected thereto, could be argued to be more parallel to the cyclical, repetitious view of history more typical of non-Christian religions.

Fourth, it could be argued that tonality, literally depending on a rational and deliberate bending of the natural overtone series, is a primary example of nature eating up grace. The overtone series is made up of an unnumbered sequence of pitches which, as one proceeds upward through them, gradually become out of tune with the bottom pitches. In daily practice this means that if we were to tune a piano according to what the natural law actually dictates, the instrument would be in tune for only one or two keys and would gradually go more out of tune as we proceed from a close to a more distant key, say from C Major to E Major. All keyboard instruments are nowadays tuned to what is known as "equal temperament," achieved by making certain notes flatter or sharper than their natural occurrence allows them to be, and out of tune with what the sensitive musical ear really calls for.

In this sense, what Schoenberg was able to achieve could be argued to be based on a concept of pitch relationships more in accord with the way natural law really works: once one begins moving away from a given pitch, there is no way to return to it. Schoenberg's concept of nonreturn could just as easily be philosophically based on a desire to be true to natural law with its lack of closure than on a denial of absolutes through a questioning of tonality.

These hypotheses are shown, not because they have any necessary basis in historical thought, but because they make a certain kind of philosophical sense and thereby exemplify the ways we can read into a situation.

Schaeffer's linking of Schoenberg to John Cage overlooks the radical difference in their approaches. Schoenberg's system involved tight, nearly legalistic controls, whereas Cage sought out the opportunities of pure chance (HSWTL: 193). There is no question about the error in Cage's world view, nor need anyone be too alarmed about the ways in which he has decided to make music. Cage is as much a maverick, a musical gadfly, as he is a radical. Many of his insights are as refreshing as they are disturbing. They should be used as we use salt, to add flavor only. In his "compositions" in which there is total silence, we can infer an element of protest against the way the average person has lost his ability to truly listen to the music he professes to hear. He is asked to face and respond to silence, not at all an evil idea, considering how much contemporary man is afraid of silence—continually seeking out ways to cover it with activity that itself is not really valued.

Schaeffer and the "Fragmentation" in Modern Music

In commenting on French music, Schaeffer links Debussy's compositional process to the concept of fragmentation (HSWTL: 194). He does not define musical fragmentation at all, nor does he show how it is particularly realized in Debussy's music. He simply makes the statement, leaving the reader to sort the evidence out for himself.

The issue is further complicated when in a sweeping statement he links Debussy to

. . . most composers since, not only in classical music but in popular music and rock as well. Even the music which is one of the glories of America—black jazz and black spirituals—was gradually infiltrated (HSWTL: 194).

We can only guess what is meant by this statement. Schaeffer may possibly be referring to Debussy's preference for using harmony in ways that did not conform to common classical practice. Although Debussy's music certainly fits the concept of tonality and his harmonic language is most pleasant to listen to, he uses it as much for its coloristic purposes as for its procedural leverage, thereby bringing a new freedom to concepts of consonance, dissonance, their preparation, and their resolution. His consummate musicianship imparts a rightness and integrity to this new process that no one can question. Debussy then linked these procedures to concepts of musical form that set the closed classical concepts aside in favor of a more open, freely narrative, though entirely logical approach.

It seems that Schaeffer fails to make an important distinction in his criticism of Debussy and, for that matter, most twentieth-century artists: the distinction between language and linguistic process. For something to work as a language it must internally, or linguistically, cohere. Even though French makes no sense to a speaker of Finnish, each language makes sense to itself and to its own speakers. And all languages make sense to a linguist because each can be found to cohere internally and to communicate on the basis of that coherence. Lacking this, there would be nothing more than phonic chaos; and chaos never "means." But something not thought to mean is not necessarily chaotic unless through linguistic scrutiny no internal coherence can be found.

Debussy simply used a different language than his forebears. His grammar is complete and the syntax clear. It is no more mysterious than that. There are no more grounds for construing it to be a shift from wholeness to fragmentation, than the transition from modality to tonality (which took place roughly from A.D. 1300 to 1600) should be construed to be an exegesis of the shift from salvation by works to *sola fide*.

A few remarks are necessary about Pierre Shafer and *musique concrète* (GWIT: 37, 38). Once again, the question is not whether one must immediately appreciate this music, but whether it is described and contextualized correctly by Schaeffer. He describes this music as being based on real sounds, but "seriously distorted." The composer is described as inventing a machine by which the distortions can be carefully controlled, reversed, split up, slowed down, or speeded up. Schaeffer likens the result to the illusionary effects of Op Art. Just as Op Art causes us to distrust one's eyes, *musique concrète* causes the listener to distrust his ears.

Even if this were a good comparison, the claim would still be open to question. Is distrusting our ears an evidence that something in the art is bad, if we are hearing something never heard before? How can Schaeffer say, a few sentences later, that *musique concrète* is an example that "all is relative, nothing is sure, nothing is fixed, all is in flux" when he has just described the music as being the result of the *careful* control of "distortions"? If *musique concrète* is the result of manipulating naturally and culturally occurring sound, what is wrong with making a new language of it, as long as it is neither equated with previous languages nor meant to supplant them?

Schaeffer and the Beatles

In both *The God Who Is There* and *How Should We Then Live?* Schaeffer alludes to popular music, jazz, rock, and modern jazz. Without going into detail about any of these genres, their stylistic evolutions, the various folk musics of the West, the interchange between popular and classical musics, he concentrates his attention on the Beatles, beginning with another sweeping linkage of the jazz of the forties to the door of despair, to the Beatles (GWIT: 37, including footnotes 1, 42, 43; HSWTL: 170).

Even though his sense of context and musical lineage is not clear, Schaeffer is quite right in highlighting the Beatles because of their profound influence, musical inventiveness, and stylistic eclecticism. Furthermore, there is abundant evidence that their world view was a far cry from a biblical one, and lamentable evidence that this was transmitted to a whole generation of young and even some older listeners. However, the evidence came, not uniquely through the music, but through a larger statement of what the Beatles said about themselves, their lifestyle, and what they eventually chose for many of their lyrics.

The Beatles' music by itself is creative and eclectic, showing distinct influences from Gilbert and Sullivan to English folk,

Russo-European romanticism, a variety of ethnic popular styles, and of course, Bach. Schaeffer uses the record entitled *Sergeant Pepper's Lonely Hearts Club Band* to describe the Beatles' influence. It is difficult to know exactly what he means by what he calls the "pantheism" of their music (GWIT: 42), unless he is again referring to lyrics. Even then, we do not exactly find pantheism in them, but an array of images and messages that go all the way from the doubly intended fantasy-hallucinative lyrics to those of broken relationships, repaired relationships, and outright festivity.

Schaeffer shows particular concern over the merging of one composition into the next, making each side of the record into a single sonic unit. He calls this a form of "total art," indicating that ". . . the words, the syntax, the music and the unity of the way the individual songs are arranged, form a unity of infiltration" (GWIT: 43).

Actually, the Sergeant Pepper record has more sectionalism, discreet musical separation, and structural clarity than many classical works—or sermons. Schaeffer's point about infiltrative communication is a serious one, but it deserves to be developed in a far more fundamental, detailed, and scriptural way than by use of the present example. Any such study must include attention not only to what events do to people but to what people are predisposed to want them to do.

ANALYSIS OF *ART AND THE BIBLE*

The first of the two essays in this booklet has a gentle, pastoral touch to it. Schaeffer affirms that artistic creativity is not peripheral to the Christian and must be brought under the lordship of Christ. Then, from various Scripture passages, he builds a case from which the reader can draw several inferences. With one exception they parallel those set forth in the second essay. Since these will be discussed subsequently, it will not be necessary to list them here. Only the exception will be dealt with.

According to Schaeffer, the commandment to Moses to fashion the tabernacle comprised an authorization to represent many things, including unseen beings—in this case, cherubim. God was the architect, not man, and told Moses what to do in detail (AB: 12). Moreover, Moses was allowed to go somewhat beyond representation, for example, by stylizing the color of the pomegranates on the robes. In other words, art need not be photographic "in the poor sense of photographic" (AB: 14).

Although Schaeffer allows some breathing room for the difference between representation and direct imitation, he raises other questions. First, his statement that God told Moses what to do in detail seems to attach a plenary inspiration to creativity, seemingly disallowing opportunity for personal style—a question similar to that raised in terms of the inspiration of the Scriptures allowing for personal writing styles. Actually, the Exodus passage describing the plans for the tabernacle repeatedly uses the words "after the pattern," in describing what is to be made, but it does not say anything about the artistic style employed in representing them. This task is obviously left to Bezalel and his colleagues, to whom the Lord had given wisdom and skill to do the actual designing (Exodus 31:4).

Second, although Schaeffer leaves room for the stylization of real things (pomegranates), he does not open up the question of nonrepresentation, a crucial question for the twentieth-century artist. This will be discussed in some detail in the last section, so it is sufficient to say here that there are biblical grounds for nonrepresentative art.

Probably the most winsome statement about Schaeffer's personal love for art and its healing effect on him is found in his description of the music of Handel's *Dettingen Te Deum*. Here, in two brief sentences, rather than trying to philosophize or struggling to bring all of the elements of man's doing and being together, Schaeffer simply opens his heart:

> And when you begin to understand this sort of thing [creativity in praise of God], suddenly you can begin to breathe, and all the terrible pressure that has been put on us by making art something less than spiritual suddenly begins to disappear. And with this truth comes beauty and with this beauty a freedom before God (AB: 27).

We would wish, as much for Schaeffer's sake, that he would have allowed himself and his readers more of this kind of communication. It is moving, warm, and positive.

Essay II, "Some Perspectives on Art," is given over to listing and commenting on eleven principles or perspectives by which a Christian can approach and evaluate art. The principles are listed below without any of Schaeffer's comments, so that they can be seen for what they are.

1. A work of art has value in itself.

2. Art forms add strength to the world view that shows through, no matter what the world view is or whether the world view is true or false.

3. In all forms of writing, both poetry and prose, it makes a tremendous difference whether there is a continuity or a discontinuity with the normal definitions of words in normal syntax.

4. The fact that something is a work of art does not make it sacred.

5. There are four basic standards by which to judge art: (a) technical excellence, (b) validity, (c) intellectual content, the world view which comes through, and (d) the integration of content and vehicle.

6. Art forms can be used for any type of message from pure fantasy to detailed history.

7. Styles of art form change, and there is nothing wrong with this.

8. There is no such thing as a godly style or an ungodly style.

9. The Christian world view can be divided into . . . a major and minor theme (not connected in meaning to major and minor in music, but to redemption and fallenness, including sin in the Christian's life).

10. Christian art is by no means always religious art, that is, art that deals with religious themes.

11. Every artist has the problem of making an individual work of art, and, as well, building up a total body of work.

These principles combine easily into two strands of thought—a kind of credo—one dealing with the intrinsic content of art, the other with the referential and exterior. (The parenthesized numbers correspond to the principles already listed.)

> A work of art, having value in itself (1), can be judged for its technical excellence, validity and the integration of content and vehicle (5: 1,2,4). The fact that something is art does not make it sacred (4); by the same token, Christian art is by no means always religious art (10) and there is no such thing as a godly or ungodly style (8). Stylistic change is quite

normal (7), although too much distance between the artistic symbol and the world around may decrease, or even do away with, communication (3).

Besides having intrinsic content, art has intellectual content (5:3) and can communicate this, showing and adding strength to the artist's world view, whatever it is, true or false (2). Since both sin and redemption, despair and hope, have entered the world, it is possible to show these in art works, although not at the expense of one another (9). Moreover, the world view shown is one of the criteria by which art is judged (5:3). While every artist is responsible for the individuality of each work, it is to the complete body of his output that one must look in order to judge performance and world view (11).

Stated in this fashion, it can be seen that Schaeffer's thought can be systematized in principle. The first section carries with it intelligent, understandable, and widely acceptable ideas. Furthermore, it is most refreshing to hear an evangelical say that art has value in and of itself, that style is neither godly nor ungodly, and that Christian art—better yet, art done by Christians—need not always be religious art. This is the kind of thinking that Schaeffer, to his credit, has brought to many evangelicals who have for too long accepted only a narrow sort of romanticized, often tawdry, religious art as the only legitimate kind. The second part of the credo, even though more at issue, also has a consistent ring to it, and falls in line with a significant strand of thought in art criticism.

However, the principles themselves and the way Schaeffer develops them are two different matters. Instead of the clean separation between the intrinsic and the referential, and a clear-cut development of each of the principles, Schaeffer seems to be overwhelmed with the need to introduce into almost every principle the idea of world view. Consequently the original intensity of many of the principles is dulled. Moreover, when he does try to follow through on a given principle, he occasionally loses himself in extraneities and contradictions. Instead of having a succinct and convincing essay from start to finish, the reader is left basically with just three ideas: (1) art must be technically excellent; (2) art not only shows a world view but empowers it; (3) the twentieth century is largely suspect despite the enunciations of certain principles to the contrary and specific encouragement that contemporary Christian art should be twentieth-century art (AB: 51).

In discussing validity (5:2), Schaeffer does not deal with the integrity of the entirety of an art work, but solely with the motivation of the artist. How can an outsider so link content to intent that he can say that making art to please someone—a patron—invalidates it (AB: 42)? Pleasing someone and compromising oneself are two different matters.

In explaining content (5:3), Schaeffer describes it only as that which reflects the world view of the artist. This, even if correct, is jumping the gun. There is much more to content than world view, for in the second principle Schaeffer says that art forms empower world view. From his description of art forms, we can take this to mean content. But between these two principles there is confusion. He uses Rembrandt's *Side of Beef Hanging in a Butcher Shop* as an example of how art causes one ". . . to see the side of beef in a concentrated way" (AB: 38). But a side of beef, though content, is not a world view. And Schaeffer does not tell us what Rembrandt's world view is by the way he paints the beef, nor does the beef tell us what it is. In this instance Schaeffer only describes the ability of art to empower content by saying that he had always taken a side of beef for granted until he saw the painting. But this may only speak of Schaeffer's somewhat indifference to the world around him, instead of Rembrandt's capability to empower it. If we carried this illustration to an extreme, we would have to say that the creation (a side of beef, or a daisy, or a galaxy) is less interesting than artistic representations of it, in which case we would then bespeak a preference for human handiwork over God's.

As to the principle that there is no such thing as a godly style or an ungodly style, Schaeffer begins well and then gradually allows the principle to unravel. In the following statement the last sentence contradicts both the principle and the first part of the first sentence:

> Yet, while there is no such thing as a godly or ungodly style, we must not be misled or naïve in thinking that style has no relation whatsoever to the content or the message of the work of art. *Styles themselves are developed as symbol systems or vehicles for certain world view or messages* (AB: 52).

Further on, he says this:

> Therefore, while we must use twentieth century styles, we must not use them in such a way as to be dominated by the world view out of which they have arisen. Christianity is a

message with its own distinctive propositional content, not a
set of "religious" truths in an upper story. . . . Therefore, an
art form or style that is no longer able to carry content cannot
be used to give the Christian message. I am not saying that
the style is in itself wrong but that "it has limitations" (AB:
54).

This is "both/and" writing. It seems to be locked up in the
truth/beauty equation, yet it tries to break out. Form and
content, content and intent, seem both to be equated and
separated. With the encouragement to the young artist to use
twentieth-century styles, Schaeffer does not provide one example in *Art and the Bible* or *How Should We Then Live?* of twentieth-
century styles that to him would be appropriate and useful. The
reader is left with a bare concept, qualified and often confused
by its subsequent development.

There is one more matter regarding style neutrality that
Schaeffer draws outside of the arts and that deserves comment.
Schaeffer appears to acquiesce to linguistic determinism in his
use of the following illustration. Since Sanskrit developed as a
perfect vehicle for Hindu philosophy, according to some
scholars at least, there is doubt that Christianity could be
preached in it (AB: 51). This implies a linking of truth to
language, to culture, of such magnitude that the latter two are
perceived to bind and silence the former. This thereby overlooks the metalinguistic aspect of truth, along with the power of
God and the gospel to break into and recode any linguistic or
cultural system there is.

It bypasses the theological meaning of Pentecost—that the
gospel can be heard in any language—and ignores the flexibi-
lity and evolutionary aspect of language, without which words
would be forever frozen in singular meaning. Because Schaeffer
so strongly connects world view to content, he is forced into
implying that truth is susceptible to artifact. If Sanskrit is
incompatible with the gospel because of its Hindu-shaped
processes, it follows that other artistic styles and forms will not
fit the Christian message.

Here Schaeffer comes dangerously close to equating certain
approved segments of Western art with the Christian gospel. If
world view shows in artifact, and if only occasionally Western
art is said to be Christian; if complex artistic systems have
developed in civilizations that have no clue about Christianity—how then can the Christian message be carried by these
systems without radically Christianizing the systems? Yet this

very thing happens all the time in the strategies of indigeniza-
tion and contextualization in world missions. In short, indigeni-
zation insists that a radical world view can be comfortable in an
"alien" system. Furthermore, Schaeffer seems to allow for this
elsewhere when he says, "Christian art should differ from
country to country. . . . if a Christian artist is Japanese, his
painting should be Japanese, if Indian, Indian" (AB: 51).

Conclusion

Despite Schaeffer's pleas for artistic quality and integrity
and his desire to see the aesthetic side of godliness take full
blossom, there is a pervading quality of emptiness and
suspicion throughout his writings. While he talks about this or
that occasional artist who brightens the Christian horizon, he
brings a far greater portion of artistic practice under judgment,
especially that of the twentieth century.

Unfortunately, this may only serve to keep the already
artistically disinterested evangelical where he is, or more
tragically, to turn his disinterest to outright suspicion. And for
those who may be both excited about contemporary art and
spiritually sensitive, Schaeffer's linking content to intent is so
unyielding as to leave them with a sense of doubt, if not guilt
and, in some cases, anger. And it may be quite possible that
they are left with no other conclusion than that to continue to
be Christian is to continue as always, wary of newness and
persuaded that the best visual art is the most overtly spiritual
and the best music is patently the most familiar. They may be
forced to end up moralizing where they could be celebrating
and conclude that artistic creativity, with rare exception, is
largely suspect.

Furthermore, many young artists, sensitive in their Christian sojourn, have been led to question the existence of any real
role models in the twentieth century. Consequently they may
do their art with a sense of doubt or, if angered by what
Schaeffer says, with outright defiance. They simply cannot be
dismissed as examples of Christians who, in Schaeffer's words,
produce art that embodies a non-Christian world view (AB: 46).

It has to be stressed that Francis Schaeffer did not want this
to happen. He was a caring and compassionate man. He loved
art and he loved young artists, and in a peculiar way he was
fascinated by the twentieth century. But unhappily this never
really showed through with consistency. If he would only have

spent as much time constructing a thoroughgoing, profoundly Christian alternative for art and music as he did in bringing judgment to it, his whole approach, the "body of his work"— to use one of his own phrases—would have had immeasurably greater value. The final irony is that as much as Schaeffer treasured the importance of having a world view, he failed to show his own with clarity and integrative prowess—at least for the arts.

None of this is meant to imply that art and music are not be be criticized, nor does it mean that all twentieth-century art is somehow to be protected simply because it is the only living art that Western culture has. It does not mean that artists live in a world of procedural and structural amorality, allowed to do whatever they creatively wish, protected by the sacrament of the artness of art.

Somewhere between the detached, sterile, positivist viewpoint that art is art, to which one can neither bring anything nor take anything away except an outrightly aesthetic experience, and the other extreme—Schaeffer's extreme—that art is a literal exegesis of a belief system, there is another position to be taken—one that does not excuse the inexcusable, nor bring suspicion to the noble, whatever the historical frame in which it appears.

In the presence of increasing numbers of young Christians going into the arts, evangelicalism stands in need of the kind of thinking about artistic responsibility that carries with it the love of culture, human creativity, and artistic excellence, all of which were so cherished by Francis Schaeffer. These must be undertaken with a more careful concept of what art really is, how it really works, and where it fits into the whole scheme of human doing and being.

SOME OBSERVATIONS ON ART AND MEANING

Francis Schaeffer, in his belief that art propositionally exegetes a world view, does not raise a new question. However, he is probably the first to raise it among so many evangelicals in so short a time, in a framework of intellectual thought, with such general acceptance and so little focused response. There are also evangelicals who hold the alternative view that art, though richly expressive, is not capable of the moral and ethical disclosures that Schaeffer insists on. It is ironic that two opposing camps within evangelicalism end up disregarding world view. The makers of high art, weary of sacred-secular dichotomies and facile moral pronouncements, simply say that art is art; the evangelical pragmatists, whose behavioral view of the arts has led them to borrow and legitimize every artistic style that fits the context and brings the desired results, simply says that art is a tool.

In *Art and Act*, Peter Gay attempts to attach historical cause to the works of Manet, Gropius, and Mondrian. He devotes a long introductory chapter to the difficulties faced by the art historians in locating cause and effect. After citing numerous artists who claim a relationship between the world around them and their art, he says,

> Most artists, then, are convinced that art somehow "expresses" the world in which it was made and most historians agree. Their argument, however they formulate it, employs, openly or covertly, the language of cause: it understands art to be an effect. But plain and persuasive as this claim may sound, I confess that its vagueness and its high handedness make me uneasy.[6]

Gay then speaks of the complexity of cause:

> . . . a historical event is always the product of numerous causes, immediate and remote, public and private, patent and concealed. The inquirer's impulse to fasten on a single cause appears to be practically irresistible: fame, it seems, awaits that historian who can find one cause where there had been two causes before. But this says more about the explainer and the values of his discipline than about the event he is explaining.[7]

This is a strong statement. Apart from the reference to a quest for fame (which is not being imputed here to Francis Schaeffer), one would think that Gay had read not only Schaeffer, but many others who have devoted themselves to one-cause-one-effect thinking and, in the process, have overlooked the Scriptures in their multiple strategies for stating problems and solutions: the unequivocal Yes and No, the mysteries shown but not explained, and the calls for discernment, in which the strength of one's and his brother's faith determine answers that vary from situation to situation.

In the matter of belief and artifact, Scripture does not articulate the kind of straightforward connection that Schaeffer alleges. This is not because the Scriptures are silent about handiwork. There is abundant writing about both God's and man's. But when it comes to a discussion of who God is, who man is, and what each is to the other, handiwork gives way to truth, law, gospel, and accountability. There are instructions about God's perception of his handiwork (it is good and entirely useful) and man's (beyond its usefulness, it can be turned either to praise or idolatry).

The nearest the Scriptures come to the question of the relationship of artifact and belief is, curiously enough, in the discussion of idolatry. Here, where man most flagrantly misuses his creative gifts and fabricates the most evil of connections between what he makes and what he believes, both Isaiah (ch. 44) and Paul (1 Corinthians 8:4) conclude that idols, when stripped of what man reads into them, turn out to be meaningless.

Creation and Revelation

To discuss the ways in which revelation and creation relate to, without meaning, each other it is necessary first to uncouple the classical paradigm of truth and beauty and replace it with another. This being done, it will be possible to arrive at more positive alternatives in the matter of art and meaning.

Truth and beauty are not equational. Beauty is a quality, an essence in search of a quantity, an abstraction in quest of a reality. Truth is not an abstraction, an essence, or simply a quality. It is real, revealed, self-enclosed, useful, propositional, and absolute. There is no such thing as an ideal truth and a real truth, a heavenly truth and an earthly truth. Nor is truth simply a quality applied to something else to make it truthful. It is a fullness to which all must apply.

There may be degrees of beauty, but not of truth. Something is either true or it is false, whereas something can be simply less beautiful than something else, each in some profound way remaining desirable. Even though there is legitimate debate over whether Bach's music is more beautiful than Mozart's—just as there is debate over whether the Bible is more truthful than the Koran—with truth there is a final reference point; with beauty there is none, other than the *concept* that there is one. But with truth there is more than an idea that there is truth. There is One who is himself the Truth, who has revealed himself in the Scriptures and incarnationally in the person of Christ and calls each Christian to be a living epistle. The beauty of God is not aesthetic beauty, but moral beauty. The beauty of creation is not moral beauty, but aesthetic beauty. Aesthetic beauty is the way something is made. Truth is not the way something is said—aesthetics determines that—but what is said.

A more useful model than truth and beauty is simply that of revelation and creation, at the highest level, and belief and artifact, at the human level. In this respect, the aesthetic is not just reserved for the arts. Beauty the noun becomes beautiful the adjective, applicable to all things that we are responsible for doing. Truth can be beautifully stated and things can be beautifully made. And whereas something less than truthfully done must be dealt with as sin, something less than beautifully done, as undesirable as it might be, is to be dealt with only as a lapse in aesthetic judgment.

If beauty and truth were equal, then aesthetic error, or ugliness, would be the equivalent of untruth. If this were so, an artistically inferior gospel song, while stating a truth about salvation, would have to be rejected out of hand because of its aesthetic error. People may come to a full knowledge of the truth even though what they have heard has been embedded in aesthetic poverty and mediocrity, or even envy, as attested to by Saint Paul. Truth will not ignore an aesthetic lapse, though it can override it. On the other hand, the aesthetic lapse cannot cancel Truth. It will stand apart, pure and unadulterated. Likewise, error, however beautifully stated, remains error. Beauty cannot redeem it.

Spreading aesthetic responsibility to the whole of human endeavor is to be preferred to limiting it only to artistic activity. It may even be argued that the concept of art for art's sake, with its institutions of the separately beautiful, is simply another way to journey into Platonism. It is ironic that many practitioners of a particular discipline in the fine arts often have little or no sensitivity to the work in the other arts disciplines, and often commit serious lapses in aesthetic judgment when they move out of their own particular chosen mode of expression. But when one contemplates the possibility of all things straining for aesthetic credibility, one enters a far more meaningful arena of reality, of which art is only a specialized activity. Otherwise it can quickly elevate itself above other things and attain to the level of the gods—mystically oracular and other. One of the major tasks of Christian thought is to demythologize art. As noble as it can be, it is not a little lower than the angels, but lower than the creation. And asking how the creation stands in relation to the mind of the Creator offers the best example of how man's handiwork relates to his mind.

Among the many passages of Scripture relating the creation to the Creator, the key ones may be found in Romans (1:19–20) and Psalms (19:1–13). The Romans passage is the more direct of the two: God's handiwork, his artifacts, tell enough of what is on his mind to leave mankind without excuse:

> For since the creation of the world God's invisible qualities—his eternal power and divine nature—have been clearly seen, being understood from what has been made.

Psalm 19 speaks of the creation telling the glory of God and the firmament proclaiming his handiwork: day and night pour forth speech and knowledge.

We could infer from these passages that God's handiwork does in fact tell what is on his mind: there is speech, there is knowledge, there is no excuse. We could also infer that since the Creator and the creation provide the model and raw materials for human creativity and since man is created *imago dei,* then human artifacts do show the mind, the world view of the maker. And Schaeffer's basic thesis would thereby be granted.

However, these passages do not make that kind of case. Each casts a different light on the subject, and each assists in contextualizing the other. The Romans passage is the stronger of the two because it is coupled directly to man's suppression of truth and holds him accountable for not listening to the voice of creation. The Psalm passage simply and clearly shows the difference between the speech of creation and the speech of the Law.

In each case it becomes clear that the handiwork is limited in what it can say. The Romans passage argues for the existence and supremacy of a Maker, his power, and his deity. It does *not* say that when we view the creation in unsuppressed conscience, we can tell what is on the Maker's mind or what his character or world view is. We cannot infer truthfulness, mercy, grace, justice, or holiness, all of which have moved toward mankind in saving acts. But there is this: those who see the creation for what it is certainly must face up to the supremacy of the Maker and are responsible to turn to him for what he says and are to do so worshipfully.

The Romans passage makes mention of God's handiwork

as bearing a message *of* the Creator rather than a message *about* the Creator. The implication is that once we turn from the handiwork to the Creator, we then hear the Creator speaking directly, revelationally, and truthfully in ways of which the creation is incapable. If the handiwork had the capability that truth does, there would be no need for the Scriptures, the Incarnation, or for that matter, a denial of pantheism.

Psalm 19 adds a further dimension. The heavens declare the Creator's glory. The days and nights pour forth speech and knowledge, a sure parallel to Romans 1. But an element of ambiguity is introduced. The Hebrew is not clear at this point— by intention, one might think. The days and nights pour forth speech, yet, as some translations go, there is no speech nor words; their voice is not heard. Other translations put it that there is no place where their speech is not heard. The first implies an ambiguity in the way God's handiwork communicates; the second, more parallel to the Romans passage, implies that no one can escape the speech, whatever it is.

The second third of the Psalm (vv. 7–13) introduces a dramatic change. Whatever the creation says, the Creator—the Law—says it better. There is a noticeable shift in language, from ambiguity to precision, unequivocalness, and directness.

> The law of the Lord is perfect,
>   reviving the soul.
> The statutes of the Lord are trustworthy,
>   making wise the simple.
> The precepts of the Lord are right,
>   giving joy to the heart. . . .
> The ordinances of the Lord are sure
>   and altogether righteous.
> They are more precious than gold [the creation itself]; . . .
> they are sweeter than honey.

The speech of God in the Law is undeniably clear. The handiwork with its own peculiar glory is, by contrast, in awe and in waiting. It speaks of itself with clarity, but at most it can only lisp the truth.

The lesson is clear. If we desire to know what the Maker is like, we must turn from the lisping handiwork to the Maker himself to hear his mind in no uncertain terms. The creation is not there to speak propositionally for Someone other than itself. Rather, it says, "I have been created; I have a glory of a certain kind; I have been created in myriad ways; there is richness; but I cannot speak for my Maker except to point to His infinitely greater glory. I am less than He and of a different kind. Go to Him for truth that you may know." Handiwork only points; truth converts.

Moreover, it seems obvious that in the distinction between creation and revelation God has provided a proper place in the whole of being and doing for the relative and the absolute. The creation—and by extension, human creativity—is legitimately the place for relativity, nuance, variegated meaning, and proper ambiguity: speech, but no speech; all in relation to all else, no single focal point. But revelation, the truth, the Law, morality and ethics, word and deed, are the places for absolutes, nonequivocation. The realm of creativity is freely relative, while the realm of truth is eternally fixed.

If all of this is true of the incredibly variegated splendor of God's handiwork, it can be no less true of man in his own limited handiwork. Art work after art work utters speech; there is knowledge of a kind; it is heard everywhere. But this is not the speech of the maker; we must go to him to inquire as to what is truly on his mind. His response should be direct and clear. His handiwork is another glory—not to be overlooked, certainly to be celebrated—but its speech is limited to declaring itself and pointing to its maker. The confusion comes when revelation and creation, world view and artifact, are forced into equality. When we attempt to make art act as truth, truth is diffused, made to lisp. When truth is made to act as art, art becomes slick, obvious, caricatured. This is why so much of today's "witness art" just does not work. In the rush to make the message clear, the aesthetic qualities are blunted; or, if the artistic process is given its rightful due, the truth message, to the frustration of many, cannot be that easily located.

The Creation and Human Creativity

This essay is far too short to allow for a full exploration of the relation of creation to creativity.[8] However, a few examples should be cited, dealing particularly with issues that twentieth-century art has brought to the fore. Emphasis will be on the visual arts, primarily because what is seen in the creation and how it purportedly affects the visual arts has always been more of an issue than what has been heard in the creation and how it affects the musical arts.

The evolution of music has not carried the burden of

imitation nearly to the extent that the visual arts have. Suffice it to say, the music of the twentieth century, including *musique concrète* and certain aspects of randomness, do in fact reach into the creation for precedent: sounds, pitches, transitions from one to the other, heard in any natural setting in unstructured occurrence both simultaneously and sequentially; the range of softness and loudness, including extremes too high and too low to be humanly heard, the exotic and exquisitely complex bird songs, the grunts and cacophonies of singly and multiply heard beasts and creatures. These and more were all here to enjoy long before the Cages, the Messiaens, the Shafers, and the electronicists came along to stylize and manipulate them. The return to natural sound, to nontraditional pitch combinations, to so-called fragmentative constructions, is in fact quite creational. It need not signal a shift in world view as much as a recognition and use of the large pentecost of languages that surrounds all creatures.

There is order, precision, and symmetry of such a magnitude as to cause the most sophisticated technologist to bow in worship, but this is not all. A forest is not arranged row upon row; it is a random collection and distribution of vegetation. Seeds fall where they may, unpatternistically, and they grow where they can. Mountain ranges, continental boundaries, coral reefs have no symmetry; natural sounds are polyphonic in the freest sense of the word. There are levels of attractiveness among things: orchids are more appealing to most than earthworms. Within categories there are levels of quality: one maple tree is more aesthetically pleasing than another; one sunset brings a rapture, another barely a second glance.

Is the Creator—the One holding this great panoply together, swinging asymmetrical galaxies through a universe which, unlike the garden of Versailles, has not been arranged row upon row—aesthetically dull or possessed of a questionable world view? Since the creation has no predecessor— nothing with which to compare it, with which to balance it— since it is a onceness, neither an *A* section of a binary form nor the recapitulative *A* section of a ternary, who can say if it is right?

Why is Africa or the Polar Ice Cap or a cloud a free form? Why are many crystals just enough asymmetrical to show that they are handmade? Did God do stellar number painting in order to make what man calls the Great Dipper; or did man, sequestered for a geometrical moment in his larger history, impose this on a greater mystery? In short, the creation not just allows for but displays free form, free distribution, and asymmetry.

Then there is the question of representation and abstraction, alluded to earlier. Before the creation appeared it was thought up. Dolphins, strawberries, giraffes, tortoises, gravity, sexual reproduction, and natural law had to be imagined. God neither needs any of these nor is any of these, and there were none around for him to copy. He imagined what was not. In this sense he was the first abstract nonrepresentationalist. Each thing he made was purely and simply without reference.

If a hypothetical onlooker, seeing the first rabbit, were to ask God what "that" represented, God's only reply would have been that it represented itself. It did not "look like" a preexisting rabbit. The onlooker would simply have had to trust the integrity of the rabbit itself rather than look to an idea for authentication. Transferring this over to the way people look at art, this same onlooker viewing a painting of a rabbit would be expected to see the painting for what it is, not for what it referred to. Once the viewer observed that the object in a painting looks like a rabbit, the more important question remains, "What does a rabbit look like?" The answer simply is, "It looks like itself."

This is not art for art's sake, but art as task: of the artist having to create, and the viewer having to perceive something complete and pleasing in itself without need of an exterior object to which it can be compared before it can be approved. This concept of abstraction is not enough, nor is it meant to discourage or downgrade representational art. It simply pleads for the integrity of the artist who attempts to live in the first day of Creation, to participate in what Paul Klee called "Genesis eternal."

Something else, just as important, happens in the Creation: it was not only imagined but continued. There was not just a first rabbit, but countless ones to follow, no two of which are exactly alike. Thus, as with the first rabbit, there is still no imitation, but re-presentation. The hyphen is crucial in order to highlight the difference between re-presentation and representation. Re-presenting, in the most creative sense of the word, is every bit as difficult as not re-presenting. The true artist knows he should not replicate; he also knows that he cannot hide behind visual anarchy. He must re-present. This is quite different from the ideal–real polarity of Platonism. In the creational scheme, there is not one ideal essential rabbit of which the rest are shadows. Each is essential, individual, and real. Form is not "out there" and content "right here"; both are fused in everything made.

Two ideas are clear so far:

1. Since the Creation was imagined and did not represent anything, the artist is free to imagine nonrepresentationally and nontraditionally.

2. Since the Creation is replete with re-presentations rather than imitations, the artist may re-present without imitating and remain free to continue traditionally.

However, this is still not sufficient. The artist is bound by his finitude and by the creation itself. He is part and parcel of that which, in every conceivable texture, color, shape, nuance and quality, has first of all been imagined by the uncreated Creator. Anything ever painted, sculpted, danced, or chiseled may well be nothing more than a personal stylization of something already in existence, whether seen or not yet seen by the artist, because all this is in his "dust," and he is of the dust of all these things.

Thus we discover that this or that work of art initially thought to be nonrepresentational turns out to refer to, say, the cross section of a cell under intense magnification, the topography of a distant planetary moon, or the courting rites of a tropical bird. In other words, all art is somehow re-presentative of something already in existence. Man cannot outthink God, but because he is an individual made in God's image, capable of participating most profoundly in the creation, he does not necessarily have to see something before he can imagine it. This is as close as he can ever come to creating *ex nihilo*, but how delightfully close!

Common Grace and Artistic Action

The doctrine of common grace is a pleasant one. Quite simply, it holds that God brings provision to unregenerated man which, along with the benefits of creation itself, allows him to perform noble deeds, to express profound societal, brotherly, familial, and sexual love, and to submit himself to and show understanding for moral and ethical codes of behavior, and in the areas of technology, craftsmanship, and the arts, to make beautiful, useful, and lasting artifacts.

Through common grace, both regenerate and unregenerate man are enabled to consort, to be partners, and to act as one in countless endeavors. Regenerate man can learn from unregenerate man. Words and ideas pass between them; wisdom can be shared; artistic influence can be commonly exchanged. Whereas special grace justifies man before God, common grace allows, enables, and restrains both nature and mankind in the face of fallenness, rebellion, and outright travail. Though the creation is broken and hurting, there is still beauty, efficiency, provision, and overarching mystery; though creativity has fallen and man is at cross purposes with God, there are still art pieces, symphonies, Taj Mahals, sonnets, and dances that bring praise to God even though they may have issued from unbelief.

By the same token, special grace in no way guarantees birth or increase of creativity in a person once he becomes a believer. Regenerate man, possessed of a biblical world view, quite commonly makes technological mistakes and creates artistic monstrosities. In that sense, common grace is not replaced by special grace; the former continues in its ongoing enablement, while the latter saves, irrespective of the presence or absence of the other. While common grace allows the flawed to bring splendor to mankind, special grace covers the flaws of the redeemed. While common grace allows man to rejoice in the handiwork of the sinner, it in no way calls for excusing his sinfulness. So as man sins, he astonishes and benedicts the world around him with his creativity, unmindful of the praise he brings to God, though he may gloat in the praise of fellowman.

However flawed man's world view, common grace unties it from much of his handiwork and restrains sinfulness from intruding into it. The world view is rendered impotent for a season in order that other things may show through in all of their charm and elegance. Thus, man's artifacts go in one direction, his heart in another. God is praised with the one while grieved by the other.

There is a further reach, perhaps somewhat speculative, but worth considering. Perhaps art itself is actually mandated by common grace, bringing relief to man himself from the overwhelming thickness and weight of the whole of his sinfulness and the travail in all of the creation. If man's fallenness showed here with the same ugliness and constancy as it does in what he really is and how he often behaves, there would be ugliness upon ugliness. In this sense, it is not just that sinful man is enabled to do beautiful things; it is that God in his mercy causes man to bring relief to himself and his fellows, in order to lift some of the weight, to bring a measure of light and delight, where there would otherwise be despair. This shows as well in the creation itself which, though groaning and in travail, still shows consummate imagination and brings sustenance to man.

None of this means that the artist is excused; nor does it mean by any stretch of the theological imagination that art is redemptive or even sacramental. It is only too obvious that the creature is easier to worship than the Creator and that salvation by works—among them, artistic works—is as old as mankind. Despite the risk, God has graciously brought upon man the solemn task of bringing joy to him, even though man might seduce himself and lose his own soul in the process. The glory of this same provision for redeemed man is that he can turn his creativity, along with that of his unredeemed brothers, into worship, sacrifices of praise, upon which Yahweh himself is enthroned (Psalms 22:3).

If there is error in assuming that a twisted world view inevitably issues in twisted art, there is equal error in assuming that a Christian world view inevitably issues in Christian art. However thoroughly Christian a person is, however biblically elegant his world view, he, along with all of his doing, is still flawed. As long as there is sojourn on this side of the darkened glass, there will be mistake, distortion, inefficiency, technical lapse, structural ambiguity, and procedural awkwardness.

Artistic Meaning, Linguistics, and Context

It is not accurate to say that all the arts, even those occurring in the same chronological span or geographic location, speak the same meaning. As suggested earlier, this can be explained by the difference between language and linguistics. A sentence in Spanish and a football play do not mean each other, although they may proceed similarly. For the Spanish sentence to be understood and the football play to work, certain syntactical, relational events have to take place that guarantee understanding for the one and a first down for the other. This is another way of looking at the difference between truth and artifact. What is believable—the sentence in Spanish—and what is done—the football play—are not meaningfully equal even though they may be procedurally similar.

Spoken languages are no doubt the most accurate carriers of truth that man has. But they proceed no differently than nonverbal languages do. Whatever man does, in order to make sense of any kind he must discover and adhere to relational, syntactical processes whereby he can go from point A to point B and transmit this action meaningfully to others who already understand or can be taught the process. Thus, for a composer of music to happen upon the same procedural technique used by a painter, writer, or systems analyst does not at all guarantee that the four are saying the same thing. They are simply proceeding the same way.

Limiting the illustration to language itself, we can say, "God is eternal and eternally in control"; or, "God is dead, and the universe somehow continues." There could be no more contrasting world views than in these two sentences, yet the linguistic process used to bring sense to these is exactly the same. Or, in the disjunct literary style of *Finnegans Wake*, we could even find a way to state either world view. The presence of so-called fragmentation or the so-called syntactical discontinuity of Schaeffer's third principle is quite relative, *as long as a firm linguistic process for communicating in this style is located*. Once it has been—and one could conjecture that the author of *Finnegans Wake* attempted this—communication is restored.

Thus it is wrong to say that this way of communicating signals a change in world view. Certainly one must distinguish between word-and-deed art forms and others that are not. The former will communicate beliefs and ideas far more accurately than the latter, although there still may be no proof that the writer is communicating his own personal world view.

Moreover, there is a significant difference in how we use words. A physicist writing a paper on an aspect of quantum mechanics must strive for objective accuracy; he cannot allow what he says to mean more than one thing. The poet, on the other hand, cannot afford singularity; instead, he strives for variegation, nuance, multiple and integrative imagery, and polymeaningfulness. In the Scriptures themselves we can see this principle at work. The Epistle to the Romans and Leviticus are more like the scientific monographs, whereas most of Psalms or the Song of Songs tend the other way.

The more an art form contains words and deeds, the more intrinsic meaning it may carry. The more it employs other symbols, the more contextual or associative meaning it can absorb. Thus, with the nonverbal forms it becomes quite

170 I Harold M. Best

tempting to turn immediately to context for meaning, or to actually insert context eisegetically and create meaning. Since the best art and music are open to context, the more they can be made to mean almost any context. Music, of all the arts, is the most neutral. Debussy's *Claire de lune*, for example, separated from its title can be heard in a variety of social, cultural, and geographic settings, and in almost every case a "fit" will take place, as long as the listener has not by association already unconditionally narrowed the meaning down to that of its title.

This can be stated in the form of a principle: The more an art piece is done or located in the same context, the more it will "mean" that context. This is how we can construe a concept of sacred or secular art and explain how an art piece—say a drinking song or a pagan symbol—can be adapted to church use. It explains why, in tribal societies in which art is organically linked to the activities of everyday life, musical, gestural, and visual formulae are perceived to be a part of the belief systems. The links between belief and artifact are intimately known and adhered to by the insider and are as powerfully meaningful as the meat offered to idols was to the New Testament Christians. They were warned away from it only until they were spiritually strong enough to see the artificiality of the linkage. This being accomplished, they could do the disengaging and see meat for what it was—nourishment—and the idol for what it was—nothing.

This is exactly what must take place in the evangelization of a tribal people. As long as their faith is too weak to untie belief and artifact, they should be allowed to abstain artifactually from that which brings offense or stumbling. If they are not then patiently taught that artifacts and artifactual systems are theologically nothing—even though they may have forgotten their old songs and dances and made new ones for themselves and their worship—they will still be locked up in a dangerous dualism, which will be hidden for a season, only to reappear when the next reformation or cultural change comes along.

Finally, there is a difference between an art piece being expressive and expressing belief. Whether more narrowly defined by a certain culture or somehow contained within a larger flow of transcultural deep structure, there are expressive qualities arising out of tempo, rhythm, texture, hue, length, tension, and release. Art pieces can be described as energetic, morose, vigorous, lighthearted, muscular, or sad; qualities of intellect and soul are described as mystical, transcendental, earthy, profound. There are pictorially representational qualities in music: flowing water, thunder, bird song, battle, or wind. Art forms are said to be rhythmically alive or resonant; music can be monochromatic, brightly hued, etched, or broad-stroked. And so on. However, it is important to remember that all of these, whether highly visible or partially hidden, are qualities that are comfortable in any belief system and are not to be confused with belief itself. Art has a wide reach, but it also has its limits.

The Christian, freed by truth and mandated to do all things well, is the freest of all to see art in all this variegation, richness, integration, and expressivity. The Christian understands that he is free of art in order to be free with it, thus to celebrate, to worship, to offer sacrifices of praise. The Christian artist—in the same freedom, looking back into the first day of creation, schooled by God's handiwork and his creative fellowman, transformed by the blood of Christ, called to a life of holiness, gathering the gifts that he has been given, along with all the wisdom he can pray for—glorifies his Creator and stretches his brother with new songs and art pieces.

The greatest art will always strive toward the mystery and richness of the creation itself. It will speak countless ways. This is not moral relativity, but artifactual expanse. Those who truly love the arts will recognize that they exist to bring incredible nuance to human experience—to widen, refresh, and invigorate it. Those who wish to shut the arts down to narrow meaning and singularity impute to them a function that both demeans them and risks misleading those who might otherwise rejoice.

NOTES

[1] Ronald W. Ruegsegger, "Francis Schaeffer on Philosophy," *Christian Scholar's Review* X (1981), 246–47.

[2] Robert L. Herbert, ed., *Modern Artists on Art* (Englewood Cliffs, N. J.: Prentice-Hall, 1964), 87ff.

[3] Donald Jay Grout, *A History of Western Music* (New York: W. W. Norton, 1960).

[4] Joseph Machlis, *Introduction to Contemporary Music* (New York: W. W. Norton, 1961).

[5] Specifically, "For Unto Us A Child Is Born," "And He Shall Purify," "His Yoke is Easy," "All We Like Sheep." Also, "O Death, Where Is Thy Sting?" was musically based on an earlier amorous Italian madrigal.

[6]Peter Gay, *Art and Act: On Causes in History—Manet, Gropius, Mondrian* (New York: Harper and Row, 1976), 4–5.

[7]Ibid., 7.

[8]For a fuller treatment see Harold M. Best, "God's Creation and Human Creativity," in *The Reality of Christian Learning,* ed. David L. Wolfe and Harold Heie (Washington: Christian University, 1986).

6

SCHAEFFER ON MODERN
THEOLOGY

CLARK H. PINNOCK

INTRODUCTION

It is plain from Schaeffer's published work that he regarded modern theology as a largely sick and misguided project. It is also clear that he thought he had the analysis which would explain how it went wrong and the alternative to put it right again. These are some of the claims we will want to examine.

But first let me indicate what it was about his interaction with modern theology that attracted me during the period before the publication of any of his books. When I think back on the years before 1968, when the books started rolling off the presses, two impressions stand out in my memory. First, Francis Schaeffer showed the young evangelicals who came to L'Abri that fundamentalism was intellectually respectable. He made orthodox Protestant theology live and have relevance in the twentieth century. Furthermore, he devastated liberal theology, not with the fiery rhetoric of the redneck preacher, but by means of intellectual analysis. He was a kind of evangelical Paul Tillich, moving back and forth between the questions of the culture and the answers of Christianity.

Clark H. Pinnock is Professor of Systematic Theology at McMaster Divinity College, Hamilton, Ontario, Canada. He earned the B.A. at the University of Toronto and the Ph.D. at the University of Manchester, England. Among his numerous books are Biblical Revelation *and* The Scriptural Principle.

I myself was one of these young converts of the postwar period in North America who were on the lookout for a well-reasoned biblical faith. I was already pretty sure that the traditional faith was superior to the liberal revisions, but I needed a teacher like Schaeffer to make sense of my own instincts.

This explains, I think, the continued popular success of Francis Schaeffer among conservative Christians: he vindicated orthodoxy and put down liberalism in academically interesting ways, and tied the whole discussion into cultural issues of the greatest importance. He may even have done a lot to change the nature of fundamentalism in America. If we listen to Jerry Falwell, Schaeffer's friend in the latter years, is it not obvious that fundamentalism has grown in intellectual confidence and come forward to challenge the cultural elite? One of the points of appeal in Schaeffer for me was his claim to be able to vindicate conservative theology in dialogue with the best and the brightest in the liberal camp. There were exciting ideas at L'Abri, and we flocked to hear the new scholar–prophet in droves.

Second, we liked some of what we heard when we got there. Schaeffer seemed to understand what the new existential theology was saying and why. He talked about the "leap of faith" and the "upper story." There were long discussions of the later Heidegger and avant garde painting. We were presented a scenario in which theology had shifted from a realism in which God's reality was affirmed to a fictive standpoint in which religious beliefs are existential symbols rather than cognitive claims. Schaeffer saw in the latest theology of the early sixties, in the books by John Robinson and Thomas Altizer, proof of the fact that theology had gone mad. Instead of affirming the objective verities that give men and women hope, these neologians were engaged in transforming Christianity into useful fiction, into existential symbols, themselves the products of man's own fertile imagination.

I would have to say that to this day Schaeffer seems to me to have discerned better than most evangelical leaders the true proportions of the challenge that biblical Christianity faces in our time. He may not have been the best educated and polished of these leaders, but he possessed a gift of discernment that enabled him to articulate a great many truths. We sensed at L'Abri that we were in the presence of someone who really understood the spirits at work in contemporary theology.

THE BASIC EXPOSITION

Turning now to Schaeffer's published opinions, let me sketch the standpoint he took in relation to modern theology. Here in a nutshell is a basic summary of his outlook:

First and foremost, Schaeffer believes that sound theology must be grounded in an inerrant Bible if it is to be able to give solid answers to modern people.

Second, he traces many of the problems in modern theology to autonomous reason, which Thomas Aquinas was supposed to have let loose in the church. This resulted in—to use Schaeffer's colorful phrase—"reason eating up faith, and nature eating up grace."

Third, once loosed, autonomous reason devastated the basis for holding firmly to biblical absolutes, and this led theology to an awful choice between despair on the one hand and a leap of faith in the dark on the other. Modern theology is characterized now by this upper story or existential quality that Schaeffer finds first in Kierkegaard and then in Barth.

Fourth, the only hope for theology lies in a return to what he called biblical presuppositionalism. This is not only the single hope for theology, but beyond it for Western civilization itself.

In filling in the details of this summary, let us consider what Schaeffer writes about modern theology in his books from the earliest to the latest. On the very first page of *Escape From Reason* (1968) we see a facet of Schaeffer's appeal. He says that the theologian ought to understand thoroughly how people think in modern culture just as a missionary has to learn the language and culture of the country to which he is going. Only in this way can we communicate effectively to people. We have to be open to dialogue and be prepared to correlate biblical answers and existential questions in a meaningful way (EFR: 7).

The book proceeds to blame Aquinas for setting up a bifurcation of reality in which reason was granted autonomy in the realm of nature. Although the "Angelic Doctor" intended nature to serve as an apologetic stepping stone to grace, it did not turn out that way, according to Schaeffer. Rational autonomy was taken further and further until in the hands of men like Kant and Hegel it threatened the very foundations of faith and led Søren Kierkegaard to see that the only way to salvage Christianity was to propose a leap of faith. To Schaeffer the two key theologians are Aquinas, who let autonomous reason loose, and Kierkegaard, who proposed the leap of faith.

In chapter 2 Schaeffer indicates what modern theology ought to do: it ought to return to the biblical presuppositionalism of the Reformation. As he explains it, according to this position man, including his reason, is seen to be fallen, and all reality is to be viewed under the norm of God's inscripturated Word. With the authority of the Bible in hand, theology is in a position to offer modern man a solid basis of meaning along with ethical absolutes to guide him. Schaeffer evidently did not think that commitment to biblical authority itself involves an upper story leap of faith, though the extreme brevity of his remarks could give rise to such an interpretation. It is likely that he saw it after the manner of a commitment to a rational axiom such as one would make in geometry. Such axioms are always chosen and then become the basis for subsequent logical deductions. But if this is so, the point about reason being fallen could prove to be awkward. Already the question of coherence in Schaeffer's own discussion arises.

Hegel is the villain of the piece in *The God Who Is There* (1968). Autonomous reason has taken its toll, and a new concept of truth is being born. Schaeffer credits Hegel with effecting a basic change in the way truth is regarded now. Instead of thinking of truth as involving the principle of noncontradiction, Hegel introduced the idea of synthesis in which opposites can be reconciled dialectically. By doing this Hegel gave further impetus to placing religious truth in the upper story, where existential symbols are everything and rational truth nothing (GWIT: 20).

Thereupon Schaeffer again points his finger at Kierkegaard as the father of modern theology, who made the fatal separation of faith and reason and launched the process of upper-story theology. For Schaeffer all modern theology is existential theology; this is the unity that binds all its expression together (GWIT: 51). Theology has made the leap into the irrational. Reason has reached the end of its tether, and a leap of faith is all there is left to do. Karl Barth is interpreted in these terms. Schaeffer sees him as pawning off biblical categories in existential terms. He abhors the way Barth holds to errors in the Bible on the level of history and doctrine and then advances biblical symbols in the upper story of the existential (GWIT: 54, 80).

Again, in terms of his alternative, Schaeffer points to biblical presuppositionalism (GWIT: 15). Unless we posit the inerrant Bible and all that it yields in terms of the Christian world-and-life view, Christianity is meaningless and there are no answers. Only an inerrant Bible supplies the framework, with its absolutes, that modern man needs. Schaeffer does not see this commitment as a leap in the dark, of course, but as the unargued starting point all truth systems adopt in order to begin. In this Schaeffer shows his clear preference for a rationalist rather than an empiricist mode of argument.

The book *He Is There and He Is Not Silent* (1972) sheds further light on Schaeffer's critical vantage point. Theology cannot be sound unless it starts with the proper presuppositions. One must begin with an objective God who speaks to man and then go on to identify the Bible with God's Word to humanity. Beginning with this presupposition, "one can move along and find that every area of life is touched by truth and a song" (HIT: ix, 65). But if one does not start there, the alternative will turn out to be a choice between despair and a theology of the upper story. The tenor of the book clearly shows Schaeffer to be a rational presuppositionalist rather than a straight authoritarian one. He puts his axioms in place and then, like a Gordon Clark or a Carl Henry, he ventures out onto common ground with sinners and offers to debate the issues with anyone on the basis of the superior coherence of the Christian system as compared with any alternative world view.

In his pamphlet *No Final Conflict* (1975) Schaeffer underlines how crucially important it is to hold fast to the full inerrancy of the Bible in this context. He senses that unless the truth of the Bible in the lower story—that is, in the area of objective truth and historical fact—is upheld, the biblical message might be mistaken for an existential solution itself. If that should happen, we would of course find ourselves occupying the same existential upper story with all those religious liberals Schaeffer is critiquing. We would have no alternative to offer and would be operating under the line of despair.

Therefore Schaeffer feels it is crucial to defend the inerrancy of the Bible in exhaustive detail: for example, vindicating the correctness of the Genesis 5 genealogy and the special creation of Eve from Adam's rib. He argues not so much on empirical grounds that these things are objectively true (how could he?), but rather on the basis of the coherent system. Cain and Abel *have* to be historical because of the apologetical agenda Schaeffer is employing. Were he to dub them legendary, for instance, he would seem to be interpreting the Bible existentially himself.

In a truly rationalist manner Schaeffer argues that unless every biblical fact is indeed a fact, no other biblical fact is safe. Exegesis aside, the system calls for an across-the-board consistency on this point. It is easy to see how Schaeffer will have problems not only with the great majority of nonconservative theologians, but also with those conservatives currently experimenting with biblical criticism and hermeneutics.

How Should We Then Live? (1976) adds nothing to what we already know about Schaeffer's assessment of modern theology, but it marks his move into a new media instrument, the cultural film–book spectacular, after the manner of Kenneth Clark's *Civilisation*. Aquinas gets the blame again for letting autonomous reason loose on the church and theology (HSWTL: 43, 52, 81). The Reformation is credited for holding to biblical presuppositionalism (HSWTL: 81). Kant is now mentioned for his part in splitting reality up into two sections (HSWTL: 160). We hear again how Hegel invented a new meaning for truth (HSWTL: 162) and how Kierkegaard inaugurated the leap-of-faith theology (HSWTL: 163, 174). Barth is again interpreted in these terms (HSWTL: 176), while Tillich gets a mention for alleged theological agnosticism (HSWTL: 178). In a special note appended to the book Schaeffer darkly warns of the danger of evangelicals themselves drifting off into the upper story, a theme that preoccupies him during the final years of his life (HSWTL: 255).

The fear that conservative Christians might fall into the pattern of thinking which Schaeffer calls the existential methodology is confronted in *The Great Evangelical Disaster* (1984). Evangelicals are accommodating themselves to the same cultural directions and developing what Schaeffer calls "evangelical neoorthodoxy" (GED: 49). These people no longer hold to the full view of Scripture, as Schaeffer defines it, in terms of total inerrancy and seem willing to engage in some exploratory upper-story theologizing.

To Schaeffer, given his analysis of the situation, this is indeed a disaster. He sounds the alarm: the evangelicals are going liberal! They are surrendering the opportunity to give solid answers to modern man. Alarmed, Schaeffer announces that it is necessary to draw the line between those who take the full view of Scripture and those who do not (GED: 51). The gospel itself is at stake, he says. Thus, in his last statements Schaeffer seems to judge all theology on the other side of the strict reading of the inerrancy of the Bible as deeply flawed if not apostate.

THE BASIC EVALUATION

Let us now evaluate Schaeffer's view of modern theology along with his antidote to its many ailments.

A Lone Voice

One of the sources of Schaeffer's strength and appeal is his ability to make a cultural analysis in which the gospel becomes very crucial to mankind's salvation and restoration. Leaning on the Dutch school, symbolized by Abraham Kuyper and mediated to Schaeffer by his close friend and collaborator Hans Rookmaaker, he traces a breakdown in Western civilization in the autonomy of modern man which leads inexorably to a crisis of meaning and values. He sees a growing hopelessness in the culture, and traces it back to a death of God in modern consciousness. In doing so he is obviously in touch with some basic themes in contemporary life and able to open up a fruitful dialogue with unbelievers, many of whom became Christians at L'Abri.

So successful did this effort become that Schaeffer's ministry broadened out to become a crusade to save the church and Western civilization, particularly in the United States. He enlisted in this task fundamentalists like Jerry Falwell and Tim LaHaye who, although they were world-denying dispensationalists at first, quickly became culture-reclaiming activists under Schaeffer's influence. One of the startling turnarounds in contemporary church history is the way in which a wave of neo-Puritans has been recruited from the ranks of separatist fundamentalists. They have *in effect* become culture-reclaiming postmillennialists, determined to reverse the decline brought about in modern times by the secular humanists.

Though premillennial and initially deeply pessimistic himself, Schaeffer seemed to grown in confidence that it is still possible to turn the tide in America. He became increasingly victory- and not defeat-oriented and was able to appeal to a host of Americans who evidently felt the same way. Modern man needs the undiluted gospel, and regenerated people are in a position to regain an influence in public affairs they had lost early in this century.[1]

As for modern theology, Schaeffer is deeply disappointed with it for not holding forth the saving message of the Bible and challenging the secularizing drift in the culture. Instead, as he sees it, most modern theologians have accommodated the gospel to these apostate directions and failed to make a difference in their generation. In fact, they have not only refused to preach the gospel, but have also brought the church nigh unto death. A great opportunity has been squandered. Instead of challenging the cultural drift into humanism, modern theology has played along with it and sought to reconceptualize the Christian message in humanistic terms.

Even the evangelicals, in Schaeffer's view, show signs of following in this weak-kneed direction. So Schaeffer sees it as his duty to speak out boldly, even if his is a lone voice, to stem the tide of humanist thinking.

And in a sense he was a lone voice. The modern theologians who did see the handwriting on the wall of Western civilization did not present a fundamentalist theology, while the conservatives often were content to couch their message in nonintellectual terms. Schaeffer's appeal to many of us was precisely his ability to deliver the strong message of historic Reformed theology in academically intelligent ways. He opened up to us a new way to see modern theology and new ways to move in communicating the saving message.

Even here, there was, however, a tendency to force modern theology and culture onto a Procrustean bed of Schaeffer's own making. Certainly there is a good deal of despairing in modern life, owing to the logical implications of rejecting the God who gives hope and meaning. But behind the decision to do without God lies a kind of scientific thinking that believes the world is all there is.

There has been a broad shift in the way we tend to regard reality so that now it is not very clear what role if any God plays, with the result that many people have decided to live on the basis of their own resources—realistically and without despairing. They are not so much rebels who want God not to exist so they can be God themselves, as they are nostalgic former theists whose belief in God has faded somewhat reluctantly away. When we look at a man dying of cancer, we do not think of demons or predestination, but of a biological process affecting the functioning of his cells.

Schaeffer does not appear to recognize this kind of problem in modern culture and therefore is not prepared to grant that nonfundamentalist theology might be trying to cope with it. Very little of what Schaeffer says is likely to help a person with this sort of problem.

A Great Gulf Fixed

A second area where Schaeffer is quite right about contemporary theology relates to the enormity of the gulf he sees between the message preached by the Reformers and the one preached by many modern theologians. This is not a point denominational leaders like attention called to. Schaeffer is certain that the theology of the old Reformation—based as it was on the infallible Word of God in the Bible—and the theology of the new Reformation, whether liberal or neo-orthodox—based as it ultimately is in human experience—are two very different things. Between Luther–Calvin and Schleier-macher–Bultmann there is a great gulf fixed. On this point surely Schaeffer is dead right.[2]

Religious liberalism accepted as normative the leading notions of secular modernity and presented Christian faith as normative because of this capacity to transform secular life by infusing religious values into it. It changed the concept of Christian truth from one of divinely revealed propositions into a set of relative human symbols that elucidate human life but do not compete with scientific or historical knowledge. Although neo-orthodoxy challenged liberal theology at several points—for example, its facile optimism and rational confidence—the new theology still came across extremely vague when it came to locating the Word of God. It sounded to Schaeffer like a new modernism which, when all was said and done, grounded theology in an existential encounter. Were not all these liberals pretty much the same in making Christianity an interior thing, an experience of faith rather than the objective truth of the self-revealing God? I would award Schaeffer a lot of credit for having seen this.[3]

But in doing so, Schaeffer was more than just a fundamentalist. Though he agreed with the theology and even the need to separate from compromising religionists, Schaeffer, like other so-called evangelicals, deplored the anti-intellectual approach taken by so many fundamentalists. He himself wanted to recover the kind of theology that had been done at the old Princeton Seminary by the likes of Warfield and Machen, in which high standards of scholarship were maintained and intellectual challenges were calmly faced. He also deplored the lack of love often displayed among the fundamentalists and deplored their failure to see that Christianity applies to the whole of life and society and not just to the spiritual realm.

What enabled Schaeffer to retain the admiration of these fundamentalists was his combination of intellect and passion. Here was a man who would weep over the condition of the church and the culture and would pray fervently for revival with anyone. The fundamentalists were impressed by this and therefore remained open to the new ideas they heard coming from his mouth.[4]

The problem for Schaeffer here is the one I have mentioned: did he wholly grasp *why* modern theology made the shift to the interior that it did? He saw it in terms of giving up the proper presuppositions and losing a rationally coherent system of truth, which led to a line of despair and the leap of faith. But he did not seem to take into account the difficulties a thoughtful person has nowadays believing what he is commending. Have we not replaced providence with scientific explanation? Is not the New Testament world view mythical? Has not criticism shown that the Bible is mistaken at points and in some ways cultural conditioned? How can one just follow Schaeffer's advice and swallow the Bible as God's verbally inspired Word simply on the grounds that the orthodox system requires it? In the view of most modern theologians, orthodoxy has become unbelievable precisely because these questions are not properly faced.

Schaeffer was so certain that a tight rational system with an inerrant Bible would give us the answers we need to live meaningfully that he blithely overlooked the nitty-gritty reasons why such a system lacks credibility. Nevertheless, to some extent the more holistic witness of L'Abri itself made up for the gaps that were left by Schaeffer's orientation to rational presuppositionalism.

Theology in the Upper Story

Probably the finest single insight Schaeffer ever had in regard to modern theology has to do with what he calls its upper-story character. Though one can wonder if he explains it adequately, I do not think he can be denied credit for discerning a fundamental characteristic in contemporary theology. Schaeffer sensed that theology had steadily moved away from theological realism, in which it is important that God objectively exists and Christ was factually raised from death, to fictive theology in which all that matters is that theology expresses human needs and aspirations.

Under this rendering, religion is the activity in which man imaginatively creates meaning for himself in an objectively meaningless world. Theological truths then are not universally valid but on the order of moral convictions about what is right. They are the belief of the human community to which we belong, beliefs which guide our behavior and give us hope. But they are not to be thought of as objectively true, or to be considered binding upon other communities. Our beliefs are the symbolic expression of the values we have chosen and nothing more. Theology is good fiction—it grants us useful illusions whose validity we have no way to test. In their theology, people fictively frame a surreal world beyond the rational which, though it has no cognitive significance, fills life with meaning and hope.[5]

It is true, of course, that many modern theologians would hotly deny that this is the game they are playing. Schaeffer may be describing the work of Lonnie Kliever or Don Cupitt, but not Rudolf Bultmann and Jurgen Moltmann. Surely this is the kind of cynical view we would expect to come from a fundamentalist newly educated. Certainly Bultmann, for all his demythologizing and turning theology into anthropology, would not accept that he is an upper-story theologian of the fictive variety. He claims to be nothing other than a twentieth-century Lutheran!

But Schaeffer's point is not to say modern theologians agree with him about what they are doing, but only to give insight as to what is in fact going on. Modern theology at large is trying to declare things to be religiously true that are actually historically or metaphysically false. I happen to agree with Schaeffer that the direction of modern theology since Kant has been in the direction of the fictive upper story. Reason gives us no basis for meaning and value, so why not look to practical reason (i.e., experience) and create your own?

I would go further with Schaeffer and say that this is not only the overall direction of modern theology, but also a fatal mistake in terms of what modern man needs to hear from us. People will not be delivered from hopelessness and relativism by learning about religious symbols created by others like ourselves. What they need are solid answers that present the God who really is there and who raised Jesus from death for our sakes. Without that, all the self-generated faith in the world will not help much.

But there are some difficulties even with Schaeffer's finest point. First, the polemics behind Schaeffer's strong point against upper-story theology leads him to deny some senses in which theology is about meaning and values that do lie outside the realm of the scientific. He is so worried about a divided field of knowledge that he tends to equate science and theology in a way that cannot be sustained. He refuses, for example, to grant that the main point of early Genesis is not to teach in the area of geology and biology but rather to instruct us in the broader area of world view. This is to invite instant warfare between science and religion of the kind that has vexed the church for more than a century. The very strength of Schaeffer's analysis of the upper story lands him in a morass from which I cannot see him being able to escape.

Second, to repeat myself, Schaeffer does not seem to have an adequate grasp of the precise attraction of the upper story for modern theologians. He seems to miss the fact that the emphasis on subjectivity and inwardness arose in response to the pervasive scientific detachment of the Enlightenment and to the sense of alienation and dehumanization that followed. He can see the superiority of Christianity as a system over secular humanism as a system, and why logically people have been driven to fictive theology, but he is very slow to understand the problem of empirical doubt. Many modern people experience the feel of Christianity as mythical and do not know how else to do theology except as demythologizing and existential rein-terpretation. What other choice is there? They know that there are voices like Schaeffer's which exhort them to return to theology for the premodern period, but they do not see how they can do so. And very little of what Schaeffer says helps them to get over this problem.

Third, what Schaeffer recommends as an alternative to upper-story theology is sometimes hard to distinguish from it. In calling for biblical presuppositionalism he seems to be asking us to accept the Bible as inerrantly true because it would be pragmatically wise to do so and because it would give us a rational system of truth to depend on. But this invitation sounds a lot like voluntarism in religion, as if ultimates are chosen in the final analysis, as if religion is a wager or a leap of faith. Schaeffer never hints that he is in the least aware than someone might wonder where presuppositional theology dif-fers from existential theology? Both of them tell us to choose our ultimate axioms and refuse to give evidence on behalf of them that is really independent of them.

Frankly, Schaeffer does too little to help me understand

just how what he is proposing is not in the final analysis itself an upper-story theology. My own early solution to this problem, while still under Schaeffer's direct influence, was to wed evidentialist apologetics to his presuppositional approach, but this is something Schaeffer never was willing to do.[6]

Gaps in the Details

On the negative side of the ledger is Schaeffer's lack of credible scholarship when it comes to details. One gets the impression when reviewing his sketching in of the data base on which his grander claims are mounted that much of the time Schaeffer is beyond his depth. He has, as I have already suggested, some astute instincts about the general flow of intellectual and theological history, but when it comes to specific knowledge about Aquinas or Kant or Kierkegaard, there are large gaps. What he says about them is minimal, and even then his judgments are controversial and undefended in the face of alternative readings. For whatever reasons, Francis Schaeffer is poorly informed about the historical side of the topics he elects to talk about. This explains, of course, why he is loved by the crowds and ignored by many evangelical scholars.

First, on a general level all we have to do is to pick up practically any history of philosophy or theology (e.g., Colin Brown, *Philosophy and the Christian Faith*, 1968) and see what responsible summaries of the opinions of the great thinkers are like. Then when we turn to Schaeffer, what we find are fuzzy and blurred presentations, cryptic in the extreme, which tend to be pseudohistorical and leave us with the distinct impression that he has not read the original works themselves. Even when he tries to trace the evolution of the upper story from Aquinas through Kant and Hegel, one has little confidence that he has more than a hunch to back up his analysis. My impression is supported by my having been at L'Abri and knowing the lack of literary resources there and the fact that Schaeffer tended to work from newspaper clippings in his lectures and discussions.[7]

Second, in terms of specifics there are difficulties wherever we look. In the case of Aquinas, for example, Schaeffer is not consistent. On the one hand he complains that Aquinas uses reason as if sin had not affected it adversely, and then uses reason freely himself in dialogue with fallen men and women in his own apologetics. As Van Til says in his syllabus about

Schaeffer, you cannot have it both ways. The only real difference between Aquinas and Schaeffer when it comes to reason is that Aquinas is an empiricist while Schaeffer is a rationalist—but both use reason as if it works as God meant it to.

Indeed, even as a rationalist Schaeffer is not consistent. He argues in *He Is There and He Is Not Silent* that "no one has ever demonstrated how time plus chance, beginning with an impersonal, can produce the needed complexity of the universe, let alone the personality of man" (GED: 9). But what is this if not a rudimentary form of the teleological argument, an empirical argument of the very kind that made Aquinas justly famous? We would not find a consistent theological rationalist like Gordon H. Clark ever engaging in natural theology of this type.[8]

We could add one further observation to this and say that Aquinas is more than likely not the source of the upper-story theology but the best antidote to it. Surely what led to the upper-story shift was the loss of confidence in metaphysical theism, thanks in part to Hume and Kant. What we need most is a new incarnation of Aquinas who would give us the intellectual defense of theism that would sweep away the loss of faith which the upper story bespeaks. I see little truth in anything Schaeffer says about Aquinas, either by way of description or evaluation.

As for Luther and Calvin, Schaeffer wants us to return to their outlook of biblical presuppositionalism. They used no such terminology, of course, so we are taxed to discover what he means. He seems to think that they presupposed the authority of the Bible in an authoritarian way and subjected all reasoning to the Scriptures (EFR: ch. 2). But he does not seem to be aware of the difficulties in interpreting Luther and Calvin on matters that touch on the philosophy of religion. They were not very interested in apologetics in the first place and do not seem to offer a coherent viewpoint. Therefore we have some like Barth interpreting them as fideists, and others like Warfield interpreting them as if they were rationalists. The fact is that not a lot of light is shed on Schaeffer's apologetic agenda from their writings. In fact, what with the stress both Luther and Calvin made on the witness of the Spirit to the Word, I think a decent case could be made out for the neo-orthodox interpretation of Reformation theology, in preference to Schaeffer's own rationalism. Again, he shows no profundity in speaking about the Reformers.

Schaeffer is definitely unfair to Søren Kierkegaard. While it is true that Kierkegaard began the trend to speak of faith as risk and encounter, it is not true that he was unorthodox on that account. He cannot be equated, say, with Bultmann later. He was a thoroughly orthodox believer who happened to believe that classical apologetics had failed and that stress on faith as inner passion is what is called for. He may have been wrong about that (I am not sure he was), but we cannot charge him with being theologically in the upper story. He believed in the triune God who is there every bit as much as Schaeffer did, but believed that access to God is along the lines of a faith decision. I would not minimize the importance of Kierkegaard's apologetic move or deny that it invited extending the principle into theological heresy. I simply object to Schaeffer's depicting Kierkegaard as a theological liberal when he was not.[9]

The way in which conservatives like Schaeffer handle Karl Barth is also disturbing. They seem to see him as incarnating all that is bad in modern theology, even though the liberals see him as some kind of fundamentalist on account of his doctrinal orthodoxy.

I believe there are two basic reasons for this. First, Barth was not a rationalist at any time in his career and therefore fails to articulate the system Schaeffer thinks is needed for a theology to be and to remain sound. Second, in the early twenties Barth did express an existentialist theology of the Bultmann type, which could honestly be called a new modernism, as Van Til and Schaeffer called it. But Barth forsook that early position in the late twenties and launched the *Church Dogmatics* on a fideistic and basically biblicist basis. Yet Schaeffer, having pegged Barth as a new modernist, will not hear of this change of direction and insists on portraying him in the darkest colors. To my mind, Schaeffer is unfair to the Barth of the *Church Dogmatics* and misses the fact that the mature Barth is in many ways an ally in the work of defending the orthodox faith in our generation.[10]

Schaeffer does not really discuss other modern theologians. He is already persuaded that they are upper story to a man and does not bother to treat them. I believe that the process theologians, the Pannenberg circle, and the liberationists do not fit the upper-story pattern at all and belie Schaeffer's sweeping claims.

When we enquire into Schaeffer's treatment of individual thinkers, the questions pour forth. What kind of open dialogue is this when the other views are distorted or not heard? How can one justify forcing the evidence to fit a preconceived pattern? Is it right to promote Schaeffer as a great scholar who, like Kenneth Clark, can open up intellectual history to the common man? I wish we could say that Schaeffer was just an evangelist and ward off this criticism, but his own claims and those made for him in the books and on film will not allow it. If I were to speak of Schaeffer's greatness it would be in terms of what this man did with a very unpromising background and set of tools. This fundamentalist came a long way from the Machen–McIntire circle, but cannot reasonably even be placed in a league with Carl Henry or E. J. Carnell in evangelical scholarship.

And yet I would want to speak about the genuine insights that Schaeffer had despite all his limitations. How is that possible? How can a person swim so far beyond his depth into the realms of philosophy and theology and still be able to put his finger on matters of importance? I think the answer lies in the gifts that God gave him. Although Schaeffer is not a guide to intellectual history, he possesses a keen discernment and sound intuition into the spirit and texture of much of modern life and theology. One often finds a person not formally trained who has deep insight into difficult issues and has wrestled with them genuinely in his own terms. Schaeffer may not have been a great scholar, but he was a wise man, steeped in the Scriptures and aware of the pain of modern life. Using the gifts he had been given by God, he went a long way toward relating that pain to the Balm of Gilead.

Inevitably his good ideas were rendered ineffective for many by their inadequate presentation, but they were good ideas nevertheless and he made them available to other Christian minds who can now take them and use them to better advantage than Schaeffer himself could.

The Presuppositionalist Pitfall

A few slips and errors are forgivable if Schaeffer's own methodology contrasts properly with the upper-story method he is criticizing, but this is not the case. First of all, his own alternative seems at first sight to lie in the upper story itself. We are asked to assume that God exists and that the Bible is God's inerrant Word and at the same time are told to reject any theology that calls for a leap of faith. We are exhorted to take early Genesis as simple fact, not because hermeneutically it must be or because the evidence is mounting that it should be, but because Schaeffer's system requires it. Even the Bible must conform to his apologetic agenda—how can we condemn the upper story if we allow the Bible at times to commend such a thing? Schaeffer's bottom line is that we *choose* the Christian presuppositions. How then can he criticize voluntarism in theology so harshly?

Second, Schaeffer is so enamored with his analysis of the history of recent theology in terms of the line of despair and the upper story that he does not identify accurately what the situation calls for. If reason has been used to undercut the rationality of Christian theism, then surely Christians ought to use their minds to reestablish its cogency and solidity. By accepting presuppositionalism himself, Schaeffer adopts an upper-story-like solution and does nothing to rectify the situation.

The problem we face is secular thinking, and to combat that it is not sufficient to predict where humanism will lead us if we follow it out. At some point one has to refute it. We have to mount arguments that show how close attention to reality will reveal not only the intelligibility of theism but also the truth of the Incarnation and of the Bible itself as a linguistic vehicle of divine revelation. If we cannot do that (and Schaeffer scarcely attempts to do it), it is safe to say we will never regain the position of influence in the culture that evangelical Christianity once had in North America.

Until we present a nonpresuppositional apologetic for the Christian faith—one that does not require a person to start with the right religious assumptions, but offers to justify the truth of Christianity apart from such a leap of faith—we will never convince modern theologians to forsake the upper story. It will continue to offer them a false haven from the storms of intellectual criticism. Little that Schaeffer says is designed to lessen the appeal of the upper-story safe haven when what he offers is a great deal like a refuge from intellectual storms itself.[11]

Third, even as a presuppositionalist Schaeffer is inconsistent. At one time he will speak like Cornelius Van Til, asserting the fallenness of reason and attacking the neutrality of thought. But normally and regularly Schaeffer will proceed as if he thought reason is an instrument both sides of the discussion can safely use. In this he reveals his affinity to the old Princeton school and its empiricist apologetic approach. Schaeffer tries unsuccessfully to combine two incompatibles: presupposition-alism, which holds that reality is constituted by the prior commitments one holds, and the classical apologetic model, which believes reality out there can dictate which ultimate commitments are the best and most reasonable. Schaeffer floats back and forth between these two very different standpoints as suits him. He will appeal to presuppositions when it pleases him, or he will (rarely) hold out a piece of evidence or two when it feels appropriate. This serious lack of consistency threatens Schaeffer's reputation to be a foremost critic of other modern theologies.[12]

Wagging the Theological Dog

One of the great dangers of any apologetics is that its intellectual requirements will tend to make demands on the theology it is supposed to be defining. Bultmann's judgment about what modern man is going to be able to *accept* clearly influences his hermeneutic of what the gospel *is*. The same has happened to Schaeffer. He has chosen a rationalist type of apologetic to defend Christianity, a style that counts on Christianity's being a system of truth based on certain axioms and involving a certain set of absolutes. The apologetic tail has a way of wagging the theological dog. Once one is committed to a rationalist apologetic, he will inevitably seek to construe Christianity after the manner of a rational truth system wherever possible, stressing the parts of Scripture that lend themselves to that reading and underemphasizing the rest. This can lead to rather serious consequences, as it has done in Schaeffer's case.

The clearest and most serious example is the emphasis Schaeffer places on the inerrancy of the Bible. Whereas at the Reformation justification by faith in Christ was the article of the standing or falling church, now according to Schaeffer iner-rancy is the watershed and the foundation of theology. It sounds as if the vehicle of the saving message has taken over the center stage and pushed to the side the message itself. Now, presumably, the key issue to determine is not, Do we trust in Jesus Christ for salvation? but, What view about inerrancy do we hold?

Obviously Schaeffer made a distinction between Christ as the material foundation and Scripture as the epistemological foundation, even if he did not always pause to make it clear. He knew perfectly well that a sinner can be justified only through faith in the shed blood of Christ. Nevertheless, his apologetic did not allow him to begin preaching Christ; rather, he had to being talking about the need for absolutes and proper presuppositions. Presumably, if one gets these things right, the rest will take care of itself.

Francis Schaeffer the believer trusts in Christ, but Francis Schaeffer the thinker is preoccupied with rational methodology and propositions and inerrancy. And, as if to prove how deadly serious he is about it, he is prepared to divide Christians from one another according to whether they agree about these methodological questions. A theologian like C. S. Lewis, for example, who rejected biblical inerrancy but who defended the gospel of the Incarnation, would by Schaeffer's criteria be on the other side of the great divide that separates those who hold the "full view" of Scripture and those who do not.

How evangelical is this? How far have we come from Luther, who measured even the Bible by the standard of whether Christ was being preached, to this new scholasticism, which places the Bible on a par with Jesus Christ if not above him? Schaeffer's apologetic approach has led him to inflate the admittedly important place of the Bible in Christianity and thus to obscure the very point of the Bible, which is to bear witness to Jesus Christ. An apologetic that is appropriate to defending the New Testament message must be one that keeps the focus where the New Testament places it and does not shift the emphasis in order to placate the requirements of the system.

I realize how ironical these remarks are. Schaeffer set himself up as the defender of true biblical Christianity and condemned others for yielding to cultural pressure and surrendering essential beliefs. However, I believe that Schaeffer himself allowed his theology to be distorted by the pressures of the polemical situation, presenting a less than clear gospel himself. Yet he was not conscious of this at all and continued to call true Christians to leave the large denominations and join with him in separatist churches maintaining a pure testimony. This should be a warning to the rest of us in judging our brethren and setting ourselves up as paragons of theological virtue.

CONCLUSION

Francis Schaeffer, warts and all, was a great Christian man and a most important person in my life. I have not known another like him to this day. Here was a serious disciple of Jesus Christ, who paid a price for following his Lord and bore a courageous witness to the gospel. He was a godly man, a man of prayer, who wept and pleaded, intellectually and passionately, that people should heed the message of God's kingdom. He convinced me of the importance of keeping a balance of mind and heart and not backing down in the face of opposition whether from within the church or the culture. He cared about truth, and because he was not a prisoner to the establishment in any sense, he could speak out boldly on issues that mattered.

On the subject of modern theology, Schaeffer was an insightful interpreter. Although the details of his analysis will not bear much close scrutiny, the general lines of his intuitions need to be taken seriously. Obviously he is a stepping stone rather than a final authority. In many ways he ventured beyond his intellectual depth. One could not compare him in a class with Carl Henry or Van Til, or with Barth or Bultmann. His influence as a thinker will not last long. But what is impressive and what will last, as in the case of Bonhoeffer, is not the thought but the total quality of the man in whose face the glory of God shone.

NOTES

[1] Although some commentators try to distinguish father Francis from son Franky Schaeffer V, I am inclined to see a flow from one generation to the next. Franky is simply pursuing to greater consistency the culture-reclaiming agenda that was beginning to come from his father. The style is different, but the direction is not. The group to watch in my opinion is Christian Reconstructionism, spearheaded by Gary North.

[2] On the same point, B. A. Gerrish, though a truly great historian of Protestantism, is wrong. He tries to link Calvin and Schleiermacher together theologically even though he is honest enough to admit their methodologies in terms of biblical authority are profoundly different. *The Old Protestantism and the New* (Chicago: University of Chicago, 1982), ch. 12.

[3] Schaeffer grasps basically what Gilkey explains so much more profoundly than Schaeffer could. Langdon Gilkey, *Naming the Whirlwind* (New York: Bobbs-Merrill, 1969), 73–106.

[4] It is instructive to compare Schaeffer with another leader of American evangelicalism, Carl F. H. Henry, about whom a helpful book has been written. Bob E. Patterson, *Carl F. H. Henry* (Waco, Tex.: Word, 1983).

[5] Two current theologians who espouse just the kind of upper-story theology Schaeffer warns against are Lonnie Kliever and Don Cupitt. Kliever, *The Shattered Spectrum: A Survey of Contemporary Theology* (Atlanta: John Knox, 1981), and "Fictive Religion: Rhetoric and Play," *Journal of the American Academy of Religion* 49 (1981), 657–69. Don Cupitt, *The Sea of Faith: Christianity in Change* (London: BBC, 1984), and *Only Human* (London: SCM, 1985).

[6] Clark H. Pinnock, *Set Forth Your Case* (Nutley, N. J.: Craig Press, 1967).

[7] A lesson in how one ought to discuss the developments in modern theology can be gained from James C. Livingston, *Modern Christian Thought From the Enlightenment to Vatican II* (New York: Macmillan, 1971), and Alasdair I. C. Heron, *A Century of Protestant Theology* (Philadelphia: Westminster, 1980).

[8] For some correct insights on Aquinas see Edwin A. Burt, *Types of Religious Philosophy* (New York: Harper & Row, 1939), ch. 5, and Stuart C. Hackett, *The Resurrection of Theism* (Chicago: Moody, 1957), 117–30.

[9] See Frederick Ferré, *Basic Modern Philosophy of Religion* (New York: Scribner's, 1967), ch. 9.

[10] For the fascinating story of how evangelicals have interpreted Barth, see Gregory G. Bolich, *Karl Barth and Evangelicalism* (Downers Grove, Ill.: InterVarsity Press, 1980).

[11] If Schaeffer had done what Stuart Hackett has recently done, he would have broken the hold that the upper story has on despairing Christian minds. Hackett, *The Reconstruction of the Christian Revelation Claim: A Philosophical and Critical Apologetic* (Grand Rapids: Baker, 1984).

[12] If the reader desires to sort out the variety of evangelical approaches to Christian apologetics, see Gordon R. Lewis, *Testing Christianity's Truth Claims* (Chicago: Moody, 1976).

Part III

SCHAEFFER'S CRITIQUE OF CULTURE

7

SCHAEFFER ON HISTORY

RICHARD V. PIERARD

Francis Schaeffer was not particularly known as a historian until the appearance in 1976 of his first film series, *How Should We Then Live?* But readers had long recognized that his philosophical and theological ideas were rooted in a historical context, and they frequently found him using such concepts as the meaning and flow of history and the Bible as history. However, the publisher of the book version of *How Should We Then Live?* went much further and referred on the dust jacket to Schaeffer's "profound scholarship" in the field of history.

By this time, professional historians were beginning to pay more attention to his work, especially since the film series was touted in some quarters of the evangelical Protestant community as the Christian counterpart to Kenneth Clark's *Civilisation* and Jacob Bronowski's *Ascent of Man* projects.[1] But no one had made a systematic analysis of Schaeffer's contributions to historical thought. This essay will seek to do so, first by examining his philosophy of history and treatment of Western thought and culture, and then by assessing the strengths and shortcomings of his historical scholarship. Although his wide-

Richard V. Pierard is Professor of History at Indiana State University, Terre Haute, Indiana. He holds degrees from the California State University at Los Angeles (B.A., M.A.) and the University of Iowa (Ph.D.) and was a Fulbright professor at the University of Frankfurt, Germany, in 1984–85. He is co-author of Streams of Civilization: The Modern World to the Nuclear Age, *Vol. 2, and* Twilight of the Saints: Biblical Christianity and Civil Religion in America, *and other books.*

ranging intellectual interests and writings constantly spill over the traditional disciplinary boundaries, the discussion will seek to confine itself as much as possible to historical concerns.

SCHAEFFER'S PHILOSOPHY OF HISTORY

Although Schaeffer does not devote a specific section in any of his works to spelling out a personal philosophy of history, his understanding of the historical process is readily visible. His underlying conception is an unflinching teleological, providential view of history. God created history and acts within it; he is not suspended above it (CBWW: 80). History is going someplace; it is not a series of endless cycles. There is a flow to history. From its absolute starting point at the Creation, history flows on to its fulfillment at the establishment of Christ's reign on the earth. The past, present, and future are intimately connected in the divine plan. God works in history "on the basis of his character," and when his people and their culture turn away from him, he judges them either by "direct intervention in history" or "by the turning of the wheels of history" (NLP: 202, 226–27; GST: 29, 63–64; DIC: 17, 20, 31).

Christ stands at the center of the historical process. He existed before the creation of the "space–time continuum," an absolute event which happened at one point in time and not another and which he brought about. Then, as soon as the Fall occurred, the future coming of Jesus was promised and God proceeded to work through the lives of people as recorded in the Old Testament to prepare the way for this event.

Jesus' incarnation, death, and resurrection were so central in history that the dating system B.C.–A.D. was developed. This reflects how the divine perspective in history is Jesus, the point at which the lines from all places and times, both past and future, converge. At his return will occur the establishment of his kingdom of glory and righteousness, the creation will be restored to its original state of peace with itself, and the present era of history will end. Thus Christ's past work, continuing presence, and future coming are bound together. History has meaning and purpose because Jesus is at the center of time (NLP: 164, 202–3; GST: 63–64).

Schaeffer resolves this knotty problem of historical objectivity and factuality through an affirmation of common-sense realism. He insists that the things God made have an objective existence. The Bible stated history "in ordinary literary forms," and the events and personages recorded there existed "in space–time history." The information contained in the Bible is reliable, even when it comes down to the simplest matters of time and place. Such things as the Fall and Jesus' life on earth, death on the cross, and resurrection on the third day are historical "brute facts," i.e., space–time events that can be verified by normal processes.

Schaeffer will allow no room for hermeneutics that tries to explain these away as "theological" or "religious" statements. He says that to reject the "true truth" of history and allow the possibility of Scripture's being written in an otherworldly "religious language" is to blur the line between fantasy and reality. He is especially critical of modern theologians who use the word *history* in such a way as to manipulate biblical language in the direction of existential experience (JFBH: 181, 202–3; WHHR: 160; CBWW: 79–80, 86–87; CETC: 93; GST: 159–60; GWIT: 82).

For Schaeffer the motive force in history is ideas. What is in the inner thought world of people determines how they act, whether it be their individual value systems and creativity or corporate actions. They live on the basis of their presuppositions, which in turn provide the basis for their values, decisions, and actions. In short, "the inner thought world determines the outward action." People's "world views" or presuppositions determine the direction of their political and social institutions and their scientific endeavors. He minimizes or ignores economic, social, and psychological factors as alternative or supplementary forces in the flow of history (HSWTL: 20; DIC: 17).

God imposes structure in every human relationship because structure is needed for order, yet man is not an automaton. Because humans are made in the image of God, everything is open to them and their choices and actions do influence history. For example, when Eve chose to eat the fruit, she put her hand into history and changed the course of human events. As Schaeffer puts it: "The flow is from the internal to the external; the sin began in the thought-world and flowed outward." Sin began the moment she believed Satan, but "a history is involved" because she then ate and gave the fruit to Adam (GST: 47, 85, 97; DIC: 81).

Thus Schaeffer holds that "the Judeo-Christian world view" emphasizes "the significance of men in history" and the things they do have an effect (NLP: 129). In a vivid passage in

Death in the City Schaeffer presents a "figure of speech" to illustrate what he means about how people can influence history. "Imagine space-time history as feminine and us (all men and women) as masculine. As masculine figures we can impregnate history. We can plant into it seeds that come to fruition in the external world. Just as a man can bring forth legitimate or illegitimate children, so the Bible stresses that man is able to impregnate history with either that which is good or that which is bad" (DIC: 81).

Working from this basis, Schaeffer adopts an activist stance in his later works that essentially is in harmony with his general philosophy of history. For example, in a passage in *Whatever Happened to the Human Race?* he argues that history could be made "abnormal by men" and not everything that occurs there should be there. People could stand against that which is wrong and cruel without standing against God because he did not make the world as it presently is. The chasm that exists between what mankind and history are now and what they could have and should have been gives us a real moral framework for life (WHHR: 155).

THE DEVELOPMENT OF WESTERN CIVILIZATION

How Should We Then Live? is the fullest statement of Francis Schaeffer's view of Western civilization. Subtitling it *The Rise and Decline of Western Thought and Culture*, he affirms at the beginning that it is not "a chronological history of Western culture" but instead is "an analysis of the key moments in history which have formed our present culture, and the thinking of the people who brought those moments to pass." Its purpose is to shed light on the "major characteristics" of our age and to help find solutions "to the myriad of problems" facing people today (HSWTL: 17). Because it brought together in one coherent package the things that Schaeffer had been saying for years, his disciples enthusiastically welcomed it, and we can safely say that it did more than anything else to spread his fame beyond the confines of conservative evangelicalism.

Although passing reference is made to the earlier civilizations of the Middle East and Eastern Mediterranean, the narrative actually begins with late Republican Rome. This civilization built its society on finite gods who, as amplified humanity, lacked any permanent reference point for thinking or living. Thus the Roman experiment in social harmony failed, and an authoritarian system created by Julius Caesar and Augustus was accepted by the people. Augustus and his successors, who like him deified themselves, tried to legislate morals and family life and implement legal reforms and welfare programs, but a human god was a poor foundation. This internal weakness led to Rome's eventual fall.

The Christians, on the other hand, had a world view based on an infinite-personal God who spoke in an understandable way through the Old Testament, the life and teaching of Jesus, and the developing New Testament. They had knowledge about the universe and mankind, absolute values by which to live and to judge the society and political order in which they resided, and an understanding of the basic dignity and value of the individual person who was made in the image of God. Rome persecuted the Christians because of their refusal to engage even in a syncretic emperor worship, but even more so because they adhered to God's absolute revelation, a standard that judged not only personal morals but also the state. "Totalitarian Rome" could not tolerate such an authority. There being no sort of inward base, decadence set in as the Romans gave themselves over to violence, sensual gratification, and apathy. Finally Rome's civilization passed out of existence.

With the onset of the Middle Ages, the pristine Christianity of the early church was distorted, a development that was reflected in art (abandonment of realism), infiltration of humanistic ideas into the church (salvation resting on man's merits, and the church as the source of spiritual authority), and the manner in which local pagan and residual Greco-Roman customs shaped the emerging Christian culture.

Still, as the Middle Ages progressed, cultural and intellectual life grew by leaps and bounds in conjunction with an awakened piety. Christian baptism was spiritually, socially, and politically significant in that it denoted an individual's admittance into society, but the church consecrated the state as well. Theoretically this should have meant good government and a responsible attitude toward the use of material possessions, but in fact it enabled those holding political and economic power to betray society with impunity. There were numerous tussles between the ecclesiastical and secular rulers over the boundary between church and state power, which in turn encouraged the evolution of a political theory stressing the principle of governmental limitation and responsibility.

Meanwhile, Greek and Roman thought forms crept

through the cracks of a faith founded increasingly less on the Bible and more on the authority of church pronouncements. This led to the momentous action by Thomas Aquinas of absorbing Aristotle into Christian thought and thereby placing revelation and reason on an equal footing. Aquinas had an "incomplete view of the Fall," teaching that the human will was corrupted but not the intellect. Thus people could rely on their own human wisdom and were free to mix biblical teachings with those of non-Christian philosophers. Philosophy was gradually separated from revelation (the Bible) and thinkers began to act in an ever more independent, "autonomous" manner. Aquinas brought the Aristotelian emphasis on "individual things" or "particulars" into philosophy (the "nature-versus-grace" problem so central to the Schaefferian analysis of Western thought). This in turn set the stage for Renaissance humanism, which was unable to arrive at the "universals" or "absolutes" needed to give meaning to existence and morals (HSWTL: 52–55; EFR: ch. 1).

As the Renaissance dawned, the positive side of Aquinas' teaching—the emphasis on man's life in the world that God created—was clearly evident in the artistic realm. Nature was once again recognized as important, people and objects in the world around them were portrayed more realistically (as real people in a real world), and nature was regarded as something to be enjoyed.

Yet the negative side of Aquinas rapidly came to prevail. Dante led off by mixing the classical pagan and Christian worlds in *Divina Commedia* and introduced the upper–lower-story separation (spiritual and sensual aspects of life) in *La Vita Nuova*. Others, like Petrarch and Boccaccio, followed the trail he had blazed.

The enthusiasm shown by the Renaissance humanists for the non-Christian Greek and Roman classics set in motion an evolution toward modern humanism, a value system rooted in the belief that man is his own measure, autonomous, and totally independent. Looking back beyond the Middle Ages to the pre-Christian era, they visualized mankind in their own day as taking a great forward leap and regaining the position he once had.

Renaissance artists, as exemplified by Brunelleschi, contributed to humanism by using a new view of perspective that placed man in the center of space and subordinating space to mathematical principles spun out of the mind of man. Michelangelo's *David* was especially a statement of humanistic man's confidence in his own ability and strength to shape the future. Working from a humanistic standpoint, Leonardo da Vinci tried to paint the universal and give it meaning merely out of his observation of the particulars, but he failed. This revealed man's inability to solve every problem by starting from oneself, and in his own despondency Leonardo anticipated the pessimism that would be the natural conclusion of humanism.

The Pivotal Role of the Reformation

The pivotal event in Schaeffer's analysis of Western culture is the Reformation, a topic to which he devotes two full chapters in *How Should We then Live?* and one chapter in *Escape From Reason*. In contrast to the Renaissance, the Reformation provided the universal that gave unity and meaning to life and morals. The Reformers accepted the Bible as the only final authority rather than the autonomy of human reason, which acted as though the mind is infinite with all knowledge within its realm. Unlike Aquinas, they held to the biblical concept of the Fall and recognized that people could not begin from within themselves and think out the answers to the great questions confronting mankind.

By challenging church and tradition and restoring biblical authority, the Reformation removed the humanistic distortion that had entered the church. The Reformers also rejected "Christian humanism," typified by Erasmus, because it only espoused a limited reform of the church and did not go back to New Testament times where only the Bible was authoritative. While the Renaissance "centered in autonomous man," the Reformation "centered in the infinite-personal God who had spoken in the Bible" and thereby had the answers to the problems of meaning (HSWTL: 84).

Culturally the Reformation enhanced art, music, and literature and regarded nature and the whole of life as things of dignity and beauty. Politically it brought "freedom without chaos" because it provided a consensus based on biblical absolutes and real values. The Bible was the foundation on which law was built, and flowing from that was the idea of the responsibility of all people, including monarchs, to adhere to God's law.

The political tide turned toward representative government in those countries where the Reformation emphasis on the Bible as the ultimate authority took root. Although Schaeffer is vague here, he apparently sees them as lands where the Calvinist variety of the Reformation predominated, and this just happens to coincide with his own denominational preference, namely, Presbyterianism. In countries where kings sought to establish centralized, absolutistic regimes, the aid of the hierarchically structured Roman Catholic Church was welcomed.

The two principles—a government should be based on laws rather than arbitrary decisions of men, and a people should exercise political control over their sovereign—were most clearly stated by a Scottish Presbyterian divine, Samuel Rutherford, in a book published in 1644 entitled *Lex Rex* (The Law Is King). His work and the tradition it embodied had a great influence not only in Britain but even more so in America, since it was mediated across the Atlantic directly by John Witherspoon, a Presbyterian who signed the Declaration of Independence, and indirectly by John Locke, who secularized the tradition. The American doctrines of inalienable rights, government by consent, separation of powers, and the right of revolution all had a "biblical" or "Christian" base. Schaeffer devotes only four pages to this development in *How Should We Then Live?* but it is a major theme of *A Christian Manifesto.*

In short, the Reformation provided both an interest in culture and a true basis for form and freedom in society and government. Christians who identified with the Reformation tradition had great influence "on the consensus in the northern European culture" (he includes in this the United States, Canada, Australia, and New Zealand); since they understood the Fall and the sinfulness of man, the governments in their lands were characterized by checks and balances. However, these people were inconsistent with the biblical teaching they professed to follow in two important areas. They had a "twisted view of race" (the slavery question), and they engaged in the "noncompassionate use of accumulated wealth" (the ills of the Industrial Revolution).

The "bloodless" English Revolution of 1688 and the American Revolution were both founded on a Reformation base, but the Enlightenment ensured that the French Revolution in 1789 would flow from other premises and result in a bloodbath and the authoritarian rule of Napoleon Bonaparte. The utopian dream of the Enlightenment was thoroughly secular, and the humanistic elements that had arisen in the Renaissance reached flood tide here. The Enlightenment taught the perfectability of man and society and looked on God as the Creator who had no contact with people now (deism). The revolution in France was founded on the humanistic base of the "general will of the people" and ended up in anarchy and repression.

The parallel to this was the Russian Revolution of 1917, which was built on a Marxist–Leninist materialist foundation and produced only repression, which continues even to this day. No country with a communistic base has produced freedom of the kind brought forth under the Reformation in northern Europe, because such regimes, as is the case with all humanistic polities, have no ultimate standard to turn to that determines what right and wrong are. Laws have their ground only in the changing historic situation.

The rise of modern science paralleled the Renaissance and Reformation. To be sure, the latter did not cause the Scientific Revolution, but modern science did not conflict with the Bible's teaching, and in fact it was born out of the Christian world view. The natural order was reasonable because it was created by a reasonable God, an objective reality was there for researchers to examine, and the world was worth finding out about, for in so doing one was investigating God's creation. Francis Bacon, Isaac Newton, and other great men of science took the Bible seriously. They did not see science as autonomous, and they held to the concept of the uniformity of natural causes in an open system.

Schaeffer sees the breakdown in science, philosophy, and theology as occurring in the early nineteenth century, and he devotes a considerable portion of four books to this development: *How Should We Then Live?*, *Escape From Reason*, *The God Who Is There*, and *He Is There and He Is Not Silent*.

First, scientists pushed God to the edge of their system until it became a completely closed one that leaves no place for deity or the role of man himself. Everything becomes part of a cosmic cause-and-effect machine. When Darwinian evolution excluded both man and deity from their places in the creative process, humanistic men responded by applying the theory to society, leading to Social Darwinism. This made possible the sanctioning of racism and noncompassionate use of accumulated wealth by "science" and led eventually to such evils as National Socialism and genetic engineering.

The ideas of Rousseau, Kant, Hegel, and Kierkegaard shattered the optimism of earlier philosophy and produced the modern outlook of hopelessness and despair. Modern man was left in a dichotomous situation where total separation exists between reason and the area of meaning and values. They put various things "upstairs" in the compartment of "nonreason" in a desperate attempt to find some optimism about meaning and values. However, in the realm of humanistic reason ("downstairs"), man is a machine, there are no values, and life is meaningless. After articulating these concepts, Schaeffer leads readers on a whirlwind tour of modern philosophers, theologians, scientists, musicians, artists, and films to demonstrate their fragmented conception of reality, i.e., the universe and life, and the hopelessness of their search for meaning.

Schaeffer concludes that modern man has lost all sense of objectivity and certainty. In the West there are now no absolute moral values or categories to distinguish between reality and fantasy. In response, most adults have adopted two impoverished values: personal peace and affluence. They just want to be left alone and not be bothered with the troubles of others, and to have more and more material prosperity. Young people, meanwhile, seek meaning in drugs, rock music, and the New Left, but to no avail. For them the only remaining options are apathy or accepting the values of their parents.

The numerical majority has become the new absolute. Civil law based on biblical absolutes has been replaced by sociological law, a jurisprudence that depends on the whims of transient majorities. Now anything goes—abortion, infanticide, euthanasia, hedonism, what have you. New elites are jockeying for position to fill the vacuum in our culture, offering arbitrary, totalitarian absolutes. Under the authoritarian state they intend to establish, they will use techniques of psychological control, biological engineering, and manipulation of the media to influence behavior and extinguish liberties. Most people will accept the elitist, totalitarian regimes because of apathy, a desire for personal peace and affluence, or a yearning for order to ensure the functioning of business and everyday life. The only way out of this desperate situation is for man to affirm God's revelation in the Bible and to turn to Christ, who will provide the values and purpose in life that humanism has denied to him.

TOWARD A CRITIQUE

The overwhelming mass of source material now available has impelled historians to focus more and more on narrow topics, but Francis Schaeffer boldly set out to develop an integrating scheme that tries to pull together the complex story of the West and give it meaning within a Christian framework. He offered what at first glance seems to be a plausible explanation for the dehumanization that so characterizes the twentieth century in spite of all its technological and social progress. Like a modern-day Amos or Jeremiah, Schaeffer's prophetic voice thundered forth from the mountains of Switzerland and in the lecture halls of Great Britain and the United States against the forces that were cheapening the value of human life and rendering the Christian message impotent. Because of the deep longing for some interpretation of the West that would provide meaning and show where we are going, scholars and laypeople alike greeted his endeavor with enthusiasm.

In terms of his own work, it is important to remember that Schaeffer early spoke out against racism, environmental pollution, and the improper use of wealth by Christians. He stood firmly for an inerrant Scripture at a time when destructive criticism was diminishing its importance and undermining the faith of many sincere believers. L'Abri was a sterling example of a caring community, and through his intense desire to help others he demonstrated a sense of warmth, compassion, and selflessness that has seldom been equaled within evangelicalism. His lifestyle was itself a word of judgment on modern man's quest for personal peace and affluence.

Schaeffer was not reticent to declare that his principal calling was that of an evangelist, a preacher of the Word of God. His approach was to confront aimless, drifting, despairing young people with the claims of the Christ in the context of their own thought world. He had taken the time to inform himself about the history of Western thought and culture, and he used the implications of that history as a vehicle for conveying the gospel message. Through his many books he introduced a largely anti-intellectual evangelical community to the wider realm of culture, art, and ideas, and he helped innumerable people, including this writer, to see that it was not necessary to abandon the life of the mind in order to be a Christian.

However, his historical analysis is not without problems, and evangelical scholars have been among his most severe critics. One criticized *How Should We Then Live?* as offering an explanation of events that never occurred and thoughts that were never thought until the Schaeffer troupe portrayed them before cameras. Others said that the work would not impress a thoughtful reader and it had not used history fairly or accurately. A well-known historian observed that "if an undergraduate made such assertions in an essay he would be in serious trouble because of his lack of evidence."[2]

Various reviewers called attention to significant omissions from Schaeffer's discussion of cultural history, for example, Classical and Hellenistic Greece, the Byzantine Empire, the Crusades, the voyages of discovery, European imperialism, southern Europe after the Renaissance, tsarist Russia, and the development of nationalism in nineteenth-century Europe. Schaeffer's view of science as a completely predictable cause-and-effect system was that of the eighteenth and not the twentieth century.[3]

Most of Schaeffer's knowledge was acquired from secondary sources, and he all too often prooftexted from writers and philosophers whose works he had not mastered in order to fit them into his preconceived interpretation. In his books, footnotes are a rare occurrence (and often refer to other pieces by him). One wonders if during the writing of *How Should We Then Live?* Schaeffer ever consulted with any academically trained historians besides Jeremy C. Jackson, who holds the same views as his mentor.[4]

This sampling of the critical response to Schaeffer's work should not be dismissed out of hand as professional jealousy on the part of scholars whose own published works never attracted the attention that his did. Rather, the comments reflect deep concern on the part of people who identify with him as an evangelical that his enterprise may have failed. They realize that the possible result would be inestimable harm to the larger cause of Christian scholarship and an undermining of confidence in biblical inerrancy as well, because the latter is so central to Schaeffer's theological explanation of culture. Unfortunately, the flaws in his treatment of cultural history are indeed serious, and these place his whole interpretive system in jeopardy.

THE GREAT PRESUPPOSITIONAL DISASTER

Schaeffer's foray into the realm of historical scholarship was fraught with difficulty from the very beginning. Not only does his commitment to presuppositionalism place him far from the mainstream of twentieth-century historical scholarship, but also his philosophical idealism leaves him without many of the necessary tools to carry out rigorous historical analysis. His starting point—people are what they think, and accordingly the inner thought world determines their outward actions—is far too simplistic. His stance is that people's presuppositions determine how they act, and as these change or are modified, they affect both individuals and the society they construct. One starts from the mind, brings forth actions in the external world, and thus influences it. In other words, the inner thought world governs the outward action.

But where does the ideational impulse have its origin? Schaeffer says that most people "catch their presuppositions from their family and surrounding society the way a child catches measles," but he believes it would be better if they chose their presuppositions "after a careful consideration of what world view is true" (HSWTL: 19–20). In the Schaefferian schema, "world view" and "presuppositions" are exact synonyms, and he uses the terms interchangeably in his writings. Thus a person's ideational starting point can be a matter of individual choice.

Few historians today will accept such a hard-nosed idealism. For one thing, presuppositions are shaped by our cultural, social, economic, religious, and political environment. We do not just "catch" them. Also problematic is the inherent voluntarism in such a view. Can we overhaul our entire presuppositional framework, our life-orienting world view, simply by an act of will? Certainly Christian conversion in and of itself does not accomplish that, as the apostle Paul's injunction in Ephesians 4 to put off "the old man" brings out.

Much more serious, however, is Schaeffer's ideational emphasis. His interpretation centers on the impact that ideas have on life, and such an idealist reductionism essentially excludes as crucial or even significant the other forces that impinge on human behavior, such as economic and geographical factors, social conditions, natural disasters, and personal charisma. Stanford Reid astutely observes,

Like Karl Marx in his insistence on the economic interpretation of history, he believes that the ideational is basic to all
else, and consequently the more mundane matters of economics and the like can be ignored.[5]

The history of ideas is a vital component of the larger
discipline of history, but no respectable intellectual historian
today believes that ideas operate in a vacuum.[6] The social
contexts of ideas are extremely important for understanding
their functional role, development, and change in meaning over
long periods of time. Schaeffer's obsession with the propositional affirmation of absolutes and his fear of sociological factors
relativizing those universals blind him to this fundamental
reality, and thus he cannot cope with the methodological or
functional character of ideas. The result is that he oversimplifies
or distorts important concepts and lays himself open to
damaging criticism by the experts who do know them well. In
his essay in this volume and in the *Reformed Journal*, Ronald
Wells points out the problems with regard to humanism; Kent
Hill shows that Schaeffer's treatment of the terms *reason*,
rational, and *rationalism* is confusing and deficient.[7]

I will not pursue these, but instead focus on a concept with
which I am quite familiar: totalitarianism. The term itself is of
recent origin, having been popularized by Mussolini in the
early 1930s as the doctrine that the state is the master and end
of life and society. The notion was picked up in Nazi Germany,
where the "movement" as expressing the true will of the
people and the racial elite was seen as the totalitarian center.
But the Soviet communists refused to identify their systems as
such because that would have been degrading.

Social scientists who use the term *totalitarian* emphasize
that totalitarianism goes far beyond traditional monarchical
absolutism or despotism and that it is essentially a phenomenon of the twentieth century. It involves an official ideology to
which all living in the society must adhere, a single party that
professes to be the true consciousness of the masses and not a
ruling elite apart from them, an efficient system of terroristic
police control, manipulation of the mass media by the state or
party, and central direction of the economy. Technology and
ideology link the totalitarian dictatorship to modern mass
democracy, hence the ever-present emphasis on the "people"
in such systems. Above all, they are socio-political, secularized
religions that replace God and religious institutions with the

state and its leaders, rituals, and institutions, and that claim the ultimate allegiance of the populace.

On the other hand, some point out that no state has ever succeeded in establishing permanent governmental control over the totality of life. Because so many exceptions to the defined characteristics exist, they question whether the concept as an analytical tool even has validity. Also of great importance is that the major scholarly discussion that refined the concept and used it to describe current political systems occurred in the late 1940s–early 1950s, and thus it functioned as an ideological weapon in the Cold War. Even today in the United States the political right appropriates the term *democracy* for the American system and refers to the Soviets and their sympathizers as *totalitarians*. In short, the social origins and use of the concept have great importance in comprehending its meaning.[8]

Schaeffer is unaware of this theoretical discussion, as evidenced by the manner in which he interchanges it with authoritarianism. For example, the regime of the wicked King Ahab of Israel was a "totalitarian structure," or Imperial Rome was "totalitarian" (NLP: 147; HSWTL: 26). He joins in the Cold War struggle by linking his theory "if there are no absolutes by which to judge society, then society is absolute" to communism, where he alleges the elite has its way and lays down arbitrary absolutes that "can be *this* way today and *that* tomorrow." This elite filled the vacuum "left by the loss of the Christian consensus which originally gave us form and freedom in northern Europe and in the West," and now is in charge in communist countries like Mao's China (HSWTL: 224). To be sure, the critique makes sense in western Europe, but neither China nor Soviet Russia ever experienced Schaeffer's "Reformation base." It appears to me that Schaeffer is suggesting that without first Christianizing such lands, any attempt to import or impose Western democratic institutions there would lead to totalitarianism (CM: 29).

Nevertheless, Schaeffer deserves to be lauded for some insights here. He courageously called attention to totalitarian tendencies within the church itself that were arising from those caught up in the mechanics of leadership, and by implication from the anti-intellectual passivity of some in neo-Pentecostal movements (NLP: 207; NSS: 14–23). He is correct in saying that totalitarian states see themselves as the integrating point of life, that there is no difference between the systems of the right and left (fascism and communism), and ambitious elites can manipulate people whose only desire is for personal peace and affluence.

Having in his last years moved rather far to the political right, Schaeffer would undoubtedly have been shocked to learn that the last point unwittingly fits quite well with the contention made by Professor Bertram Gross that Americans are subject to the allurements of a self-centered, benign, "friendly" fascism, one that is

> a more concentrated, unscrupulous, repressive, and militaristic control by a Big Business–Big Government partnership that, in order to preserve the privileges of the ultra-rich, the corporate overseers, and the military brass, squelches the rights and liberties of other people both at home and abroad.[9]

Unlike the "unfriendly fascism" of the 1930s that relied on repression and mobilization of the masses, the new fascism will depend more on public apathy and the use of scapegoats (such as racial conflict, school-busing, homosexuality, abortion, and women's rights) to distract attention from the increasing integration of big government and big business. According to Gross, the totalitarian order will be ushered in by stealth while the "silent" or "moral" majority is being manipulated to fight over tangential issues that do not impinge significantly on the vital interests of those who occupy the bastions of power within the country.

BAD HISTORY IS BAD HISTORY

That Schaeffer's ideational approach ignores other factors in the historical process and contributes to conceptual weakness is not his only flaw. Another is that his effort to force the ideas into predetermined channels leads to distortion of the past and outright myth-making.

Lex Rex Lackings

Perhaps the most egregious example is his thesis that a direct link exists between Calvinist Reformation political theory and the American constitutional system. As mentioned above, Schaeffer maintains that Samuel Rutherford in Lex Rex advanced the position that a sovereign may not rule arbitrarily but must be subject to the higher law of God, and he may be overthrown if he violates his responsibility to do so. The law is king, and if the king and the government deviate from this, they are to be disobeyed. This idea was transmitted to America through John Locke and John Witherspoon and provided the religio-legal consensus for the new nation. America was founded on a biblical or Christian base and today needs to return to it. Ronald Wells deals with the implications of this in chapter 8, but I will give attention to the historical methodology Schaeffer uses in establishing the intellectual tie between Calvin and the Constitution.

A task of intellectual history is to draw connections between ideas and to show the influence of thinkers on other thinkers. The procedures for doing this are clear-cut. One studies the writings and speeches of individuals to see whom they cite as sources for ideas they express and what works they have read. Close correspondence between their statements and those of earlier or contemporary thinkers may be dug out and identified even though they are not attributed to the individuals in question. Also, the "climate of opinion" of a given era is analyzed and its components factored out.

However, when this methodology is applied to the *Lex Rex* thesis, it is found wanting. Nowhere does Schaeffer directly footnote the connection between Rutherford and the American revolutionaries or show specific ways in which any drew from Rutherford; he simply posits its existence. He flatly declares, "Locke took *Lex Rex* and secularized it." He "drew heavily from it." Then, "Witherspoon certainly knew Samuel Rutherford's writing well. The other Founding Fathers may have known him" (CM: 105–6). Where Schaeffer picked up the idea is not certain, but he was saying as far back as 1962 that Rutherford's book "brought the total cultural view of the Reformation into the 'practical world' of Law."[10]

Using the method of historical analysis described above, Timothy D. Hall carefully examined the connection with respect to Locke and found that the differences separating the two were so great that they must be placed in disparate strands of the constitutional tradition in Britain. As a student and lecturer at Oxford, Locke's views were influenced not by Scottish Presbyterian political theory but by English Independents and Royalists. Later he served as adviser to the First Earl of Shaftesbury and further developed his ideas. Locke never refers to Rutherford in his writings, and a catalogue of his personal library made toward the end of his life does not include a single book by the Scottish divine.

A content analysis of *Lex Rex* and Locke's *Two Treatises on Government* reveals important differences concerning natural law, man's depravity, equality, and social nature, religious toleration, social contract, and the right of resistance. Moreover, the ideas of limited government and consent of the governed found in both writers clearly antedate the Reformation. They stem from such sources as the Magna Carta, John of Salisbury, and William of Ockham. And for Locke the basis of the social compact is not God or revelatory law, but natural law and human reason. Hall concludes, correctly I believe, that because Locke's theory underlies the American republican experiment, Schaeffer's appeal in *A Christian Manifesto* to revelation as a basis for the use of force involves a shift from America's historic conception of government to the Puritan covenantal views of civil society. There such an appeal to revelation on its own merits could occur.[11]

Thus the Rutherford–Locke connection can be consigned to the scrap heap of history.

But what about Witherspoon? In 1768, at the height of his career as a Presbyterian minister and theologian in Scotland, John Witherspoon was called to America to become president of the College of New Jersey (later Princeton University). He later played a major role in the Revolution and was the only clergyman among the signers of the Declaration of Independence.

Schaeffer's only source of information is a slight biography done in 1906 by David Walker Woods, and he seems unaware of the corpus of Witherspoon scholarship (CM: 31). Those who have studied Witherspoon find that although he held the standard Calvinist views about the nature of man, his thinking on natural rights, social contract, mixed government, the right of resistance, and the moral advantage of civil liberty drew heavily from the Scottish Enlightenment and its principal spokesman, Francis Hutcheson. Witherspoon's public statements during the revolution indicated that he derived his political ideas from nature and the natural human conscience and that the Bible played almost no role in his teaching about law and liberty.[12]

As for Rutherford's influence, nothing by him was published in colonial America, and there is no reference to him in the four-volume published works of Witherspoon, not even in the crucial lectures on ethics and politics.[13] So much for the Witherspoon connection. It is not unfair to conclude that accepting the argument of the transmission of *Lex Rex* as proof of America's Christian historical underpinnings will involve an enormous "leap of faith," to use a favorite phrase of Schaeffer's.

From Rome to Reformation

This is only one example of bad historical scholarship. Many more could be cited. For example, Schaeffer provides an inadequate treatment of the "fall" of Rome that is reminiscent of Gibbon—a moralistic explanation of the decline of the western empire complete with analogies to present-day conditions. Rome allegedly fell because it worshiped a finite god and thus lacked an "inward base," yet it had largely acquired one by the fifth century through the process of Christianization that had been occurring. Also, there were other ancient civilizations, most notably in India and China, that had endured for thousands of years without such a base.

If Schaeffer had consulted the vast body of literature on the topic,[14] he would have learned that Christianity had contributed to undermining the imperial structure, the rapid expansion of the Germanic peoples along the borders in western and central Europe had become more of a problem than Rome could cope with, and the eastern portion of the empire continued in existence for another millennium. In fact, he seems to have forgotten almost completely about Byzantium.

Schaeffer's handling of medieval thought has made Christian scholars of that era nervous. Professor of philosophy Arvin Vos, a Reformed evangelical, shows convincingly that Schaeffer seriously misrepresents Thomas Aquinas. In spite of what Schaeffer says, the "Angelic Doctor" did give primacy to faith over reason, grace over nature, and the Bible over Aristotle, and he influenced Calvin more than many people think. Moreover, contrary to Schaeffer, there had been an interest in "particulars" for a least a century before Aquinas, and the twelfth century from Abelard onward showed a growing nominalism.[15]

The treatment of the Reformation satisfies virtually no one who knows the period well, but to deal adequately with the defects here would require a long essay. Certainly the Reformers' views of government (and there was a variety of these) were not derived solely from Scripture, and the ideal of many whom Schaeffer admires most was some form of theocracy.

Regardless of his disclaimers, one gains the impression that the Reformation pattern of government Schaeffer would have liked to see instituted today is a moderate theocracy in the guise of the "Judeo-Christian" tradition.[16]

Schaeffer stretches the historical record beyond all reasonable bounds when he compares the civil disobedience of the early church with the use of force in Reformation countries. Also, he overlooks the Reformation movements of Italy, Spain, and east-central Europe, forgets about developments in Germany after Luther, ignores the authoritarian elements of the Reformation—i.e., the burning of Servetus and harsh treatment of the Anabaptists—and for that matter is completely oblivious to the Anabaptist contribution.

Missing Pieces in Modern Times

Approaching modern times, Schaeffer finds a direct link between the Enlightenment and the French and Russian revolutions that cannot be supported historically. Since he does not touch on eastern Europe, he is unaware of the fundamental tension in Russian history between the Slavophilic and Westernizing elements that is a crucial factor in understanding the revolution there. He neglects the technological development of the Industrial Revolution and its social impact. He does not comprehend that Marxism claims to be *more* rational than any other theory, because history confirms it, and thus requires no more of a leap of faith than in Schaeffer's own system.

As for Germany, Schaeffer makes inaccurate references to "the Germans' loss of confidence in the Weimar Republic just before Hitler, which was caused by unacceptable inflation" and to Heinrich Himmler as "leader of the Gestapo" (HSWTL: 246, 151). He is correct in assigning liberal theology part of the responsibility for laying the groundwork for Hitler,[17] but he refuses to give any positive credit to the theological outlook of Karl Barth, who was one of the strongest voices of resistance to Nazism. Barth probably came closer to having a "Reformation base" in his theology than most of his contemporaries. Though Schaeffer grudgingly expresses "profound admiration" for Barth's stand in the Barmen Declaration of 1934, he does not deal at all with this, the most important statement criticizing the Third Reich made by the German Protestant churches (HSWTL: 174).

Although Schaeffer cites Nazi Germany as primary evidence for the evil of abortion, he fails to acknowledge both the role that conservative Protestants played in bringing in the Third Reich and the fact that they welcomed Hitler's movement as a kind of "moral majority" which would sweep away the immorality, lack of patriotism, and socialism of the hated Weimar Republic and restore Germany's national greatness.[18] Moreover, in none of his books does Schaeffer examine Hitler's social and racial policies in order to put abortion and euthanasia in context. After all, the Führer can be quoted as favoring or opposing abortion, depending on the situation.[19] And Schaeffer ought to know that for Jews it is the height of insensitivity for anyone to identify the *Holocaust*, a very special and meaningful event in the Jewish experience, with abortion and euthanasia (WHHR: 13, 16, 91, 102, 207).

Missing from his discussion of contemporary history are perceptive treatments of some of the most important happenings of the time. Feminism and the women's liberation movement are not mentioned in *How Should We then Live?* and receive only barbed comments about their anti-family stance and attitude toward abortion in *Whatever Happened to the Human Race?* (53, 115–16, 208, 214). Schaeffer does not talk about the Vietnam War and its implications for America, is highly critical of pacifism, strongly supports the United States' maintaining nuclear supremacy over the Soviet Union, and equates the campaign for nuclear disarmament with pre–World War II appeasement.[20]

Schaeffer condemns slavery and racism, but overlooks the civil rights movement in the United States (Martin Luther King, Jr. is not referred to in any of his books) and apartheid in South Africa. Although he does not address the matter, one could argue logically from Schaeffer's premises that the South African regime has a Reformation base, since it comprises Dutch Calvinist and English liberal elements.

CONCLUSION

The foregoing shows clearly that Francis Schaeffer failed in his noble effort to construct a unified history of Western culture from a Christian perspective. His overemphasis on ideational factors and deficiencies in factual and interpretive accuracy doomed the venture. It is regrettable that he did not carry over the methodological aspects of his firm commitment to biblical inerrancy into his treatment of the historical process. He deeply wanted to produce a Christian explanation of where we are going, one that could provide a basis on which to call America and other Western countries to corporate repentance; but unfortunately he neglected to apply the same rigorous standards of accuracy to historical analysis that he demanded (quite properly I would add) in the realm of biblical scholarship.

The result is that despite what he said about the rationality of his approach, it requires a "large leap" of faith to accept it. Given its weak evidential basis, I question whether very many non-Christians will do this.

NOTES

[1] Evangelical writer Philip Yancey asked Schaeffer in an interview whether he was satisfied with the film series. Schaeffer responded affirmatively, saying, "We've got something that is useful, obviously. I think it answers both Clark and Bronowski. Technically, I think *Civilisation* is poorer than ours, but Bronowski's was good, though I hated the message. . . . [If you] compare their objectivity to my objectivity, there's no comparison. I think they loaded everything for their thesis." *Christianity Today* 23 (April 6, 1979): 26.

[2] From reviews by Robert W. Matson, *Wittenburg Door* 37 (June–July 1977): 28; James Daane, *Christian Century* 94 (October 12, 1977): 923; George Giacumakis, Jr., and Gerald C. Tiffin, *Fides et Historia* 9 (Spring 1977): 57; and W. Stanford Reid, *Westminster Theological Journal* 40 (Spring 1978): 381.

[3] Jack Rogers, "Francis Schaeffer: The Promise and the Problem," *Reformed Journal* 28 (June 1977): 16.

[4] Jeremy C. Jackson, *No Other Foundation: The Church Through Twenty Centuries* (Westchester, Ill.: Crossway, 1980), is a history of Christianity that uses Schaefferian concepts as its interpretive schema. According to Schaeffer, Jackson was the "chief historical researcher" for HSWTL and gave "timely help and suggestions"(HSWTL: 13). He prepared the study guides for HSWTL and WHHR.

[5] Reid, *Westminster Theological Journal*, 380-81. See also Stuart Cunningham, "Towards a Critique of Francis Schaeffer's Thought," *Interchange* 24 (1979): 218-19; David W. Gill, "Jacques Ellul and Francis Schaeffer: Two Views of Western Civilization," *Fides et Historia* 13 (Spring 1981): 26.

[6] Although some scholars distinguish between the history of ideas and intellectual history, I am not convinced that it makes all that much difference, and I shall use the terms interchangeably.

[7] Ronald A. Wells, "Francis Schaeffer's Jeremiad," *Reformed Journal* 32 (May 1982): 17–18; Kent R. Hill, "Francis Schaeffer: An Evaluation of His Life and Thought," in *Faith and Imagination: Essays on Evangelicals and Literature*, ed. Noel Riley Fitch and Richard W. Etulain (Albuquerque: Far West Books, 1985), 144–48. When confronted with Wells' arguments, Schaeffer did not attempt to answer them but merely reaffirmed his original stance and accused the writer of devaluing the Reformation and urging evangelicals to look at the Social Gospel as their basis for having something to say to modern culture (GED: 118, 190).

For a concise but insightful treatment of humanism that avoids the Schaefferian pitfalls, see the entries by Robert G. Clouse, "Christian Humanism," and David W. Gill, "Secular Humanism," in *Evangelical Dictionary of Theology*, ed. Walter A. Elwell (Grand Rapids: Baker, 1984).

[8] For an introduction to the definitional and interpretive problems see Carl J. Friedrich, ed., *Totalitarianism* (Cambridge: Harvard University, 1954); Carl J. Friedrich and Zbigniew K. Brzezinski, *Totalitarian Dictatorship and Autocracy* (Cambridge: Harvard University, 1956); and Paul T. Mason, ed., *Totalitarianism: Temporary Madness or Permanent Danger?* (Boston: D.C. Heath, 1967).

[9] Bertram Gross, *Friendly Fascism: The New Face of Power in America* (New York: M. Evans, 1980), 161.

[10] Francis A. Schaeffer, "Christianity and Culture," *Themelios* 2 (1962): 8.

[11] Timothy D. Hall, "Rutherford, Locke, and the Declaration: The Connection," unpublished Th.M. thesis, Dallas Theological Seminary, 1984.

[12] Roger Fechner, "The Godly and Virtuous Republic of John Witherspoon," in *Ideas in America's Cultures: From Republic to Mass Society*, ed. Hamilton Cravens (Ames: Iowa State University, 1982), 17–20; Mark A. Noll, Nathan O. Hatch, and George M. Marsden, *The Search for Christian America* (Westchester, Ill.: Crossway Books, 1983), 90–93.

[13] Noll, Hatch, and Marsden, *The Search for Christian America*, 142. Witherspoon scholar Roger Fechner told me that he had gone through more than four hundred of his pamphlets and found virtually no reference to Rutherford. Telephone interview with the author, August 29, 1985.

[14] Alden M. Rollins, *The Fall of Rome: A Reference Guide* (Jefferson, N. C.: McFarland, 1983), contains 260 references to scholarly and popular literature published in the twentieth century on the demise of the Western empire.

[15] Arvin Vos, *Aquinas, Calvin, and Contemporary Protestant Thought: A Critique of Protestant Views on the Thought of Thomas Aquinas* (Grand Rapids: Eerdmans, 1985); G. J. C. Marchant, review of HIT in *The Churchman* 88 (January–March 1974): 63.

[16] It is important to mention that scholars are becoming increasingly uneasy with the concept of "Judeo-Christian," and some now reject it entirely. See Mark Silk, "Notes on the Judeo-Christian Tradition in America," *American Quarterly* 36 (Spring 1984): 65–85. Ronald Wells calls attention in his essay to the work of David K. Watson, who shows that Schaeffer relied heavily on the writings of Rousas J. Rushdoony. Rushdoony's school of thought, theonomy, does advocate theocracy. For more on this movement see the articles by David A. Rausch and Douglas E. Chismar, "The New Puritans and Their Theonomic Paradise," *Christian Century* 100 (August 3–10, 1983): 712–15, and "Regarding Theonomy: An Essay of Concern," *Journal of the Evangelical Theological Society* 27(September 1984): 315–23.

[17] HSWTL: 151; GED: 35. Well worth reading on this even today are the comments of Franklin H. Littell in his essay "The Protestant Churches and Totalitarianism (Germany 1933–1945)," in Friedrich, *Totalitarianism*, 108-119.

[18] See Richard V. Pierard, "Why Did German Protestants Welcome Hitler?" *Fides et Historia* 10 (Spring 1978): 8–29, and "Implications of the German Church Struggle for Christians Today," *Covenant Quarterly* 39 (February 1981): 3–16.

[19] For an introduction to this see Jill Stephenson, *Women in Nazi Society* (New York: Barnes & Noble, 1975); and Marc Hillel and Clarissa Henry, *Of Pure Blood* (New York: McGraw-Hill, 1976).

[20] Yancey, *Christianity Today*, 22; Francis A. Schaeffer, Vladimir Bukovsky, and James Hitchcock, *Who Is for Peace?* (Nashville: Nelson, 1983), 19–31.

8

SCHAEFFER ON AMERICA

RONALD A. WELLS

INTRODUCTION

When Francis Schaeffer's book *The God Who Is There* appeared in Britain in 1968, I was serving with the United States Army in Germany. Harold O. J. Brown, then theological secretary of the International Fellowship of Theological Students, asked me to review the book for the IFES journal, *Themelios*.

Having recently completed a Ph.D. in American intellectual history, I was predisposed to read the book with an "American" eye. It struck me quite forcibly that this was a "European" book. The setting was European, and the important examples given were European. Even when a good American example was possible, Schaeffer seemed to prefer a European one. The most outstanding instance was Schaeffer's repeated references to the Armory Show of 1913, in which "the line of despair" could be illustrated as having come to America in the form of "modern" art.

What struck me then was Schaeffer's passing over a better example. While the arrival of the "new" paintings in New York were an important sign of things to come, Schaeffer's own

Ronald A. Wells is Professor of History at Calvin College, Grand Rapids, Michigan. He holds the M.A. and Ph.D. degrees from Boston University. In addition to publishing several articles, he has edited The Wars of America: Christian Views.

typology of a "line of despair" had philosophy before art. In philosophy, the path-breaking book, *Pragmatism,* was published by William James in 1906. Here we have a philosophical statement of prime importance, yet Schaeffer chose—in what I thought was his European centrism—to pass it by. In 1968 I honestly wondered if Schaeffer would have much impact in, and on, America with this sort of European orientation.

In fact, Francis Schaeffer was to have his main impact in America, as it is now widely known. Other contributors in this book comment on the transition of Schaeffer from philosophical theology in his early career to the emphasis on practical socio-moral matters in his later career. I wonder if, contrary to my initial impression, Schaeffer was always looking toward America—as a place where his impact would be most pronounced, and as a place where his main concerns lay when it came time to concretize his theories.

A Christian Manifesto (1981) was, to my mind, Schaeffer's last book. (To be sure, *The Great Evangelical Disaster* came out later, but that book was largely written by others in Schaeffer's name. And, in any case, *Manifesto* was thought to be his final book when his publishers decided to issue his *Complete Works,* which implies that no more works are expected.)

As Schaeffer says in the preface, *Manifesto* is an outgrowth of his earlier work. In claiming the lordship of Christ for all areas of life, he began with philosophical theology for foundations, then moved to other areas—the environment, the nature of life, and now government. He asks, "What is the Christian's relationship to government, law and civil disobedience?" (CM: 10). It is a book written, he says, not as a philosophical treatise or theoretical exercise, but as a manifesto. Where he intends this book to be placed is quite clear: on an open page after the preface and before the beginning of the text, we read, "The Communist Manifesto, 1847; Humanist Manifesto I, 1933; Humanist Manifesto II, 1973" (CM: 13). It is clear that Schaeffer intends his manifesto to stand in the great tradition of manifesto writing and to provide a Christian reply to the supposed shortcomings of the earlier writings.

This essay devotes itself to, first, a description of Schaeffer's *Christian Manifesto* and, second, a critique of it.

A DESCRIPTION OF *A CHRISTIAN MANIFESTO*

Schaeffer asks his readers to see the picture of what has happened to America, not in fragments but in the totality of a world view. This is his initial and foundational point: that Christian disquiet about the tendency of things in America (permissiveness, pornography, family breakdown, abortion) can only be understood if Christians realize that all of this has come about because of a shift in world view.

> This shift has been *away from* a world view that was at least vaguely Christian in people's memory (even if they were not individually Christian) *toward* something completely different—toward a world view based upon the idea that the final reality is impersonal matter or energy shaped into its present form by impersonal chance (CM: 18) [Schaeffer's emphasis].

These two world views stand in complete antithesis to each other, according to Schaeffer, and they *inevitably* produce different social results (Schaeffer's emphasis). Most notably the differences are pronounced in the areas of society, government, and law. The real danger for Christians, it is said, is to try to merge these world views or to blur the distinctions between them.

Martin E. Marty is singled out for special criticism for his attempts to blur the argumentative distinctions between types of humanism (CM: 22–23). No, according to Schaeffer, "Humanism is the placing of Man at the center of all things and making him the measure of all things" (CM: 23). With this "standard" definition of humanism in hand, Schaeffer can assert that Christianity cannot be synthesized with such a world view. The Christian world view was formative in the development of government and law in northern Europe and North America in which liberty was rooted in the law, which came from God, not man.

Schaeffer quickly moves to the establishment of a Christian world view in government and law in the United States. A major case is made for the conjunction of Christian values and the legal-governmental structure of the United States by citing the career of John Witherspoon (1723–1794), to whom we were introduced by Richard Pierard in chapter 7. According to Schaeffer, this linking of Christian thinking and concept of government was fundamental. Witherspoon, in turn, stood in the tradition of the thinking of Samuel Rutherford (1600–1661), who wrote the pamphlet *Lex Rex* in 1644. To make "law" the sovereign over earthly sovereigns was, to Schaeffer, "absolutely earthshaking. Prior to that it had been *rex lex*, the king is law. . . . Therefore, the heads of government are under the law, not a law unto themselves" (CM: 32).

Even noted deists like Jefferson understood this notion of *lex rex*, albeit in a secularized form. Schaeffer writes, "We cannot say too strongly that they really understood the basis of the government which they were founding" (CM: 32). The great phrases were linked: a belief in "inalienable rights" turned on a prior affirmation of "in God we trust." So, for Schaeffer, it is foundational to his later argument that there was a religio-legal consensus among the founding fathers of the United States. He cites many other sources throughout American history to document, to his satisfaction, that consensus of values centered on the notion that the Anglo-Saxon common law and the structures of government developed within a recognition that law and society are based on the law derived from the Bible. This was "the base of government and law" until "the takeover of our government and law by this other entity, the materialistic, humanistic, chance world view" (CM: 39).

Both faith and freedom are said by Schaeffer to have been destroyed by the conquests of this new world view, because the secular society of our time is founded, not on the principles of God's law, but on "sociological law." The work of Oliver Wendell Holmes (1841–1935) in developing this sort of legal theory is said to parallel the movement away from the science of Copernicus and Galileo to the materialist science which "took over" in the last century. This shift, or takeover, Schaeffer contends, was not based on new knowledge but on a philosophical shift.

The galling part of this takeover, at least for Schaeffer, is that it is stated with such arrogance. Similar arrogance is also characteristic of those who supplant the Christian legal-governmental consensus with that based on "the materialistic concept of reality" (CM: 45). This new sort of law is justified in the name of "pluralism," a doctrine developed in democratic society to protect the freedoms of those people not belonging to majority denominations.

Schaeffer champions one side of this pluralism because he agrees that freedom must be extended to all citizens; but he laments the other half of pluralism because it inescapably means that "other" people are present in society. He cites the year 1848 as a turning point, when emigrants from nations not shaped by "Reformation Christianity" began to come to the United States in large numbers, thus diminishing the dominance of evangelical and reformational Protestantism (CM: 46). Without that dominance in society, there has been no check against the movement of "pluralism," which means that in law there is no basic moral code and that our descent into a "humanistic culture" is paralleled in law as much as in art and philosophy. Schaeffer utters his greatest lament for Christians in law, theology, and education, who, he observes, did not "blow a loud horn" when this "titanic shift" was going on over the past eighty years (CM: 47–51).

Schaeffer goes on to point out that humanism is a religion in that it functions on the level of ultimate beliefs. He quotes a few lines from Supreme Court cases to illustrate what he calls "the shift" from law grounded in Judeo-Christian religion to humanist religion. This is also reflected, Schaeffer believes, in the media, where, in the name of pluralism and free choice, society is presented with a bewildering welter of choices because the humanist view of reality precisely believes that there are no normative choices. Schaeffer believes we should use the little freedom we still have to oppose "the other total view."

Turning his attention to evangelical church leadership in the United States, Schaeffer finds an unhappy picture here too, insofar as church leaders have been so busy "spiritualizing" reality that they have allowed the whole culture to "go so far down the road" (CM: 63). In a kind of latter-day Platonism, evangelical leaders have tended to make "the spiritual" realm the reality, but in doing so they forget the heritage of evangelical revivalism in the eighteenth and nineteenth centuries, which linked spiritual and social gospels into an integrative whole. So, for Schaeffer, the situation has almost reached its nadir, because leadership in evangelical churches, from whom one might have expected more, has joined other societal leaders in not blowing the trumpet against the takeover of society by the other totality.

Is there no hope, in Schaeffer's view? Against this encroaching—the takeover—which is nearly complete, Schaeffer can see some hope. He evokes "an open window" through which one can see the way forward. The fact that the ray of hope coming through the window is the "conservative swing"

(CM: 73) in American political life, the way forward may very well be the way back, because Schaeffer's great hope is to "roll back" the societal workings of the "material-energy, chance world view." But Schaeffer, following George Will, wonders how many people are actually principled conservatives, or merely people wanting the bourgeois ideal of prosperity and of being left alone from the troubles of the world. Schaeffer suggests that if government can no longer deliver prosperity and security, most people will turn to an elite to govern them.

Despite this guarded hope, then, Schaeffer presses his readers onward to inquire about the times and places in which Christians must oppose the institutions of their society and engage in civil disobedience. Relying once again on Samuel Rutherford's *Lex Rex*, Schaeffer lays out the case for civil disobedience. He clearly and forthrightly distinguishes the various theoretical instances in which Christians may, or must, resist evil, both individually and corporately—through protest and remedies at law in the first instance, and then by force in the last extreme.

A real case in the United States is said by Schaeffer to fit Rutherford's theories exactly: the "creation science" case in Arkansas in 1981. The State of Arkansas passed a law that, according to Schaeffer, "allowed" the story of creation to be taught in the public schools. The American Civil Liberties Union (ACLU) brought suit to have this law disallowed on the grounds that it violated the separation of church and state. The Moral Majority Legal Defense Fund entered the case opposing the ACLU.

For Schaeffer, this defense is an appropriate response because it seeks remedy at law. Until this remedy has been sought, and potentially negated, Christians should go no further in disobedience. But if this is negated (which it was in Arkansas, after *A Christian Manifesto* was written) Schaeffer suggests that other forms of disobedience are appropriate. (And in suggesting this he hints darkly at the parallel cases of "humanist" dominance in education in the United States and the Soviet Union alike.) Since humanists have no God at the center of their lives, says Schaeffer, they must put something else there, and that usually is the nation state. Again he makes an analogy to the Soviet Union, a completely statist society, which the United States mirrors too closely to suit Schaeffer. By citing the alarming parallel with the Russians, Schaeffer adds pungency to the statement that Christians must realize that we are "at war, and there are no neutral parties in the struggle" (CM: 115).

In the end, of course, the remedies of flight and protest can be exhausted, and physical force becomes appropriate. Schaeffer uses the case of the American Revolution as a good example of the appropriate use of force:

> The colonists used force in defending themselves. Great Britain, because of its policy toward the colonies, was seen as a foreign power. The colonists defended their homeland. As such, the American Revolution was a conservative counter-revolution. The colonists saw the British as the revolutionaries trying to overthrow the legitimate colonial governments (CM: 117).

In the very next paragraph after the line quoted above, Schaeffer suggests a controversial analogy in which Nazi Germany is cited as an appropriate case for legitimate, Christian overthrow of an illegitimate government. In the paragraph after that one he cites the case of abortion in America, insinuating that the cases—the American Revolution, resistance to Nazi Germany, and resistance to "legal" abortion—are all of one theme: resisting illegitimate government and its actions in the name of "law which is or ought to be 'king'" (CM: 118–23). Schaeffer seals this part of the discussion with long quotations from the "radical" parts of the American Declaration of Independence in which the right of revolution is articulated in the counterrevolutionary terms of responding to a "long train of abuses and usurpations."

In short, if the government attacks people, people should first try to reform it, and (if flight is inappropriate) they should abolish the government and institute a new one—as Jefferson wrote, "laying its foundations on such principles, and organizing its power in such a form, as to them shall seem most likely to effect their safety and happiness." Schaeffer quotes at length from the venerable colonial historian, Perry Miller. That quotation is reproduced here because we will return to it in my analysis of Schaeffer's views.

> [We] still do not realize how effective were generations of Protestant preaching in evoking patriotic enthusiasm. No interpretation of the religious utterances as being merely sanctimonious window dressing will do justice to the facts or to the character of the populace. Circumstances and the nature of the dominant opinion in Europe made it necessary

for the official statement [that is, Declaration of Independence] to be released in primarily "political" terms—the social compact, inalienable rights, the right of revolution. But those terms, in and by themselves, would never have supplied the drive to victory, however mightily they weighed with the literate minority. What carried the ranks of militia and citizens was the universal persuasion that they, by administering to themselves a spiritual purge, acquired the energies God has always, in the manner of the Old Testament, been ready to impart to His repentant children.[1]

For Schaeffer, the American Revolution is acceptable revolution because it was a "conservative" revolution and because it was religiously formulated.

The conclusion of A Christian Manifesto restates the main themes of the book and restates the call for action, in Schaeffer's terms, a "blowing of the trumpet." He clearly hopes to energize the Christian community into resolute action.

A CRITIQUE OF A CHRISTIAN MANIFESTO

Finding something wrong with modern Western culture has not been an exclusive concern of Christians. Social commentators from all ideological persuasions seem agreed on a central proposition: there is something dreadfully wrong with modern society, especially in the United States. Whether it be Robert Heilbroner,[2] speaking out of the liberal humanist tradition, or Christopher Lasch,[3] speaking out of the radical tradition, intellectuals of note seem agreed that we moderns are adrift in a sea of indecision and that the malaise of the human spirit has nearly reached its nadir. It is no longer necessary for intellectuals to demonstrate that something is fundamentally wrong with Western culture.

Thus Schaeffer's contribution is that he is speaking out of an evangelical-Reformed perspective. He offers nothing essentially new in the basic thrust of the argument that "we can't go on like this" in modern American culture, but he is to be commended for joining the discussion on a Christian basis. The remainder of this essay offers a critique of some of the themes raised by Schaeffer in his Manifesto.

Humanism and the Reformation

Throughout Schaeffer's work there has been a constant theme—that "humanism" is the antithesis to Christianity. What he calls "the other totality" has been constantly at war with the "total" ideology of Christianity. If humanism is the enemy, it would be helpful to define just what humanism is. But that is the difficult point: historians, encumbered by reality, not the idea of reality, will not accept a definition of humanism that fits all times and places. In short, no historian will accept an ahistorical and propositional definition of humanism.

At the same time, historians cannot accept ahistorical and propositional definitions of the Reformation. Indeed, the very problem turns on the connection between Renaissance humanism and the Reformation. For Schaeffer and many Protestant apologists, the Reformation offers "a base" from which to judge humanistic culture. Because this point is so important to all of Schaeffer's writings, no less to the *Manifesto*, we must clear up this matter before going any further in discussing the book.

Humanism in the Renaissance was not so much a philosophy or world view as a methodology by which a number of philosophies, both sacred and profane, were possible. At basis, humanism was about the right of private conscience to govern action and belief. Crane Brinton helps us by making an important distinction between types of Renaissance humanisms.[4] "Spare" humanism exerted the right corporately and with historical discipline. "Exuberant" humanists did so individually and contemporaneously and were clearly the forerunners of the democratic individualists of our time whom Schaeffer deplores.

But most Renaissance humanists, especially in northern Europe, come under the rubric of "spare." For them, their rebellion against the authority of the medieval synthesis was not a rebellion against authority itself (as with the "exuberants"), but against "wrong" authority as they saw it. But how was one to know "wrong" from "right" authority? Herein is the basis of the humanist methodology at least in its "spare" form: that a better prescription for "right" authority can be found in antique sources, hence the insistence that scholars learn Greek, Latin, and Hebrew. The majority of intellectuals in the Renaissance employed the humanist methodology insofar as they judged their contemporary culture (art, music, literature, government, theology) by the standards of the past, to which they had access through the writings of past wisdom, "the classics."

Let it be restated that humanism was not so much a philosophy as a method by which a number of philosophies were possible. Let it also be said that, while the methodology of referring to antique sources united the users, it is of fundamental difference that one referred to the "wisdom" of Greece and Rome and the other to the Christian Scriptures as authoritative. In the Reformation the Protestants employed the "humanist methodology" insofar as they objected to then-current religious doctrine and practice.

The protest from most of the Reformers was not against religious authority itself, but against "wrong" authority as they saw it. The antique source to which they repaired, via the ancient languages, was the Christian Scriptures. This led to the Protestant slogan "Scripture alone," by which it was meant that the Bible was the source for Christian believing and behaving. So most Protestants conformed methodologically to the spare tradition of humanism. But like any movement based on free choice and selective reading of text, they could not agree on much more than that the Bible was "authoritative" and they were no longer content to remain within the historical church. Moreover, even though Lutherans and Mennonites were both Protestants, they shared very little; indeed, if Lutherans had to choose, they would find much more in common with the Roman pontiff than with Menno Simons.

Protestant Christianity, then, is Christianity synthesized with the spare tradition of humanism. The Protestant Reformation is an extremely complex and paradoxical movement, and it cannot be wrenched out of its time and context to be made a repository of timeless truth. This is all the more difficult because of the relative distinctions between the types of Protestantism. Schaeffer seems to think that Calvinism *is* the Reformation, a point that Christians in the Lutheran and "free church" traditions would dispute hotly.

In the end, the importance of all of this for Schaeffer's apologetics is that the Reformation is not a single "base," and without the whole notion of a "base" it is a far more difficult task than Schaeffer supposed to judge the merits and demerits of modern culture. This is so precisely because we Protestants have founded our religious lives on a methodology that is said by Schaeffer to form the basis of the other totality. With our religious lives founded on this synthesis, it isn't possible to think, act, and believe antithetically—unless we are prepared to return to the historical church, an act that most evangelical Protestants would find unacceptable. Calvinist triumphalism will not answer the real questions that persist.

The Meaning of America and the American Revolution

Throughout *A Christian Manifesto* Schaeffer implicitly endorses what historiographers call "the Whig theory of history." This view of history has had several incarnations, and the details vary, but in general it means that right religion and liberty are on the same side against wrong religion and tyranny. The Anglo-Saxon peoples are especially blessed in this regard, and it is the Protestant nations of northwest Europe and their overseas extensions that are cited as the righteous nations. (At one point Schaeffer becomes explicit and invokes northern Europe in this context, adding the names of the United States, Canada, Australia, and New Zealand.) But it is for the United States that the superlatives are reserved in this view of history, and Schaeffer seems to have adopted the theory as his own.

It has been said that the discovery of America was the cause of the greatest liberation of the European imagination. As the Renaissance-humanist world view drove the voyagers west to go east (they defied the "biblical" authority of a flat earth), the discovery of the Western Hemisphere was, as C. S. Lewis wrote, a great disappointment. But soon that disappointment changed to anticipation, and Thomas More's Utopia was the first mature reflection in the Old World on the potential of the New. The general idealism in Europe that mankind could begin over again was widely shared, in both secular and religious circles.[5]

Once again the Protestant movement was not immune from the impulses of its time, and as is well known, Calvinists came to the New World early in the seventeenth century. John Winthrop's sermon, "The Model of Christian Charity," offers the interpretative paradigm for American history: the meaning of America was to consist in "building the city on the hill," in which the light to the Gentiles would shine and in respect of which all would one day turn and be converted.

With this model of early American development clearly in mind, Schaeffer turns to the American Revolution. True to the Whig theory, right religion and liberty were arrayed against wrong religion and tyranny. Schaeffer correctly notes the evangelical impetus behind the Revolution, and he endorses it. But should it be endorsed? Nathan Hatch has written in *The Sacred Cause of Liberty* that evangelicals did believe that there was a British conspiracy against liberty, especially after the passage of the Quebec Act in 1774.[6]

While we might have empathy for these evangelical revolutionaries in their context, surely they were deluded if they believed that an "absolute tyranny" was about to be imposed. (Here the Whig theory argues against itself. It was supposed to be the Anglo-Saxon peoples who were on the side of right religion and liberty, especially since Schaeffer insists that the British have a "reformational base." How do they suddenly become "absolute-tyrants"?) Surely the revolutionaries acted on a pretentious view of themselves and their cause if they believed that they alone were protecting the right view of society.

As to the Declaration of Independence and the Constitution, Schaeffer is similarly muddled. The Declaration of Independence is an Enlightenment document, whereas the Constitution opposed the spirit of both the Enlightenment and the Declaration in requiring liberty to be ordered by law. Once again, Schaeffer is half-right. Jefferson was thoroughly baptized into the Enlightenment faith, but John Adams was not. Of the several books on this subject, readers would do well to consult Merrill Peterson, *Adams and Jefferson: A Revolutionary Dialogue*.[7]

Richard Hofstadter once said, "The Constitution of the United States was based on the philosophy of Hobbes and the religion of Calvin."[8] Schaeffer is on to something fundamental in suggesting the unique character of the Constitution. But his argument is substantially flawed by suggesting a moral-legal consensus among "the Founding Fathers." There were two sets of Founding Fathers, because there were two factions in the revolutionary party, advocating quite different visions of society. As John Adams said in writing the Massachusetts state constitution, the question was whether or not the government would be "a government of law or of men." While Adams clearly advocated "law," for Jefferson the meaning of America and of its revolution was that it would be "a government of men."

Not surprisingly, the main sign of hope Schaeffer sees (an "open window," in his terms) is the present-day conservative successes in American politics. One of the founding principles of the neoconservative faith is the doctrine of return to the principles of the Founding Fathers. But this simplistic view of past reality cannot accept that the same divisions which bedevil our society were there then too. Nostalgia will not help us out of our present malaise, nor will rewriting American history.

A Christian Example: John Witherspoon

In *A Christian Manifesto* Schaeffer gives the example of John Witherspoon as a prime case for linking reformational Christianity to concepts of government. Witherspoon is said to stand in the tradition of Rutherford, and for Schaeffer, that is *the* place to stand (see Pierard's discussion in chapter 7). If there is a case to be made for an actualizing of reformation action in American history, Witherspoon is clearly it.

If this is the best case for the theory, then one must state that the theory does not hold. Schaeffer's unvarnished praise for Witherspoon as a laudable Christian patriot can perhaps be explained by the source he cites. The source is a biography of Witherspoon written nearly eighty years ago and published by a self-described "inspirational Christian publisher." Had Schaeffer done more homework and read recent scholarship on the subject, it may have saved him from substantial error in interpretation.

Mark Noll, Nathan Hatch, and George Marsden have done that homework, and the picture they portray of Witherspoon is not at all as Schaeffer would have it.[9] Quoting James McAllister: "The answer to the question regarding the biblical contribution to Witherspoon's teaching about the law and liberty is: almost nothing. . . . his theory of society and civil law was based not on revelation but on the moral sense enlightened by reason and experience." And quoting from Flower and Murphey: "Thus he starts his ethics, not with premises guaranteed by religion or revelation, but from the construction of human nature as learned by observations."[10]

Noll, Hatch, and Marsden conclude,

> Yet in Witherspoon, the most self-consciously evangelical of the founding fathers, there is little of the effort which marked the work of earlier Christian thinkers to ground politics in specifically Christian propositions. . . . Witherspoon remains valuable as an example of courageous activity by a Christian in public life. . . . But it would be foolish to believe that the way in which Witherspoon reasoned about politics should ever serve as a model for Christian political thought.[11]

Calling it "foolish" is perhaps a bit strong, but surely it is misguided to see in Witherspoon, as Schaeffer does, an example in early American history of "the antithesis" at work. Witherspoon synthesized the Enlightenment and the Reformation, and his "approach to politics opened the door to secularization."[12]

The Moral Majority and Christian Reconstructionists

Schaeffer is very careful in *Manifesto* not to endorse the "Moral Majority" specifically, but he does endorse what they do. He writes, "They have carried the fact that law is king, law is above the lawmakers, and God is above the law into this area of life where it always should have been." And, "if you personally do not like some of the details of what they have done, do it better" (CM: 61–62). Jerry Falwell remarked on his television program that *A Christian Manifesto* "was probably the most important piece of literature in America today."[13] This cozy relationship between Schaeffer and "the new Christian Right" invites us to inquire briefly into that movement and its origins insofar as they relate to Francis Schaeffer.

When I first visited L'Abri I was very eager to hear how Schaeffer, then largely unpublished, would relate his world view studies to American history. I was told there that Mr. Schaeffer had not yet worked a great deal on that subject, but there was one tape in which I might be interested, a review by Schaeffer of *This Independent Republic* by Rousas J. Rushdoony. I have since learned that Rushdoony is founder-mentor of a Calvinist-oriented movement called "Christian Reconstruction."

Along with his disciples, Gary North and Greg Bahnsen, Rushdoony has produced a small library of books and pamphlets which contend that Christians in the New Testament age are still required to obey the details of the Old Covenant and to work for the establishment of Mosaic law in societal structures—in short, they believe in theonomy.[14] Theonomists are proud of their intellectual influence over the "New Christian Right," although they rarely receive the recognition due them in this respect.[15]

According to David K. Watson, *A Christian Manifesto* demonstrates how much Schaeffer relied on the writings of theonomists, most notably Rushdoony. Two noted theonomists, Gary North and David Chilton, reviewed *Manifesto* and compared it to Rushdoony's *The One and the Many* (1971). They did a side-by-side comparison of the two books, and in several instances the similarities "are more than coincidental," says Watson, who quotes North and Chilton: "Francis Schaeffer has been reading the writings of R. J. Rushdoony for twenty years. In fact, Rev. Rushdoony's thought has been a major influence on Schaeffer."[16]

Again, the theory advanced by the two theonomists, North and Chilton, as to why Schaeffer would not acknowledge his dependence on Rushdoony "is that Rushdoony is a theological hot potato . . . because he is a self-proclaimed advocate of 'theocracy.' "[17] While careful not to advocate a theocracy himself, Schaeffer apparently borrowed significantly from Rushdoony's legal-religious analysis of "secular humanism." Some of Schaeffer's disciples have not been so careful, most notably his son, Franky, who freely quotes from Rushdoony,[18] and John Whitehead, who argues a theonomic line on the bibliocentric nature of normative law[19] and whose work Schaeffer enthusiastically endorsed.

Facing Up to Modernity

A Christian Manifesto really should have been entitled *A Fundamentalist Manifesto*. By using the term "fundamentalism" I do not merely slap a label on Schaeffer and damn him with guilt by association with that unfortunate movement. Rather, before Schaeffer had read much in philosophy or law, he was predisposed (I was told repeatedly at L'Abri) to accept the notion of "the antithesis," because his early experience as a Presbyterian had taught him that the times were right to contend mightily against modernity in all its forms, especially theological liberalism. As George Marsden suggests, Fundamentalism is "militantly anti-modern," because it sees the struggle as all-or-nothing, so reality is divided by two types of people: those who "stand fast" for the truth ("true truth") and those who accommodate to "the world."[20] In short, for Schaeffer, either we are "reformational" (the antithesis) or we have accommodated to "modernity" (synthesis). This is a false antithesis.

In calling for a return to the Christian foundations of America, Schaeffer stands in a venerable tradition of Calvinist writing, "the jeremiad."[21] There is a long history of Calvinists preaching the doctrine of return to the vision of Winthrop.

Already in the seventeenth century this form of sermonizing was well-developed. The theme is familiar: the people have betrayed the faith, have fallen from grace, but there is still time to return and to recapture the vision.

Manifesto conforms to one important theme of the jeremiad: the enemy within. All that Schaeffer sees as "the base" of law in American history was built by immigrants from Protestant northern Europe. The American story begins to go wrong when substantial Catholic immigration began in the 1840s. While he does not name the Irish specifically, Schaeffer suggests that 1848 is a turning year, a year in which the mass migration from famine-ridden Ireland began. Here we may have a vestigial remain of that virulent Protestant disease: Anglo-Saxon anti-Catholicism. This is appalling, for surely Schaeffer, who knew that ideas have consequences, must have known that in endorsing such views he is endorsing by extension some of the most undemocratic acts of intolerance in American history, acts of which Protestants must be ashamed.

What Schaeffer really cannot handle is pluralism, although he says he defends it. Pluralism, he says, should mean "a general religious freedom from the control of the state for all religion. It will not mean just freedom for those who are Christians. It is then up to Christians to show that Christianity is the truth of total reality in the open marketplace of freedom" (CM: 46). But Schaeffer goes on to lament the reality of pluralism, blaming it on the "greater mixture" of peoples in America—apparently meaning that Anglo-Saxon Protestantism has lost its dominance.

No doubt Schaeffer is quite correct in suggesting that cultural pluralism has become the norm of American society and we currently live in a society in which no norm of one religious or ethnic group may be imposed on another. But Schaeffer doesn't like this: "Pluralism has come to mean that everything is acceptable. This new concept of pluralism suddenly is everywhere. There is no right or wrong; it is just a matter of your personal preference" (CM: 46).

But, one asks, what is the alternative in a democratic society? Does Schaeffer mean that, given the freedom to advocate Christianity (he means proselytization), Christians should ênforce their views by "law" if people will not accept Christian belief and behavior by choice? He singles out the striking down of the Arkansas "creation-science" law as an example of a cause justifying civil disobedience, and this suggests his tendency to favor establishing "Christian" views by law. In fact, the Arkansas law would have required the teaching of the fundamentalist scientific arguments for a young earth and flood geology, *along with* teaching "evolution science" whenever the subject of origins was taught in public schools.

This tendency to promote one's own view by "law" has always been the dangerous part of Calvinism: one sees Calvinists in power as triumphal and dictatorial. Whether in Calvin's Geneva, Knox's Edinburgh, Cromwell's London and Dublin, Winthrop's Boston, or in our own time, Vorster's Pretoria and Paisley's Belfast, Calvinists in power have wielded that power oppressively. Without doubt the above-named Calvinists *thought* they were doing God's service—restoring God's law—when they did their (in my view) intolerable, even heinous acts of repression. Before Calvinists act too quickly in following Schaeffer's call for civil disobedience in respect to restoring "God's law," they should follow the trail of Oliver Cromwell through Ireland in the 1640s and then go in person to confront their own beliefs at Drogheda, where Cromwell presided over a massacre that is at the heart of Irish Catholic oral tradition in resisting Protestantism.

To be sure, pluralism *is* a risk that any religionist takes in electing to live in a democratic society. And it may be that beliefs and behaviors opposed to ours may be enacted into law. But that is the essence of a social contract in a modern nation-state: that we try to change law and practices through the law courts and by political means. While I accept that there are cases in which civil disobedience, even revolution, is justifiable, I join most Americans in thinking that we have not reached that point.

Schaeffer would reply, immediately and with vigor, that abortion is *the* issue of our time, and it *does* demonstrate that things have gone too far. I too deplore abortion, although without the fervor that obscures consideration of all other matters. But in the end, Schaeffer's disengagement with American culture turns largely on abortion. Given his views in *Whatever Happened to the Human Race?* it is not surprising that this should occupy so prominent a place in *Manifesto.*

The fact that abortion can exist and that it is validated by law and, apparently, a substantial portion of the American people is enough for Schaeffer to question the legitimacy of the whole social contract in the United States. Again, though it is not the only matter on his agenda, the existence and social acceptance of abortion is the fundamental signal of what he repeatedly calls "the takeover of the other totality." This sort of thing, he laments, would not have happened in the America of eighty years ago, before what he calls the "titanic shift" in world view occurred. While he is not victim to a trivial nostalgia, Schaeffer genuinely believes that life in America would be better if we could restore the sort of society we had—a relatively monistic one—before we descended into cultural diversity.

Perhaps here we can begin to see the real source of anger and resentment that one reads between the lines of Schaeffer's books. Abortion is the sign, but the meaning of the sign is the displacement of the hegemony of evangelical Protestantism as the legitimizing ideology it once was. Schaeffer's anger is understandable, in that all of us share it to a degree. (What is to be done about it is another matter.) Christians feel a deep anger about modern society because it *is* the world that Max Weber described early in this century and James D. Hunter analyzed recently.[22] Gary Scott Smith gives an excellent summary paragraph on modernization that begets secularization:

> Drawing upon the work of sociologist Peter Berger, Hunter attempts to show how the processes of rationalization, cultural pluralism and structural pluralism force religious world views to make accommodations. The rationalization process, which rests upon a naturalistic world view, undermines the credibility of religious assumptions about life and the universe and encourages people to see the world in mechanistic terms. Cultural pluralism divides society into subunits with distinct cultural traditions, thus challenging the universality of traditional religious views. Pluralistic societies deprive people of the constant social confirmation they need to sustain their beliefs about ultimate reality. Structural pluralism separates life into public and private spheres. It confines religious symbols and authority to private dimensions of life—church, family, and leisure—while public institutions and structures—politics, economics, education, media and the like—come to rest upon secular values.[23]

To this, and small wonder, Schaeffer would have said that it is unacceptable. Christians *must* oppose modernization, he would declare. But the ultimate question for social theorists today is this: Can modernization be opposed or its processes stopped? It is not much believed any longer that Weber was correct in saying that religious belief would disappear in modern society. We can see now that it would continue in a less meaningfully differentiated subsphere. Religion continues, in short, to be big business in America, but it is not the essence of the whole, just one part of it. So paradoxically religion means less as society differentiates and compartmentalizes, even though there are more people being "born again."

With this structure of thought in hand, the news sounds really bad to conservative evangelicals like Francis Schaeffer who want to restore America to its "Christian foundations." The very individualism and anti-institutionalism that were the hallmark of nineteenth-century society created the social vacuum that ushered in modernization (and its partner secularization).[24] Fueled by a transportation revolution, a mobility ideology, and drawn by the frontier, Americans after about 1825 broke down what Stephan Thernstrom calls "the Federalist culture."[25]

Protestant evangelicalism, in its heyday in the nineteenth century, mirrored the social attitudes of Americans in the deinstitutionalization of American society. Evangelicals participated happily in that "liberation" from premodern social structure because they believed they were ushering in the republic of millennial Protestant virtue they so dreadfully desired.[26]

But society, like nature, abhors a vacuum, and that vacuum was soon filled with the modern state. In the generation between the breakdown of the Federalist culture and the onset of modern institutions (1825–65), the United States experienced the greatest amount of structural freedom in its history; but tragically, it was precisely the absence of institutional structures that required the debate over slavery to be resolved, not within democratic patterns, but in civil war.[27] It was in the aftermath of the Civil War that Americans created the new world characterized by the themes of industrialization, mechanization, urbanization, and nationalization. The American people groped to find the meaning of their place in the new social order. In the classic work on the subject Robert H. Wiebe tells of that groping:

> Yet to almost all of the people who created them, these
> themes meant only dislocation and bewilderment. America
> in the late nineteenth century was a society without a core. It
> lacked those national centers of authority and information

which might have given order to such swift changes. American institutions were still oriented toward a community life where family and church, education and press, professions and government, all largely found their meaning by the way they fit one with another inside a town or a detached portion of a city. As men ranged farther and farther from their communities, they tried desperately to understand the larger world in terms of their small, familiar environment. They tried, in other words, to impose the known upon the unknown, to master an impersonal world through the customs of a personal society. They failed, usually without recognizing why; and that failure to comprehend a society they were helping to make contained the essence of the nation's story.[28]

In conclusion, let it be said clearly that we do not rejoice in citing such matters as Wiebe points to. We are not happy that the world is a large, impersonal entity, with a "system" into which we all must "fit." With Schaeffer I feel rage against the sort of world I must live in, a world vastly different from my father's. With Marx I feel the alienation that is a natural outgrowth of the specialized and impersonal environment in which I must live in modern industrial society.

Schaeffer is right to say that there has been a dramatic shift in world view, but in saying that, he is only half-right. The world of modernity and secularity did not emerge merely because people began to think differently, as Schaeffer the idealist suggests. People began to think differently because "thought" (or, world view) always parallels, and is not independent of, its social context. Did Schaeffer ever read Karl Mannheim and learn about "the sociology of knowledge," in which "ideas" cannot be understood apart from their social context?[29] The point here is that the social context of America altered dramatically in the years after the Civil War. What came into being can be characterized by the phrase "the new industrial state."[30]

Modernity, then, means much more than secularity and vastly more than "secular humanism," the new cliché of the Christian Right. It means a whole pattern of social organization *and* of world view. To return to the question posed above: Can the process of modernization be stopped? Can this radically disconnected world ever be put back together again?

Evangelical Protestants, who typically have had a trivial view of evil, believe they have an answer. If they were to "preach the gospel," people would be "saved," and, since evil resides essentially in the human heart not in social structures, social evil can be eradicated when people "turn to the Lord." More thoughtful evangelicals, like Francis Schaeffer, however, realize that the gospel needs to be articulated into the social order. They are to be applauded for that, because without an integrated faith–life view, one can expect little advancement for the gospel in our time.

If modernity is as difficult to penetrate as most think it is, Christians really have only two options: to work within it and, one supposes, effect some accommodation to it, or to oppose it on every level. In general, liberal (mainline) Protestantism has accepted the reality of modernity and seeks to give gospel ministry while accommodating to the structures, even the thought patterns, of the modern world.[31] Fundamentalists, on the other hand, find the modern world view unacceptable as much in socio-political as in religio-moral terms.

Evangelicals, although arising out of fundamentalism after about 1945, have been ambivalent about how much to keep up the fundamentalist militancy or to move toward some semblances of modernist accommodation. Either course of action will exact its price. If the reality of modern culture is rationalization, cultural pluralism, and structural pluralism, then evangelicals will have to recognize this reality in significant ways in order to make their message comprehensible to modern people. James Hunter is probably correct in suggesting that such accommodation—even while keeping theology "pure"—will rob evangelicalism of its energy to sustain itself over time.

On the other hand, demographic shifts are likely to overtake evangelicals, and they will be unable to keep their movement pure enough to survive if they choose the route of resistance. The sustaining force of anti-modern evangelicalism has been that its adherents have been kept distant from modernity's most powerful agents: universities, the professions, upper social classes, and urban lifestyle. As increasing numbers of evangelicals are exposed to these modernizing agents, it is difficult to see how the movement can sustain a significant countercultural style.[32]

This kind of analysis would surely upset Francis Schaeffer if he were still alive. Nor can it be pleasing to his followers, who would insist that its "relativism" and "synthesis" are all too typical of what Richard Quebedeaux called "worldly evangelicalism."[33] But it is curious that Schaeffer thought his own work

to be an example of "the antithesis," when it is vintage
synthesis itself. He has taken abstract legal thinking from
Rushdoony, linked it to a theological style from Van Til, and
bound it all up together in the notion of a mythic American
history. In jeremiad style, he issued a manifesto, hoping it to be
a counterblast to the "Humanist Manifesto," only to create
something that is its mirror image.

In the end, the Schaeffer I thought to be too European in
his thinking turns out to be an American after all, and, as
George Marsden has reminded us, fundamentalism is a uniquely American phenomenon.[34]

NOTES

[1] Perry Miller, *Nature's Nation* (Cambridge: Harvard University, Belknap Press, 1967), 110.

[2] Robert Heilbroner, *An Inquiry Into the Human Prospect* (New York: Norton, 1976).

[3] Christopher Lasch, *The Culture of Narcissism* (New York: Norton, 1979).

[4] Crane Brinton, *The Shaping of Modern Thought* (Englewood Cliffs, N. J.: Prentice-Hall, 1963), 22–53.

[5] On this point see especially J. Martin Evans, *America: The View From Europe* (New York: Norton, 1979). For a wide-ranging analysis from a Christian perspective see Ronald A. Wells, "Viewing America: A Christian Perspective," *Fides et Historia,* 17 (1984): 56–67.

[6] Nathan Hatch, *The Sacred Cause of Liberty: Republican Thought and the Millennium in Revolutionary New England* (New Haven: Yale University, 1977).

[7] Merrill Peterson, *Adams and Jefferson: A Revolutionary Dialogue* (London and New York: Oxford University, 1978).

[8] Richard Hofstadter, *The American Political Tradition* (New York: Vintage, 1955), 3.

[9] Mark Noll, Nathan Hatch, and George Marsden, *The Search for Christian America* (Westchester, Ill.: Crossway, 1983).

[10] Both sources quoted in Noll, Hatch, and Marsden, 90–91.

[11] Noll, Hatch, and Marsden, 92–93.

[12] Ibid., 93.

[13] Quoted in Jon Zens, *Searching Together* 11 (1982): 41.

[14] Most notably in Greg L. Bahnsen, *Theonomy in Christian Ethics* (Nutley, N. J.: Craig, 1979).

[15] For these insights into the relationship of the theonomy movement to Schaeffer and the "Christian Right," I am greatly indebted to the work of David K. Watson, "Theonomy: A History of a Movement and An Evaluation of Its Primary Text," unpublished master's thesis, Calvin College, 1985.

[16] Quoted in Watson, 36.

[17] Ibid.

[18] Franky Schaeffer, *A Time for Anger* (Westchester, Ill.: Crossway, 1982).

[19] John Whitehead, *The Second American Revolution* (Elgin, Ill: David C. Cook, 1982), esp. 73–82, 181–92.

[20] *Fundamentalism and American Culture* (New York: Oxford, 1982).

[21] See especially the brilliant work on this literary genre by Sacvan Bercovitch, *The American Jeremiad* (Madison: University of Wisconsin, 1978).

[22] Max Weber, *The Theory of Social and Economic Organizations* (Glencoe, Ill.: Free Press, 1964); James D. Hunter, *American Evangelicalism: Conservative Religion and the Quandary of Modernity* (New Brunswick, N. J.: Rutgers University, 1983).

[23] Gary Scott Smith, "Can Evangelicalism Resist Modernity?" *TSF Bulletin* 8 (March–April 1985): 25.

[24] See especially Richard D. Brown, *Modernization: The Transformation of American Life, 1600–1865* (New York: Hill and Wang, 1976).

[25] Stephan Thernstrom, *Poverty and Progress* (Cambridge: Harvard University, 1964).

[26] Timothy L. Smith, *Revivalism and Social Reform: American Protestantism on the Eve of the Civil War*, 2nd ed. (Baltimore: Johns Hopkins University, 1980).

[27] Stanley Elkins, *Slavery: A Problem in American Institutional and Intellectual Life* (Chicago: University of Chicago, 1959).

[28] Robert H. Wiebe, *The Search for Order: America, 1877–1920* (New York: Hill and Wang, 1967).

[29] Karl Mannheim, *Essays on the Sociology of Knowledge* (London: Routledge and Kegan Paul, 1952).

[30] John K. Galbraith, *The New Industrial State* (Boston: Houghton, Mifflin, 1967); Glenn Porter, *The Rise of Big Business* (New York: Crowell, 1973).

[31] William Hutchinson, *The Modernist Impulse* (Cambridge: Harvard University, 1976).

[32] These points are fully illumined in Hunter, *American Evangelicalism.*

[33] Richard Quebedeaux, *The Worldly Evangelicals* (New York: Harper & Row, 1978).

[34] George M. Marsden, "Fundamentalism As an American Phenomenon," *Church History* 46 (1977): 215–32.

9

SCHAEFFER ON ETHICS

DENNIS P. HOLLINGER

Francis Schaeffer was first and foremost an apologist, a defender of the Christian faith to the twentieth-century mind. Intertwined with that role, however, was the heart of a prophet—an interpreter and critic of modern culture and society. As such, Schaeffer entered the realm of ethics (the discipline) and morals (the behavior).

Nevertheless, Schaeffer's discussion of ethical problems was primarily in the service of apologetics. As he saw it, only a Christian thought system can provide an adequate basis for dealing with moral issues and social ills. No other world view can furnish a coherent explanation for why cruelty and inhumanity exist within the world. Since the Christian has a solid philosophical base that is true to reality, "The Christian should be in the front line, fighting the results of man's cruelty" (PDM: 32).

The reason Schaeffer's focus on ethics was always secondary to his apologetics was his belief that one's world view determines subsequent behavior. In one of his earliest works he wrote, "Men act the way they think" (EFR: 27). Therefore, rather than focusing primarily on specific ethical issues, Schaef-

Dennis P. Hollinger is Associate Professor of Church and Society at the Alliance Theological Seminary, Nyack, New York. He holds degrees from Elizabethtown College, Trinity Evangelical Divinity School (M.Div.), and Drew University (M.Phil., Ph.D.). He is the author of Individualism and Social Ethics: An Evangelical Syncretism.

fer believed that one needs to assess the perspectives and ideas that give birth to human actions. For example, abortion is an evil to be fought, but more significant than the issue itself is the world view that lured society into accepting the practice. Thus, while Schaeffer's prophetic energies did propel him to address specific moral and social problems such as abortion, euthanasia, racism, economics, and ecology, his engagement with these issues should always be seen against the backdrop of his larger mission—that of an apologist attempting to show the bankruptcy of all world views and ethical systems, save Christianity.

This chapter will first explore the basis of Schaeffer's Christian ethic and secondly examine his position on specific issues. Finally, we will turn our attention to a critical assessment of his ethical methodology and content.

THE BASIS FOR CHRISTIAN ETHICS

The proper basis for ethical reflection in Schaeffer's mind is a coherent Christian world view that heralds one moral principle above all others, the dignity of human beings.

World View

Abortion, infanticide, child abuse, violence, pornography, and other social ills are not born and bred in a vacuum. Rather, says Schaeffer, they are conceived by a view of reality that directly affects human behavior. "We act in accordance with our world view, and our world view rests on what to us is the ultimate truth" (WHHR: 121).

Schaeffer never offered a clear in-depth definition of world view other than to say it entails our overall way of looking at the world. He seems to mean by this our view of God, human beings, and nature. The way we understand the essence and interrelationship of these three elements will inevitably determine our ethical commitments and the way we live. The relative impact of environment, circumstances, or social structures in shaping human behavior is of minimal interest to Schaeffer, for "people are unique in the inner life of the mind— what they are in their thought world determines how they act. . . . It is true of their corporate actions, such as political decisions, and it is true of their personal lives" (HSWTL: 19).

As Schaeffer sees it, the central moral problem today is that "in one short generation we have moved from a generally high view of life to a very low one" (WHHR: 20). What accounts for this change? He believes it is due to a dramatic shift in world view. In the Western world a Christian consensus formerly provided the basis for true morality, but that foundation has eroded under the onslaught of a mechanistic-humanistic concept of reality.

In the mechanistic dimension of this world view, only matter exists. Humans are mere "products of the impersonal plus time plus chance" and hence "all values are open to manipulation" (BFD: 15). Schaeffer contends that this mechanistic perspective destroys the significance of human beings and makes them ready prey for destructive manipulations. In critiquing the French biologist Jacques Monod's concept of chance in nature, he asks,

> How, then, if man lives in such a universe shall he decide how to live? Where will he get his moral principles? If there are no moral absolutes against which man can measure his actions, how then shall he understand what value is? (BFD: 12).

Schaeffer responds that we are not equipped to ascertain values and moral principles with such a perspective, for "the material universe in itself gives no basis for values. Those who begin with the material universe can describe but they can never define. They speak only in the indicative, never in the imperative" (WHHR: 136).

The humanistic dimension of this contemporary world view reflects "the fundamental idea that men and women can begin from themselves and derive the standards by which to judge all matters" (WHHR: 15). Though humanists attempt to define ethical values and principles, Schaeffer argues that their agenda is self-defeating. They have no basis for moral judgments apart from themselves, and as such must settle for the "51% view of morality"—what the majority thinks is morally good.

It is precisely this materialist-humanist world view that Schaeffer blames for the "loss of humanness on every level" (WHHR: 28). Taken to its logical conclusion it will totally destroy humanity, for within ourselves we have no grounds for dealing with cruelty and human evil. Only Christianity possesses such a basis. Schaeffer writes, "Modern man has no real basis for fighting evil, because he sees man as normal. . . . But the Christian—he can fight evil without fighting God" (HIT: 32).

The veracity of the Christian faith is then demonstrated by the fact that it alone can provide a foundation upon which we can make moral judgments and live. What is this world view? Schaeffer emphasizes the personal nature of an infinite God; His creation of finite persons in his image, hence distinct from the rest of nature; and their subsequent fall into human sin. This framework suggests two basic truths about humans—their dignity and their cruelty. "Man stands with all his wonder and nobility, and yet also with his horrible cruelty that runs throughout the warp and woof of man's history" (HIT: 22).

It was this Judeo-Christian system, says Schaeffer, that dominated the West for centuries and provided major answers for questions of identity, meaning, and value. He admits that "Judeo-Christian teaching was never perfectly applied, but it did lay a foundation for a high view of human life in concept and practice" (WHHR: 20).

Thus the major issue in ethics today, for Schaeffer, is not how to resolve value dilemmas, discern appropriate ethical principles in light of empirical realities, or relate moral injunctions to technical solutions. Rather, the watershed issue is that of world view, for when our perspectives are faulty, social and moral malaise is sure to follow. Therefore, the crucial ethical agenda goes beyond attacking specific problems like abortion and racism to recasting the fundamental world view that prompts them.

Human Dignity—The *Summum Bonum*

From the Christian view of reality there is one major value that Schaeffer eulogizes above all others—human dignity. In fact, although there are secondary values and concepts that he readily employs in ethical analysis, human dignity is the only moral value and principle which he sets forth systematically.

In *Back to Freedom and Dignity* Schaeffer castigates those biological and psychological theories that reduce people to a bundle of genes or a matrix of environmental conditioning. Such determinisms destroy the concept of responsible humanity, diminishing people to mere machines that are at the mercy of others' manipulation. In contrast he sees individuals as possessing a unique selfhood with inherent dignity and value: "Made in God's image, man was made to be great, he was made to be creative in life and art" (BFD: 48).

For Schaeffer, human dignity as an ethical category denotes that "each man, woman, and child is of great value, not for some utilitarian motive such as self-gratification or wealth or power . . . or the 'good of society' or the maintenance of the gene pool—but simply because of his or her origin" (WHHR: 158). Though humanity fails to live up to its dignity in a fallen state, the inherent worth of every person remains intact. This means that although cultures can be judged in many ways, "Eventually every nation in every age must be judged by this test: How did it treat people?" (WHHR: 15). Unless they adhere to this firm principle rooted in a Christian view of reality, Schaeffer believes, societies will embark on an inevitable decline in which what is morally unthinkable today will become morally thinkable tomorrow.

Most systems of Christian ethics tend to accentuate one theological category over others. Christology, soteriology, sanctification, eschatology, and revelation have all served as theological linchpins for ethical analysis. The linchpin for Schaeffer is clearly theological anthropology, since the most celebrated feature of his moral discourse is the Christian view of human beings. It is this aspect of the Christian framework that most strikingly distinguishes it from Western materialist— humanist schemes or Eastern "impersonal" views of reality. Within Schaeffer's anthropology the cruelty and sinfulness of humanity are affirmed, but more than that is his insistence on the value and dignity of every person. "First of all, we must say that we are proponents of the sanctity of human life—all human life—born and unborn; old and young; black, white, brown, and yellow" (WHHR: 110).

Schaeffer's description of this *summum bonum* of Christian ethics is not articulated with the tight precision that would characterize most academic ethicists and theologians. He does not relate the dignity principle to each issue with careful scrutiny, but merely affirms its significance and makes general application—a style not untypical of a prophet.

THE ISSUES

Schaeffer makes scattered allusions to numerous ethical issues in his writings, but there are five main areas that receive significant treatment: bioethics, ecology, race, economics, and war.

Bioethics

Schaeffer's most in-depth treatment of ethics is found in the book and film series *Whatever Happened to the Human Race?* which he co-authored with C. Everett Koop. Here he brings his prophetic edge to bear on three bioethical issues: abortion, infanticide, and euthanasia.

These three moral "travesties" have an intrinsic relationship to each other, says Schaeffer, for the acceptance of one will lead inevitably to acquiescence in the others. "Without the Judeo-Christian base which gives every individual an intrinsic dignity as made in the image of the personal-infinite Creator, each successive horror falls naturally into place" (WHHR: 87).

Schaeffer begins with abortion because he sees it as chronologically and logically first. He points to the 1973 *Roe v. Wade* decision on abortion by the United States Supreme Court as conclusive evidence that secular humanism has eclipsed Christian consensus as the philosophical base of our society and culture. The legal endorsement of abortion-on-demand not only reflects this philosophical foundation, but will lead directly to subsequent inhumanities. Schaeffer writes, "Of all the subjects relating to the erosion of the sanctity of human life, abortion is the keystone. It is the first and crucial issue that has been overwhelming in changing attitudes toward the value of life in general" (WHHR: 31).

Schaeffer claims to base his arguments against abortion on both logical and moral grounds, but it is interesting that he accentuates the logical side. In fact, he never appeals specifically to Scripture to buttress his position. The major logical argument employed involves the impossibility of saying when a developing fetus becomes viable (able to live outside the womb), for smaller and smaller premature infants are now being saved. Since the eventual possibilities for viability are staggering, "The logical approach is to go back to the sperm and the egg" (WHHR: 37). Schaeffer also outlines the biological development from conception to birth and argues that it is impossible to say that at one moment the life would be worthless and the next moment precious and worth saving. Establishing fetal viability is further complicated by genetic realities, for "all that makes up the adult is present as the ovum and the sperm are united—the whole genetic code!" (WHHR: 41).

A second logical argument for Schaeffer centers on the

after-effects of abortion on a woman. Lamenting that abortion counselors seldom discuss the physical and emotional consequences of the procedure with their clients, he contends that abortion merely exchanges one set of problems for another. He writes,

> One of the facts of being a human being is that in spite of the abnormality of human beings and the cruelty of their actions, there still exist the hopes and fears, the longings and aspirations, that can be bundled together in the word *motherliness*. To stamp out these feelings is to insure that many women will turn into the kind of hard people they may not want to be (WHHR: 52).

A third rational argument for Schaeffer is that the logical result of abortion will be the acceptance of infanticide. This then is the second bioethics issue he addresses.

Schaeffer defines infanticide as "the killing of a born child—whether that killing is accomplished by a direct act on the part of someone, or whether ordinary care vital to the child's survival, such as feeding, is refused" (WHHR: 55). While infanticide is not yet legal, he claims that it is being practiced and is likely to receive legal sanction given the acceptance of abortion and the general philosophical milieu of our times.

Since discussion of this issue centers on children with physical or mental deformities, he asserts that the person to ask regarding infanticide is the one with disabling birth defects. Schaeffer (and Koop with his extensive medical experience in surgery for pediatric defects) describes specific people who are living quality lives that demonstrate courage and dignity despite their handicaps. While acknowledging that some of these defects are so severe that there is inward relief at the child's death, Schaeffer believes that medical practice should be guided by a commitment to "save lives at any cost." Otherwise, "An erosion would take place, which over a number of years would undermine the care of all patients" (WHHR: 72).

Schaeffer's greatest concern over allowing severely deformed children to die by nontreatment is that it opens the floodgates for further abuses. The fact that such options are now being considered reflects, not real dilemmas created by medical technology, but underlying shifts of world view. He writes,

We are moving from the state of mind in which destruction of life is advocated for children who are considered to be socially useless or deemed to have nonmeaningful lives to the stance that we should perhaps destroy a child because he is socially disturbing. One wonders if the advocates of such a philosophy would espouse a total blockade and "starving out" of urban slums as a solution to poverty (WHHR: 75).

The third bioethics issue treated in *Whatever Happened to the Human Race?* is euthanasia. Schaeffer portrays life as a continuum from conception to death, and since life is now being destroyed before birth, it is only logical that there will soon be widespread tampering at the other end of the cycle as well. Abortion is linked to euthanasia because *Roe v. Wade* said that "only viable human beings who have the capacity for meaningful life may, but need not, be protected by the state" (WHHR: 90). Schaeffer sees this statement as a potential death warrant for many in the future, and asks,

> Will a society that has assumed the right to kill infants in the womb—because they are unwanted, imperfect, or merely inconvenient—have difficulty in assuming the right to kill other human beings, especially older adults who are judged unwanted, deemed imperfect physically or mentally, or considered a possible social nuisance? (WHHR: 89).

Schaeffer is willing to grant that a physician may withhold extraordinary means of treatment "once he believes that the technical gadgetry he is using is merely prolonging the experience of dying, rather than extending life" (WHHR: 91). But he insists that this is not the issue being debated today. Rather, it is advocating death of the patient by direct killing or treatment neglect when in fact death is not imminent and inevitable. He believes that what is often disguised as treatment termination is really active euthanasia based on pragmatic considerations and a low view of human life.

Contemporary discussions about euthanasia, Schaeffer claims, come perilously close to the Nazi horrors under Hitler: "It all started with the acceptance of the attitude that there is such a thing as a life not worthy to be lived. That is exactly what is being accepted today in the abortion, infanticide, and euthanasia movements" (WHHR: 107). He sees the possibilities for moral and legal sanctioning of euthanasia accelerated by hard economic realities, for "if you are a social burden and an economic burden, no matter how precious life might be to you, there will be little chance of your surviving" (WHHR: 111).

Schaeffer calls us to join the crusade against abortion, for he considers it the initial step in the slide toward euthanasia. But even more fundamental should be an attack on the materialistic-humanistic world view from which it arose. Abortion, infanticide, and euthanasia form in Schaeffer's mind a slippery-slope trilogy from which there is no return unless Christian consensus is once again reinstated as the moral and legal basis of Western culture.

Ecology

The earliest ethical issue to which Francis Schaeffer gave major attention was ecology, as seen in his 1970 treatise *Pollution and the Death of Man*. While this work attempts to address a socio-ethical issue, it is primarily an apologetic for the Christian world view. He analyzes various conceptions of reality with reference to their solutions for the ecological crisis and finds them all wanting. Only Christianity can provide a frame of reference for coming to terms with nature.

Schaeffer takes seriously the reality of the ecological crisis:

> The simple fact is that if man is not able to solve his ecological problems, then man's resources are going to die. . . . It is quite conceivable that man will soon be unable to fish the oceans as in the past, and that if the balance of the oceans is changed too much, man will even find himself without oxygen to breathe (PDM: 10).

He is particularly distressed that Christians have no better track record than non-Christians in confronting this reality. But the crux of the issue as he formulates it is not the abuse of nature and its resources, but the manner in which people think about themselves in relation to the world about them—their world view.

Schaeffer examines several alternative frameworks for approaching pollution. One is Eastern religion, more specifically Zen Buddhism with its pantheistic understanding of reality. Writing at a time when Eastern thought was beginning to flourish in the West, he contended that "pantheism will be pressed as the only answer to ecological problems and will be one more influence in the West's becoming increasingly Eastern in its thinking" (PDM: 23). He clearly recognizes the appeal of the East in its explicit connection between the human spirit and nature.

Schaeffer, however, finds pantheistic monism to be inadequate for rectifying the imbalances of nature. One problem, as he sees it, is that this world view cannot give sufficient attention to particulars like nature or human beings, since all reality is merged together. Schaeffer writes, "In true pantheism, unity has meaning, but the particulars have no meaning, including the particular of man. Also, if the particulars have no meaning, then nature has no meaning" (PDM: 30). In this Eastern paradigm he sees no basis for human dignity, nor any means of explaining the destructive side of nature.

If Eastern pantheism can not redress the ecological imbalance, neither can certain forms of Christianity—namely, Platonic versions such as Byzantine Christianity. Schaeffer's problem with this conception of faith is its claim that the "only truly valuable thing is heavenly—so high, so lifted up, so holy that one [does] not ever make a real picture of Mary. . . . this kind of Christianity will never give an answer to the problem of nature, for in this view, nature has no real importance" (PDM: 37). In this perspective nature is denigrated, serving no other use than a proof for the existence of God. Thus Schaeffer asserts,

> Any Christianity that rests upon a dichotomy—some sort of platonic concept—simply does not have an answer to nature, and we must say with tears that much orthodoxy, much evangelical Christianity, is rooted in a platonic concept, wherein the only interest is in the "upper story," in the heavenly things—only in "saving the soul" and getting it to heaven (PDM: 40).

For Schaeffer, however, there is a very different kind of Christianity that has a basis for approaching ecology—namely, Reformational Christianity. He takes issue with people like Lynn White who blame Christianity for the rape of the earth, for true (i.e., Reformation) Christianity allows no such exploitation. The key is the doctrine of Creation, which sees God as creator, human beings as significant creations in his image, and nature as a good creation of God but under human stewardship. Created things are not extensions of God as in Eastern thought, but they have a significance because God created them and intended them for proper usage and care. Schaeffer asserts that since the Fall we have exercised our dominion wrongly and hence the exploitation of nature. But the created material of this world has value, and thus he writes, "Loving the Lover who has made it, I have respect for the thing He has made" (PDM: 57).

Ecological imbalance is a real social and moral issue for Schaeffer. But "the problem is not the population explosion alone—that could be handled. The problem . . . is the philosophy with which man has looked on nature" (PDM: 70). Christianity provides the philosophical answer for this problem and Christians ought to be a "pilot plant," exhibiting to the world new attitudes and alternative approaches toward the natural world.

Economics

In the writings of Francis Schaeffer we do not find a full-orbed treatment of economic ethics, but there are several cursory analyses in his books and articles. His views can best be described as compassionate capitalism.

Since God is the author of nature, material realities are affirmed as good gifts from God. This affirmation, however, is to be understood within the context of Christian stewardship and a compassionate use of the world's resources. Schaeffer laments that since the time of the Industrial Revolution, when wealth became a pressing issue, most Christians have failed "to preach and act upon a compassionate use of accumulated wealth."[1]

A compassionate use of wealth for Schaeffer does not entail structural or state limitations on personal economic behavior, but rather an exemplary choice on the part of men and women to act compassionately and justly. Private property and the profit motive are seen as essential, for people do not work without them, and "the Bible does not say that the profit motive is wrong as such" (PDM: 87). Indeed, Schaeffer looks askance at those who call for state limitations on profit or property, favoring instead an individualistic approach based on voluntary compassion.

Love of neighbor as ourselves is to be our guide in economic and business life. Thus, he asserts, "It is perfectly right that I should have some profit, but I must not get it by treating him (or exploiting him) as a consumer object" (PDM: 87). Christians in business certainly need a profit, but they should not do everything they can in exacting all the profit possible. Because the other person is made in God's image, Schaeffer contends that "I must impose some conscious limitation upon myself" (PDM: 87).

Christians, he believes, have missed a great opportunity for witness to the world by failing to embody economic compassion. This is not to minimize the centrality of preaching the gospel, but it means that another way of proclaiming the good news has been lost. He writes,

> If at each place where the employee was a Bible believing Christian the world could see that less profit has been taken so that the workers would have appreciably more the "going rate" of pay, the Gospel would have been better proclaimed throughout the whole world than if the profits were the same as the world took and then large endowments were given to Christian schools, missions, and other projects (RE: 18).

As in other ethical issues, the impact of world view on economics is significant for Schaeffer. He sees, for example, the economic plight of India being complicated by the pantheistic system "in which the rats and cows are allowed to eat of food that man needs." He views this system of thought as a hindrance to genuine economic development, for "the rats and cows are finally given preference to man himself, and man begins to disappear into the woodwork in economics as well as in the area of personality and love" (PDM: 33).

Race

In dealing with race relations, Schaeffer begins as usual with theological anthropology as his functional frame of reference. As he puts it, "All men were made in his image, and we all come from a common ancestor. So the evangelical Christian ought to be the man who is most thoroughly opposed to racism. We have a basis."[2]

In an article in *Christianity Today*, Schaeffer acknowledges that despite the Christian consensus that controlled Western thought for years, "certain things were definitely sub-Christian" (RE: 18). Racism was one of those elements. He believes that evangelical Christians should have been the strongest champions for racial equality due to their belief in a common ancestry. Liberals, he asserts, have not accepted the historicity of a common ancestor, but evangelicals, who affirm this historicity, have not stressed its practical conclusion. Moreover, "The evangelical taught the doctrine of loving one's neighbor as oneself but failed to apply this lesson in the context in which Christ taught it, namely, in the setting of race—the Jew and the Samaritan" (RE: 18).

There is a rather interesting sidelight to this *Christianity Today* article. Several months later, in an interview with *The Other Side*, Schaeffer lamented the editorial changes in his article. The *Christianity Today* article states that in the areas of race and economics Christians were "definitely non-Christian." However, his original wording was much stronger: "I would especially point out two places where we must say that the consensus was non-Christian, repeat non-Christian."[3] He viewed the wording changes as significant evidence that we have still not come to terms with racism.

Schaeffer further forges a link between racism and abortion, in that both these evil practices view selected individuals as nonpersons:

> In our day, quite rightly, there has been great protest because society in the past viewed the black slave as a nonperson. Now, by an arbitrary absolute brought into the humanist flow, the law in similar fashion declares millions of unborn babies of every color skin to be nonpersons (WHHR: 35).

Schaeffer's brief discussions of race are highly individualistic in that he deals with racial attitudes only at the personal level. Nowhere does he explore the structural dimensions of racial justice, nor the state's responsibility in ensuring racial equality and harmony. Racism is perceived as a problem of individuals, not institutions and social structures, and hence can be eradicated by Christians treating others with human dignity.

War

Not until the end of his life did Francis Schaeffer address the issue of war and military preparedness. In 1982 he delivered a paper to government officials in Washington, D. C., which a year later was published in the volume *Who Is for Peace?* along with essays by traditional Roman Catholic James Hitchcock and Soviet dissident Vladimir Bukovsky.[4]

Schaeffer's essay, "The Secular Humanist World View Versus the Christian World View and Biblical Perspectives on Military Preparedness," begins with his usual contrast of two opposing world views—humanism and Christianity. The Soviet Union is seen to embody the materialist-humanist perspective in its most aggressive form, for in Marxism's dialectical materialism, "Final reality is merely matter, shaped by chance" (WIFP: 20). The same world view which has come to devalue human life in the Soviet Union is now creeping like a cancer across the American landscape, as evidenced in the rise of abortion and infanticide. The Soviet Union, however, remains the most consistent and coercive exemplar of humanism, for "there we may see the inevitable conclusion of the materialist view with its corollaries of relative values and arbitrary law: the value of the individual person is lost. Only the state matters" (WIFP: 20).

It is for this reason, claims Schaeffer, that Marxist countries can sign the Helsinki accords, then turn right around to violate human rights and persecute their citizens. As he views it, "Such actions are entirely reasonable for those who devalue human life as the Soviets do. For them, oppression is not incidental to the system: it is a logical, integral, and inevitable part of their system" (WIFP: 22).

In light of Soviet expansion and oppression, what should we do? Schaeffer cautions against a notion of "manifest destiny" that permits the United States to do what it pleases. Appealing to the love-of-neighbor principle, however, he goes on to argue for the necessity of nuclear parity and readiness to withstand the Soviet threat. "From my own study of Scripture I would say that to refuse to do what I can for those under the power of oppressors is nothing less than a failure of Christian love. It is to refuse to love my neighbor as myself" (WIFP: 23).

Schaeffer does not dialogue with traditional "just war" theory and offers no criteria for determining when war is appropriate (*jus ad bellum*) or how war is to be conducted (*jus in bello*). He simply argues that military action and preparedness are imperative in a fallen world. Love of neighbor means that we should do everything possible to stop aggression when an innocent party is threatened. He quotes with appreciation General Bernard Rodgers, Supreme Commander of allied forces in Europe: "To have nuclear weapons in order to deter their use from the other side, to protect your people, that is moral, but I think it is immoral for a nation that is charged with that responsibility not to have the capability to deter that kind of war" (WIFP: 24–25).

Due to the extensive proliferation of nuclear weapons on both sides, Schaeffer favors diplomacy and weapon reduction where possible; but he insists that a balance must always be maintained. "Unilateral disarmament in this fallen world, especially in the face of aggressive Soviet materialism with its anti-God basis, would be altogether utopian and romantic" (WIFP: 26).

Likewise, Schaeffer strongly rejects pacifism, for in a sinful world it "means that we desert the people who need our greatest help" (WIFP: 23). He understands the appeal of pacifism in the historic peace churches, but laments "that they have always taken Christ's command to individuals to turn the other cheek and misguidedly extend it to the state. They ignore the God-given responsibility of the state to protect its people and to stand for justice in a fallen world" (WIFP: 28). It should be noted here that Schaeffer appears to misunderstand traditional peace-church pacifism, which has always argued that Christ's teachings cannot be applied to the state. Rather, it contends that the church as God's covenant people is called to embody the teachings of Christ as salt and leaven in the world, fully realizing that Christ's way of peace will not become the way of the nations.

CRITICAL ASSESSMENT

To use a Schaefferism, how shall we then evaluate the ethical thought of this apologist-prophet to the twentieth century? There are several prominent features of Schaeffer's moral framework that need to be affirmed.

One of his greatest contributions is the emphasis on human dignity. Twentieth-century evangelical anthropology had been plagued by a decidedly one-dimensional perspective—namely, the sinful, fallen nature of humanity. There was a regrettable tendency to view people as targets for salvation with little reference to their inherent value and dignity. Francis Schaeffer contributed more than any other evangelical of this century toward balancing our understanding of human nature with his dual foci: human dignity, due to creation in God's image, and human sin, due to the Fall.

Schaeffer's balanced view of humans is more than a theological contribution, for it has provided evangelicals with a principle for ethical reflection and action. With an anthropology focused almost exclusively on sin, evangelicals of the past century tended to be limited in their attempts to scrutinize cultural and social realities. The dignity principle, however, has provided at least one moral category for ethical reflection and societal engagement. Its usefulness for issues like abortion, ecology, and racism is evident in the works of Schaeffer, and we can be grateful for his efforts in this area.

A second contribution of Schaeffer is his emphasis on the role of world view in ethics. As will be noted shortly, I believe Schaeffer has overstated its significance, but he has raised an important issue that is often neglected in ethical discourse— namely, that moral malaise does not emerge in a vacuum. Ethical and social issues must always be seen in terms of larger contexts of ideology and world view. How we think does affect how we act, and Schaeffer is to be applauded for this reminder.

But while Schaeffer has made a positive contribution to evangelical ethics, there are some serious shortcomings in both his methodology and his content. Rather than dissecting specific moral issues, I wish to examine three overarching problems that weaken his ethical analysis: reductionistic idealism, the "slippery-slope" fallacy, and the near-absence of a biblical theology. These flaws in no way nullify Schaeffer's prophetic impact, but they are significant shortcomings from which we must learn as we carry on our own ethical reasoning and prophetic ministries.

Reductionist Idealism

Underlying the ethical formulations of Francis Schaeffer is an explicit philosophical idealism. Ideas, and particularly perceptions impregnated by a world view, are the shapers and movers of history and human lives, and thus "the real battle for men is in the world of ideas, rather than in that which is outward" (TS: 121). Social evils arise, not from material or structural factors, but from particular ideas that logically produce immoral actions. Thus, in treating abortion Schaeffer contends, "It was the materialistic world view that brought in inhumanity; it must be a different world view that drives it out!" (WHHR: 125).

Furthermore, Schaeffer's idealism is frequently reductionistic and deterministic: human actions are generated solely by ideas in the mind. In *Back to Freedom and Dignity* he does acknowledge a limited role for psychological and physical conditioning (BFD: 36), but in most of his works there is little or no acknowledgment of material factors. Moreover, he is deterministic in stressing the inevitable results stemming from particular ideas. Contrasting Christian and humanist world views, he writes,

> It is not that these two world views are different only in how they understand the nature of reality and existence. They also inevitably produce totally different results. The operative word here is *inevitably*. It is not just that they happen to bring forth different results, but it is absolutely *inevitable* that they will bring forth different results (CM: 18).

It is very likely that Schaeffer is reacting to materialistic determinism that reduces history and ethics to structural explanations (e.g., Marxism). But as David Gill has noted in assessing Schaeffer's idealism,

> An idealist reductionism is not an adequate answer to a materialist or positivist reductionism. Both the Bible and commonsense experience indicate the unacceptability of this sort of reductionism. Ideas are significant—but so are earthquakes, famines, plagues, social conditions, personal charisma and so forth.[5]

Both materialistic and idealistic reductionism must be rejected, for history and human lives are shaped by ideational and material factors. As historian David Fischer puts it, "To isolate merely the rational component of human existence is to falsify both humanity and rationality."[6]

Due to his idealist reductionism, Schaeffer is unable to develop a full-orbed social ethic that can handle structural and systemic dimensions of social problems. For example, in his economic ethic he fails to treat structural elements like unjust trade patterns, vested interests, and economic dependence, which along with certain ideas inhibit justice in the market-place. Likewise, in discussing bioethical issues he fails to appreciate the genuine moral dilemmas raised by modern technology, reducing all bioethical problems instead to a flawed world view.

Schaeffer is certainly right to stress the importance of world view in shaping economic and bioethic realities. But we must always go beyond mere idealism in ethics to affirm the dialectic between ideas and material-structural factors.

The "Slippery-Slope" Fallacy

Closely linked to idealist reductionism is Schaeffer's continual use of the slippery-slope argument. He employs this line of reasoning in two ways: first, to show the inevitable slide from humanism to a low view of human life, and second, to assert the inevitable slide from abortion to infanticide to euthanasia. This style of argumentation is used again and again in *Whatever Happened to the Human Race?*

With the emergence of materialist-humanist perspectives, Schaeffer argues that "the thinkable of the eighties and nineties will certainly include things which most people today find unthinkable and immoral. . . . They will slide into each new thinkable without a jolt" (WHHR: 17). The most visible change in what was once unthinkable is the acceptance of "abortion on demand," which is now leading to infanticide. "The argument begins with people who have a so-called vegetative existence. There then follows a tendency to expand the indicators and eliminate almost any child who is unwanted for some reason" (WHHR: 68). The same logic, Schaeffer asserts, will then lead to euthanasia:

> The arguments now being put forward center on the "miserable" person in old age—one dying of cancer, for instance. But once the doors are open, there is no reason why the aged, weak and infirm will not find that as they become economic burdens they will be eliminated under one pretext or another (WHHR: 68).

Schaeffer calls upon Christians to

> not dismiss contemptuously our concern about the wedge principle. When the camel gets his nose in the tent, he will soon be in bed with you! . . . The first step is followed by the second. It is easy to see that if the first step is immoral, whatever follows it must be immoral (WHHR: 109).

Schaeffer is right to discern a relationship between humanism and unethical practices and a link between abortion, infanticide, and euthanasia. But his slippery-slope argument is flawed in two ways.

First, it becomes a fallacy when empirical realities do not support one's logical assumptions. Cause-and-effect relationships are always complex and should not be asserted without clear verification. Schaeffer's assumption that a humanistic world view inevitably leads to abortion and total loss of humanness is not indubitably warranted by the facts. For example, while it is true that many countries have liberalized their abortion laws in the past fifteen years, ethicist Thomas Shannon notes that during this same period "4 countries in Eastern Europe [where the materialist-humanist view prevails] adopted more restrictive legislation and 3 countries liberalized their policies and then made them more restrictive."[7]

Moreover, the acceptance of abortion by a society does not necessarily lead to infanticide and euthanasia. Japan, for example, which had widespread practices of infanticide before the twentieth century, now has an extremely low incidence of infanticide despite having had one of the most permissive abortion policies in the world since 1948. Indeed, the practice was specifically forbidden by the Eugenic Protection law of 1948 and continues to remain illegal. Daniel Callahan argues that, "Japan, then, provides no support for anyone who would automatically couple abortion and infanticide, much less argue that legal abortion opens the way for infanticide."[8] Similarly, we should note that widespread euthanasia has not followed in the wake of high abortion rates. This is particularly noteworthy, since contemporary Japan is probably far more materialistic and humanistic in its world view than the United States.

I point out these empirical problems, not to take issue with Schaeffer's general stance against humanism or abortion, but rather to show that we must be careful in our moral reasoning. Employing the slippery-slope fallacy may win adherents at a popular level, but it will not convince the more learned, to whom Schaeffer has targeted his message. He is certainly right to explore causal relationships, but his idealist reductionism and use of the "wedge" argument lead to simplistic connections between ideas and subsequent actions.

A second problem with Schaeffer's specific use of the slippery-slope argument relates to the issue of treatment termination. In his analysis of death and dying issues, Schaeffer appears unwilling to make a distinction between euthanasia— the intentional taking of life to end misery—and treatment termination—allowing death to take place when meaningful life is no longer possible and extraordinary treatments are being employed. He believes that a failure to save life at any cost will inevitably lead to "an erosion . . . which over a number of years would undermine the care of all patients in any institution that kills any patient placed in its care" (WHHR: 72).

Schaeffer does make one fleeting reference to the common dilemma faced by physicians regarding treatment termination and concedes that once the doctor "believes that the technical gadgetry he is using is merely prolonging the experience of dying, rather than extending life, he can withdraw the extraordinary means and let nature take its course" (WHHR: 91). However, he never enlarges on this major dilemma, nor is he willing to carry the principle over to quality-of-life cases, where death is not imminent but the prognosis is a vegetative existence. Even to entertain this type of treatment termination is viewed as part of the slippery slope from humanism to abortion to active euthanasia.

Schaeffer's use of the fallacy ends up distorting reality. Contemporary dilemmas in death and dying are not the simple by-products of humanism and abortion. Rather, medical technology has created an extraordinary situation whereby extremely deformed children (which does not include mongoloids) or suffering elderly persons are being kept alive in a fashion that was unimagined several decades ago. The onslaught of new technologies is forcing us to make life-and-death decisions that Schaeffer seems unwilling to make. His commitment to slippery-slope reasoning precludes his willingness to explore the possibility that at times medical sustenance may go too far in playing God and demanding that a person be kept alive.

To be sure, Schaeffer's prophetic injunctions against abuses like the Baby Doe case in Indiana need to be heard. But the fact that abuses occasionally occur does not warrant a wholesale commitment to treatment at any cost. With the proliferation of new technologies capable of prolonging biological life almost indefinitely, we need in the words of moral theologian Richard McCormick, "To walk a balanced middle path between medical vitalism (that preserves life at any cost) and medical pessimism (that kills when life seems frustrating, burdensome, useless)."[9]

Schaeffer's use of the slippery-slope fallacy has prevented him from seriously grappling with thorny dilemmas that cannot be swept away with generalizations about humanism and its inevitable slide to euthanasia. Christians must acknowledge the ambiguity of these complex issues and enter into the debate with empirical understanding and solid biblical and theological perspectives.

Inadequate Biblical Theology

Francis Schaeffer was a strong proponent of biblical authority and inerrancy, but in his ethical formulations the Bible is not as much a functional authority as one might hope. His moral analyses are rooted far more in logical and philosophical assumptions than in direct biblical theology. In fact, I believe it is safe to say that Christology (the doctrine of Christ) and ecclesiology (the doctrine of the church) could be totally removed from his ethical constructions without substantially altering their content and methodology.

As we have noted, the primary biblical category in his ethics is anthropology, and more specifically human dignity. Furthermore, this is the only biblical theme that receives in-depth consideration. In most of Schaeffer's moral treatises there are actually very few references to Scripture passages. For example,

— In *Back to Freedom and Dignity* there are no specific biblical references in the text, only general allusions to Christian ideas;

— In *Pollution and the Death of Man* there are eleven specific passages cited, but few of these are at the heart of his main arguments. Psalm 8, the beautiful passage on human stewardship over the works of God, is never even mentioned;

— In *Whatever Happened to the Human Race?* there are thirty-seven biblical references, but few of these are directly used to examine the issues. Eleven of these passages are contained in a content footnote regarding the Old Testament city of Lachish, which is referred to for apologetic reasons.

Rather than building his entire thought on one biblical theme and/or rational arguments such as the slippery-slope formulation, Schaeffer's ethical analyses would be greatly enhanced by the integration of other biblical theology motifs such as love, justice, the nature of the state and power, the nature of the church, sanctification, and the kingdom of God. If world view is the foundation of moral behavior, as Schaeffer contends, then more specifics from the Christian world view, revealed in Scripture, need to be employed in ethical discourse. Perhaps it is the apologist in Schaeffer that prompts him to argue more from rational themes than biblical ones. But if indeed the Christian world view is significantly distinct from all other views, then the content of our ethics must be directly informed by biblical theology.

Of particular significance is Schaeffer's failure to integrate ecclesiology into his ethic. In *The Church at the End of the Twentieth Century* and *The Church Before the Watching World*, he examines some very salient issues relative to the church's nature, function, and mission. These affirmations, however, are not integrated into his ethics. This more than any other factor propels Schaeffer's social thought in the direction of theocratic Constantinianism. While he insists that "the whole 'Constantinian mentality' from the fourth century up to our day was a mistake" (CM: 121), it is hard to see how he avoids replicating the same error with his insistence that America was founded on a Christian consensus and needs to return to that foundation. His call to build legal systems directly on Christian principles (see *A Christian Manifesto*) is clearly in the tradition of the Constantinian legacy.

The problems caused by theocratic idealism have been manifest in the history of many nations. But of even more significance for Christians is its baneful impact on the church. Theologian John Howard Yoder has shown that when Christianity dominates society (i.e., a Christian consensus, even if there is not a legal binding of church and state), ethical guidelines are eventually adjusted to accommodate the whole society. He writes,

> Once we dominate society, the way we want things to go is the way they might very well be able to go. . . . The rightness or wrongness of behavior can now be translated or interpreted in terms of good and bad outcomes.[10]

Only a solid biblical doctrine of the church enables us to assert that the kingdom of God is qualitatively different from the powers of this world, and that the latter cannot live by specific Christian principles, since they do indeed have a different view of reality. To impose Christianity on society, or seek to make it the legal basis of a social order, tends to generate undue hostility in a pluralistic context. More importantly, it undermines the uniqueness of the church. The theocratic ideal, which Schaeffer seems implicitly to support, fails to recall that it is the church, not America, that is "a chosen people, a royal priesthood, a holy nation, a people belonging to God, that you may declare the praises of him who called you out of darkness into his wonderful light" (1 Peter 2:9).

NOTES

[1]Francis A. Schaeffer, "Race and Economics," *Christianity Today* 18, no. 7 (January 4, 1974): 18. Hereafter cited in the text as RE.

[2] Francis A. Schaeffer, "Race and Reason," *The Other Side* 10, no. 3 (May–June 1974): 12.

[3] Ibid., 15.

[4] Francis Schaeffer, "The Secular Humanist World View Versus the Christian World View and Biblical Perspectives on Military Preparedness," in Francis Schaeffer, Vladimir Bukovsky, and James Hitchcock, *Who Is for Peace?* (Nashville: Thomas Nelson, 1983), 11–31. Hereafter cited in the text as WIFP.

[5] David Gill, "Jacques Ellul and Francis Schaeffer: Two Views of Western Civilization," *Fides et Historia* 13, no. 2 (Spring–Summer 1981): 26.

[6] David H. Fischer, *Historians' Fallacies* (New York: Harper & Row, 1970), 195.

[7] Thomas Shannon, "Abortion: A Review of Ethical Aspects of Public Policy," *The Annual of the Society of Christian Ethics, 1982* (Waterloo, Ontario: Council on the Study of Religion, 1982), 72.

[8] David Callahan, *Abortion: Law, Choice and Morality* (New York: Macmillan, 1970), 258.

[9] Richard McCormick, "To Save or Let Die: The Dilemma of Modern Medicine," *Ethical Issues in Death and Dying,* ed. by Robert Weir (New York: Columbia, 1977), 178.

[10] John Howard Yoder, *The Priestly Kingdom: Social Ethics as Gospel* (Notre Dame, Ind.: University of Notre Dame, 1984), 83.

10

SCHAEFFER ON
EVANGELICALISM

JAMES B. HURLEY

In the spring of 1960 I walked down a Swiss mountainside to laugh at the psychological ploys of a fundamentalist preacher. With considerable cynicism, I watched a small man with a high voice stand in front of his living room fireplace to lead a congregation of about fifteen in singing Bach chorales. The cynicism changed as he began to preach. Although I was not prepared to believe what he was saying, I recognized immediately that Francis Schaeffer's preaching was not a psychological game, but a reflection of his passionate commitment to a God whom he knew. His presentation was forceful and his message clear. To this day, whenever I preach on the serpent in the wilderness, I make use of points that Schaeffer made on that Sunday.

Over the course of the next few months I came to understand more about Christianity as I listened to him answer questions posed by hostile students. I also came to see the reality of his faith and that of others in the small community at L'Abri. In the end I came to know their God.

Francis Schaeffer's greatest gifts lay in matters of evangel-

James B. Hurley is Professor of Counseling at Reformed Theological Seminary, Jackson, Mississippi. He is a graduate of Harvard University, Westminster Theological Seminary (B.D.), and Cambridge University (Ph.D.) and is a doctoral candidate at Florida State University. He is the author of Man and Woman in Biblical Perspective.

ism and popular communication. His own deep love for God and for people whom God has made was highly infectious and reached deeply into most people who came into contact with him. He was at his best with a small group of college students. In such a group his love blended favorably with his ability to listen to people, to help them to think out the implications of their views, and to propose a Christian alternative that touched the center of their concerns. Schaeffer's alternative always stood in clear contrast to the philosophies of the time and had its foundation in his biblical world view and in the Bible as propositional, verbal revelation from God. Students generally left such sessions with a sense of having been lovingly faced with two alternatives and with a sense of the importance of making a choice between them.

Three prominent characteristics that mark Schaeffer's life and work are (1) propositional revelation in the Bible as a basis for life, (2) a clearly presented antithesis between a biblical world view and contemporary philosophies, and (3) a genuine love for all human beings. Schaeffer's personal history and these three characteristics are crucial axes for understanding his attitude toward evangelicalism. This chapter is divided into two parts. The first part looks at Schaeffer's background and method of communication. The second part looks at three central messages that he sent to the evangelical churches.

SCHAEFFER'S PERSONAL HISTORY

Intellectual and In-Life Truth Claims

Francis Schaeffer's personal history deeply affected his life. In his early years he wrestled with the truth claims of the Bible. In personal and Saturday night discussions at L'Abri he would comment on reading the Bible through and coming to the conclusion that it was to be taken straightforwardly. And his intellectual assent to the truth of the Bible did not stand alone. At various points in his life Schaeffer confronted the question of the reality of how God dealt with him in the midst of his own life history and of his willingness to obey when God did.

True Spirituality is his statement about the in-life truth of Christianity. The continuing financial and spiritual struggles of L'Abri during his life provided an ongoing test of the life-reality of his faith. His wife Edith testifies to the ongoing intellectual test, reporting the times when he concluded after struggle that the mask of biblical teaching fit the face of created reality. These were times of great excitement for him. His repeated affirmations of faith in the intellectual and existential arenas renewed his confidence in the viability of his conviction that the Bible is to be understood as "without error in all that it affirms." This conviction stood at the bottom of Schaeffer's entire approach to Christianity. It was not arrived at by accident.

The Struggle With Modernism in the 1930s

Coming from the evangelical wing of the Presbyterian church, Schaeffer came to maturity at the time when the victory of modernism within the northern branch of that denomination was becoming clear. His personal discussions about those times were always marked by a sorrow that the conservatives had allowed things to move so far before trying to check modernism, by pain over the suffering of those who were defrocked, and by regret at the division of the evangelical camp after the separation of those who were committed to what he considered the principle of the purity of the visible church.[1]

Attending Westminster Seminary and then Faith Seminary, Schaeffer was directly involved in his crucial, formative years with men who had paid a high price indeed for their commitment to an infallible Bible. His association with J. Gresham Machen and others at Westminster gave him an understanding of their commitment to the purity of the visible church and an awareness of the price that they paid for it. His association with Carl McIntire and others who left Westminster to found Faith Seminary gave him a taste of the bitter divisions that emerged as distances grew, not only between those who left the parent denomination and those who did not, but also within the ranks of those who left.

Schaeffer withdrew from McIntire's increasingly narrow focus on communism and his alienation from virtually all Christians not associated with his movement. As early as the mid-1950s Schaeffer regularly expressed, with real regret, his view that the evangelicals of the 1930s had waited too long to confront liberalism and left their churches with too much bitterness. As he approached the 1980s, he believed that the same thing was happening again.

When to "Draw the Line"

Schaeffer's conviction that too many bitter divisions existed within the evangelical camp had a direct impact on his conduct. In his books he stressed that, while differences at specific doctrinal points should not be dismissed, Bible-believing Christians should not "draw the line" between themselves but between those who submit to Scripture and those who do not. Schaeffer did not stress his denominational affiliation during the years when he was so much in the limelight, and indeed, most people were unaware of it. While he made no secret of his affiliation, he was much more interested in making his central points than in promoting his Reformed distinctives *by name*.

At one point I asked Schaeffer why he chose to mute his distinctives. His answer reflected his goal. He indicated that if he spoke of Calvinism, or of the sovereignty of God, or of predestination, many understood him to be speaking of a harsh fatalism and would not listen to anything more that he might have to say. He chose instead to avoid catchwords and to speak of the sure hand of God, of God's faithfulness to his own, of his rule over history, or of his calling of his sheep. He felt that by using such terms he could "get behind the screen" and be heard.

Eventually, if someone asked whether he was in fact speaking of predestination, Schaeffer would readily acknowledge the term. On the three or four occasions on which I heard him do this, he quickly added a note indicating that, while he considered this point important and clear in the Scriptures, he saw it as a point to be debated among those committed to Scripture rather than as a point that should cut them off from one another. In effect he was saying that "the chasm" between belief and unbelief should not be drawn at this point. His language here is reminiscent of things that Cornelius Van Til used to say in his classes at Westminster.

Schaeffer's Isolation

Swiss Study Center

Francis Schaeffer resided in a small Swiss village from the mid-1950s. His place of residence cut him off from direct participation in American culture and from all significant academic resources. The work of L'Abri involved apologetic discussions rather than lengthy academic study. I believe the importance of this relative isolation can be over- or underemphasized. Overemphasis on Schaeffer's isolation might lead to the conclusion that he was simply out of touch with American culture. His body of work belies such a conclusion. If anything, his detachment allowed him to see the outlines of the forest rather than to see only the trees. Underemphasis on his isolation might lead to a conclusion that he was always in close touch with the currents of American life. This too is a mistake. Those who participated in some of the events that he described are aware that his broad-brush analysis sometimes led him to describe events or personal attitudes in ways that were factually inaccurate.

Limited Resources

Especially during the early years, Schaeffer's primary contacts with the currents of American life were through a specific set of channels that included students, a limited number of senior academics, popular literature such as *Time* and *Newsweek,* and a selection of more substantial books and articles recommended to him or selected by him. His resources did not include any major libraries. With the exception of his time with Hans Rookmaaker of the Netherlands, Schaeffer had no continued access to a university community against which to test his conclusions.

Access to Students

Schaeffer's sources gave him good contacts with the ebb and flow of the student world. They gave him poor contact with the scholarly world. While he resided at L'Abri, his primary sources of information about the student world were the college students who went there. These reporters were being affected by the intellectual and social currents of the day. From them and from other students whom he encountered while speaking on college campuses, it was certainly possible to learn a lot about how students were thinking.

What the students could not provide, however, was a detailed analysis of the thinkers who were influencing them. By and large their grasp was simply too vague. Between the students and his constant reading about current events, Schaeffer was in a good position to speak with authority *about* the impact of twentieth-century culture on the student intellectual world. He was also tremendously effective in speaking with authority *to* that world. This was the audience that initially responded so strongly to him. In his later years he became its interpreter to a larger evangelical population.

Access to Scholars and Scholarly Resources

Schaeffer's personal priorities and the nature of his work left him little time for traditional scholarly pursuits. His commitment to communicating with people meant that he had to carve out time to study. The better he was known, the less time he had. Schaeffer never had time to spend with original sources or in prolonged contact with an academic community. His Swiss residence and brief lecture tours of major universities ensured this. As a result his conclusions were largely formed by personal study of a minimal number of primary sources, some contact with scholarly secondary sources, and a lot of contact with popular sources and with students influenced by primary and secondary sources. His conclusions were tested on the students and in brief contacts with professional academics. This situation left him without the sort of interaction that most of us need to sharpen our grasp and to cross-check our analysis of detailed material.

Other authors in this volume critique his work from their professional perspectives. My own evaluation of his work in the area of psychology is that Schaeffer was generally correct in the central thrust of his critique, but frequently in error on specific details. A hostile professional in the field would question his competence to speak on the details of the views of major psychological thinkers and might try to evade his central thrust by faulting his details. Students are less able to do this than professionals, and they comprised Schaeffer's basic audience.

Schaeffer's Communications

Intended Audience

Schaeffer's communication was geared to present the "historic Christian faith" to an unbelieving student intellectual world by contrasting Christian beliefs and their implications with other belief systems and their implications. A survey of

Schaeffer's major lecture series and of the tapes of his Saturday night open-forum discussions makes it clear that the framework of his thought and even much of the substance of his later writings was developed in the period between the mid-fifties and the mid-sixties. These lectures spoke to the existentialist, irrationalist students of the period. His books were generally developed from transcripts of his lecture series.

At one point, as a staff worker at L'Abri, I compiled an index of the questions posed to him during the early Saturday night discussions. The questions centered around fewer than twenty basic issues. After years of dealing with them, Schaeffer's answers were smooth and predictable. Virtually all of those answers worked their way into the texts of his books.

When Schaeffer became a major figure on an international scale, he added a second audience. He became an interpreter of both Christian and non-Christian beliefs to a largely ignorant evangelical-Christian population. His method of presentation was well-suited to such a task.

Schaeffer's Dramatic Method

An effective teacher must gain and keep the attention of his audience and must present his ideas at a level that the auidence can grasp. Schaeffer worked with audiences that were not professionally prepared and were often ignorant of much of the subject matter he wanted to present. He would often lay hold of a dramatic, popular article, quotation, or event and use it to gain the ear of his audience. As he presented it, he would call attention to underlying commitments which the reader might miss, but which Schaeffer considered important to understanding the direction of the item. He would generally move from the underlying commitments and values to their implications if extended or followed out into other areas. In his analysis one event or idea often "opens the door" to another. This manner of presentation left his audience with a strong sense of having been let in on a secret, of having gained insight into a hidden dynamic that the author either missed or did not want exposed.

Schaeffer's handling of the "line of despair" concept is a good example of this method. Central to Schaeffer's critique of Western Culture (and clearly reminiscent of Van Til's critique of "autonomous reason") is the idea that finite man, starting from himself, will at first be optimistic that his reason can discover truth, but will finally come to the conclusion that his finitude necessarily precludes him from discovering truth—that his former optimism can only lead to despair.

Escape From Reason and *The God Who Is There* are fascinating tours through intellectual history that illustrate this point. The reader again and again comes away with a sense of having seen the dynamic that inexorably pushed various areas of culture into despair. Schaeffer's consistent theme was that a biblical view of man allows people to live as whole beings within the real world, while the basic secular alternatives ultimately force man either to assert the meaningfulness of personality in a meaningless world (a blind leap of faith, optimistic existentialism), or to deny the meaning of persons in an equally meaningless world (pessimistic existentialism).

Real-Life Drama

The drama of Schaeffer's presentations was heightened by his visible earnestness and deep compassion. He often remarked on the need to speak various points "with tears." His expression was not just a figure of speech; he often did shed tears of concern as he spoke with people. He was not speaking about a world of abstract ideas or ideals. His goal was to bring a message that would alter the *lives* of his hearers.

His presentations were frequently illustrated with vignettes of people with whom he had dealt or with poignant illustrations of the consequences of consistently living out alternative world views. Christianity was, for him, a life as well as a belief system. In this connection he constantly talked about an orthodoxy of life as well as an orthodoxy of belief. Again and again his books call for a living demonstration of the truth. His personal life stood as a fine example of the livability of the Christian alternative that he preached.

Polar Alternatives

The views of reality that Francis Schaeffer outlined for his live or literary audiences always stood in stark contrast to one another. Over against the inevitably dismal result of modern thought Schaeffer set a biblical world view which, he proposed, allows man to be a meaningful but finite creature of an infinite Creator.

In volume after volume Schaeffer traced what he considered to be the natural implications of consistently living out a modern world view and posited a world view built on biblical revelation as a viable alternative without the disastrous consequences of humanistic thought. Along the way he pointed out the relativistic consequences of a finite stating point without an infinite reference point (no "true truth"). Also up for attention was the loss of a place for significant personal beings in a materialistic world (loss of the "mannishness" of man).

Against these dismal consequences he proposed an answer that builds on (1) an infinite, personal Creator (2) who reveals himself in person (Christ), in his creation (nature and man), and supremely and unambiguously in a propositional, verbal revelation (the Bible). According to Schaeffer, God's complex (triune) personality offers an ultimately personal universe in which finite persons can have a place (be "mannish"). God's verbal revelation (the Bible) to reasonable (although fallen) men offers absolutes ("true truth") on which to base all of life in an otherwise relativistic world. Describing his work, Schaeffer explains,

> Many [young people whom my work reached] came to understand that this new ethos—namely the concept that the final reality is.energy which has existed forever in some form and takes its present form by chance—has totally destructive consequences for life. The young people of the sixties sensed that this position left all standards in a relativistic flux and life as meaningless, and they began to think and live in these terms. . . . happily a certain number did find that L'Abri's presentation of Christianity—as touching all of thought and life, along with a life of prayer—did demonstrate Christianity's viability, and they became Bible-believing, consecrated Christians.
>
> But note: this rested upon two things: 1) being truly Bible-believing; and, 2) facing the results of the surrounding wrong worldview that was current with loving but definite confrontation (GED: 97).

The first part of this statement is a good example of the way in which Schaeffer viewed our culture and his mission. It is also a good example of his presentation of alternatives as polar opposites. The latter part reflects his view of the importance of a commitment to the Bible. In his view a move away from a commitment to Scripture as verbally inspired, propositional revelation is a move away from the foundation that provides the answers.

SCHAEFFER TO THE EVANGELICALS:
BE PURE SALT AND LIGHT

Schaeffer's message to the evangelicals can be divided into three related parts: (1) the Scripture is propositional revelation that speaks to every area of life; the manner of our obedience must reflect the holiness and the love of God ("let your *light* shine"); (2) if the church lives its faith and confronts humanism, it is possible that our culture can be saved from disintegration ("be *salt*"); (3) faithfulness to God and to his Word demands that church discipline be practiced (especially with respect to those who move away from an "evangelical" view of the Scripture), that lines be drawn ("be *pure*"; "if salt loses its saltiness . . . it is good for nothing"). These three points will frame the next part of this chapter.

Light the Whole House: The Scripture
in Every Area of Life

Francis Schaeffer emerged from the obscurity of his Alpine home in the early sixties with the publication of *Escape From Reason* and *The God Who Is There*. Those two books alone established him as an ·intellectual spokesman for evangelical Christianity. His critical analysis of modern culture and his aggressive promotion of Christianity not only as a credible, viable alternative but as a superior view gained him the enthusiastic support of many evangelicals and the ear of many skeptics.

In a time when much of the conservative church was still hiding from the challenges of modern culture and when the youth of the culture were asking if meaning could be found, Schaeffer said to the latter, "I can tell you where to find the truth"—and proceeded to do so. To the former he issued a clarion call to challenge culture with God's truth and offered a model of how to do it. The breadth of his field of analysis opened new vistas for many "anticultural" Christians and encouraged them to enter important cultural areas and to try to bring them captive to Christ. Schaeffer's own analysis of the situation was direct:

> After the denominational turmoil of the thirties, funda-
> mentalism fell increasingly into a mistaken pietism which
> saw any challenge to the surrounding culture as unspiritu-

al. . . . Thus, the changing, destructive surrounding culture tended to stand increasingly unchallenged (GED: 98).

His own work was self-consciously intended to change the attitude of the timid fundamentalist culture:

> Throughout my work there is a common unifying theme, which I would define as "the Lordship of Christ in the totality of life." If Christ is indeed Lord, he must be Lord of all of life—in spiritual matters, of course, but just as much across the whole spectrum of life, including intellectual matters and the areas of culture, law, and government (GED: 11).

Schaeffer wholeheartedly endorsed the proposition that Scripture is the only infallible rule for faith and practice. He considered himself an evangelical and used the term

> with the connotation of being Bible-believing without shutting one's self off from the full spectrum of life, and in trying to bring Christianity into effective contact with the current needs of society, government, and culture . . . [with] a connotation of leading people to Christ as Savior, but then trying to be salt and light in the culture (GED: 97).

Be Salt: Prevent Cultural Disintegration

Schaeffer viewed the church as an agent to preserve culture from disintegration and as a demonstration of the reality of God's work in the world today. His response to those who were pessimistic about the chances of seriously influencing culture reflects his optimism about the power of the salt. In *Whatever Happened to the Human Race?* he notes that it does not take a majority to change the direction of a culture. A committed minority would be sufficient. His view of the importance of the church reflects his conviction that it was meant to influence all of life. Speaking of the drift of the churches into liberalism, he wrote:

> It was this drift which laid the base for the cultural, social, moral, legal, and governmental changes from that time to the present. Without this drift in the denominations, I am convinced that the changes in our society over the last fifty years would have produced very different results from what we have now. When the Reformation churches shifted, the Reformation consensus was undercut. . . . It is interesting to note that there was a span of approximately eighty years

from the time higher critical methods originated and became
widely accepted in Germany to the disintegration of German
culture and the rise of totalitarianism under Hitler (GED: 35).

Without this drift in the churches, I am convinced that the
changes from a rural to urban society, etc. would not have
produced the same results they now have (CBWW: 65).

In Schaeffer's judgment, the drift of the German churches
into Enlightenment thinking that based values on human
reason "opened the door" for Hitler's totalitarianism. In a
similar vein, the drift of the American church into secular
humanism has led to "a nearly total moral breakdown" (GED:
36) and the threat of a totalitarian government, welcomed by a
threatened population seeking to preserve "personal peace and
affluence" in an increasingly chaotic culture (WHHR: film).

The foundations for such a government, in Schaeffer's
opinion, are in fact in the process of being laid as the
Reformation-influenced cultures of northern Europe, North
America, and parts of the Commonwealth shift from absolute
moral values based on Scripture to humanistic, relativistic
moral values based on the present consensus.

Schaeffer's View of His Own Role

It was Schaeffer's view that the failure of the churches in
the 1930s contributed greatly to the present cultural disintegration, but that it is not too late for the remaining evangelicals to
speak out and perhaps to prevent the final collapse of the
culture. In our personal conversations during the last years of
his life, Schaeffer again and again expressed to me his sense
that it was not too late and that his ministry might help to turn
the tide. This (to borrow a phrase that he generally reserved to
describe the freedoms that he believed resulted from the
Reformation obedience to the Bible) is a *titanic* mission for a
single man. This mission was a (if not *the*) central dynamic of
his last years. It takes an enormous sense of calling and ability
to embrace the view that God may be using you as a point-man
to alter the course of an entire culture.

Ronald Wells has discussed Schaeffer's literature as a
jeremiad.[2] The literary parallel is apt. I suggest that if we were
to look for a biblical character with whom to compare Schaeffer's actual functioning and self-concept, it would not be
Jeremiah. Schaeffer's functioning and self-concept were much
more in the mold of Elijah, who spoke God's message to the

nation of Israel at a turning point in its history, a time when idolatry was infiltrating the nation with the support of its leaders.

Please note: I am *not* suggesting that Schaeffer considered himself a prophet like Elijah. That would be a travesty. I am suggesting that he felt that he was preaching God's truth (revealed in the Bible) to a nation at a turning point in its history and that his preaching might be a crucial factor in preventing a departure from God's law which will ultimately bring judgment on the nation. His message to the churches might be compared to what was undoubtedly Elijah's message to the schools of the prophets: preach the Word faithfully, unsparingly, regardless of the opposition.

If I may push the analogy further than Schaeffer would probably have liked: Schaeffer, like Elijah, raised up schools of disciples, but did not appoint anyone to be Elisha. It will be interesting to see if anyone picks up the mantle as prophetic critic-exhorter.

The Change of the Later Years

Schaeffer's early teaching and preaching announced that biblical Christianity proclaims a God who is there, who deals with mankind in the present, and whose Word speaks to every area of life. His broad brush strokes shouted "relevant truth" to an aimless student generation feeling the impact of relativism, and they emboldened a generation of evangelicals, encouraging them to work out the implications of their faith in many areas.

His work gained Schaeffer a powerful voice in evangelical circles. He was explicit in seeing the results of his ministry as the Lord's work rather than his own. It pleased him to see what the Lord had done through the work of L'Abri. He considered that the Lord's blessing of the early work of L'Abri had given him a platform from which to speak to the changes that he saw taking place in the seventies and eighties.

Schaeffer's later teaching and preaching were directed to a very different audience and brought a different message, one that brought him opposition from within the evangelical camp. Whereas his earlier message announced that humanity could not survive in a world of relativism and existentialism, his later message announced that Western culture had begun to destroy the world shaped by Reformation ideas and to create an ugly, harsh world in which every man lived for self and security ("personal peace and affluence").

The First Two Film Series

The titles of his first two film series reflect the transition of Schaeffer's later years. The first series popularized his critique of culture: *How Should We Then Live?* It outlined his view of the contrast between biblical Christianity and modern thought and warned of what he believed was to come.

The second series was quite different. It was entitled *Whatever Happened to the Human Race?* It focused on the abortion issue as an expression of the way in which our culture is choosing to kill inconvenient or unwanted children rather than jeopardize personal comfort. The series was intended to do more than focus attention on the abortion issue. It was intended to confront its viewers, Christian and otherwise, with the harsh consequences of the materialist-relativist view of reality guiding Western thought.

Whatever Happened to the Human Race? received a very different reception from *How Should We Then Live?* In it Schaeffer looked at a specific issue on which the nation was divided and which the evangelical church had by and large not directly addressed. While very few were "for abortion," very few wanted to confront the issue. Churches that happily received his first series declined the second as too controversial. If his early work is viewed as gaining him currency with the conservative church, his focus on the abortion issue must be viewed as having cost him much of that capital.

Schaeffer's films were very much in keeping with the stylistic elements commented on at the start of this chapter. They showed a man with deep compassion speaking to an issue of vital importance. The subject is developed in a manner that leaves the audience with the feeling that they must decide which side to choose on a vital issue. Clear lines are drawn, connections made between historical events and philosophical views, and powerful, dramatic illustrations presented to seize the viewers' attention. Those acquainted with Francis' son Franky will recognize his hand in much of the visual presentation of the films.

Schaeffer's "polar" presentation of material did not generally leave his audience wondering which side to take. By the end of each series, most viewers were worn out from the length and intensity of the material and strongly influenced to see Schaeffer's side as the only one to make sense. When he began speaking to the abortion issue, the pro-life perspective was not as popular among evangelicals as it is now. His forceful presentation polarized church members. This made the films undesirable for many. Schaeffer was willing to pay that price.

From his point of view, the refusal of many churches to confront the abortion issue was only a symptom of a more foundational problem facing the evangelical churches as they entered the last decades of the twentieth century. The refusal pointed to what he would call "the great evangelical disaster."

The Great Evangelical Disaster

The evangelical church of the mid-twentieth century, in Schaeffer's view, has failed to notice the ideological battle between a biblical world view and the relativism of modern thought. Worse still, the church has begun to incorporate elements of relativism into itself, to accommodate to the culture instead of standing clearly for an antithesis against it. With typical drama and polarization, Schaeffer wrote:

> And now we must ask where we as evangelicals have been in the battle for truth and morality in our culture. Have we as evangelicals been on the front lines contending for the faith and confronting the moral breakdown over the last forty to sixty years? Have we even been aware that there is a battle going on—not just a heavenly battle, but a life-and-death struggle over what will happen to men and women and children in this life and the next? If the truth of the Christian faith is in fact truth, then it stands in antithesis to the ideas and immorality of our age, and it must be *practiced* both in teaching and practical action. It must be loving confrontation, but there must be confrontation nonetheless. . . .
>
> Here is the great evangelical disaster—the failure of the evangelical church to stand for truth as truth—namely *accommodation*. . . . First, there has been accommodation on Scripture . . . no longer affirm[ing] the truth of all the Bible teaches. . . . And second, there has been accommodation on the issues, with no clear stand being taken even on matters of life and death (GED: 37–38).

The church has not seen the battle, has not retained the basis from which it might have spoken, and has failed to speak on the most crucial of issues. The price of such failure is high:

> It is my firm belief that when we stand before Jesus Christ, we will find that it has been the weakness and accommodation of the evangelical group on the issues of the day that has

been largely responsible for the loss of the Christian ethos which has taken place in the area of culture in our own country over the last forty to sixty years. . . . we must say with tears that, with exceptions, the evangelical church is worldly and not faithful to the living Christ (GED: 38).

Taking a stand for God's truth was important to Schaeffer, especially at points at which it was under fire. He often quoted Luther on this issue:

If I profess with the loudest voice and clearest exposition every portion of the truth of God except precisely that little point which the world and the devil are at the moment attacking, I am not confessing Christ, however boldly I may be professing Christ. Where the battle rages, there the loyalty of the soldier is proved and to be steady on all the battle front besides, is mere flight and disgrace if he flinches at that point (GED: 50–51).

The Point of Attack Before the 1970s

In the fifties and sixties, Schaeffer considered theological liberalism and neo-orthodox theology the point of attack against historic Christianity. He did not yet see wholesale infiltration of the evangelical camp by these views. In the early 1960s he was concerned about the failure of Fuller Seminary to maintain a clear position supporting an inerrantist view of the Bible. He did not consider this symptomatic of a general trend within the evangelical camp. Nor did he consider such views within the Christian Reformed Church to be symptomatic of such a trend. He simply noted those facts and, when asked by students about which seminary to attend, would express his personal preferences and conclude with a strong encouragement that the student attend one of those, or another that held a firm view of Scripture.

As the 1970s progressed, Schaeffer was more and more convinced that this issue would become *the* issue within the evangelical camp itself. The change in his perspective is reflected in his books. *The Church at the End of the Twentieth Century* advances his program for the church's response to the collapse of Western culture. It includes as an appendix Schaeffer's discussion of the relationship between adultery and apostasy. The substance of the appendix is drawn from material that Schaeffer had used for several decades. It is in fact part of the thought process that had guided him and others in the

1930s when the conservatives opposed liberalism in the Presbyterian church. The appendix looks at text after text from the Bible to show that the church is the bride of Christ and that spiritual apostasy is as ugly as adultery. It focuses on the necessity of lovingly opposing liberal theology, but does not hint that such theology is infiltrating the evangelical church.

> I have taken care to emphasize that God does not minimize promiscuity in sexual relationships, but apostasy—spiritual apostasy—is worse. And the modern liberal theologian is in that place. . . . The liberals elevate their own humanistic theories to a position above the Word of God. . . . They make gods which are no Gods. . . . We describe their theories . . . in polite terms . . . so as not to offend. . . . In Protestantism, we call [their theories] "Liberalism." . . .We must have politeness and struggle for human relationships with liberal theologians. . . . But as to the system they teach, there is to be no toning down what it is—spiritual adultery (CETC: 124).

In 1971 the appendix became the center of a small book calling Bible-believing Christians of all kinds, within and without the liberal denominations, to practice the "purity of the visible church" (church discipline) and to stand together in opposition to neo-orthodoxy and to the theological liberalism of churches dominated by modernism. The book does not warn the evangelical churches that they have apostasy infiltrating their ranks, but seems to have in view those in mainline churches who do not believe that it is important to try to discipline neo-orthodoxy or liberalism. The conclusion summarizes Schaeffer's message:

> Let us find ways to show the world that while we maintain and do not minimize our distinctives, yet we who have bowed before God's verbalized, propositional communication—the Bible—and before the Christ of the Bible are brothers in Christ. This is what we must do in the face of liberal theology. We must practice an observable and real oneness—before God, before the elect angels, before the demonic hosts, before the watching liberals and before the watching world (CBWW: 81).

The Point of Attack in the 1980s

As the seventies moved into the eighties, Schaeffer became convinced that the point of attack on God's truth was not only the relativism of the culture but the authority of Scripture itself. And the attack was coming, not only from those outside the church, but also from many within. This attack threatened all he stood for. *The Great Evangelical Disaster* reiterates his cultural critique and his critique of the church for failing to speak God's truth to all of life; but it goes on to introduce a whole new subject. It puts the spotlight on the differences among evangelicals on the authority of Scripture:

> In our day [the point of attack] is the question of Scripture. Holding to a strong view of Scripture or not holding to it is the watershed of the evangelical world . . . (GED: 51).
> . . . inerrancy is the watershed of the evangelical world. But it is not just a theological debating point. *It is the obeying of the Scripture which is the watershed! It is believing and applying it to our lives* which demonstrate whether we in fact believe it (GED: 61).

For Schaeffer, the question of the view of Scripture is so important that he was willing to draw a line within the Christian camp on the issue:

> But unhappily, it is not only the avowedly neo-orthodox existential theologians who now hold [the separation of faith and history], but some who call themselves evangelicals as well. . . . This may come from the theological side in saying that not all of the Bible is revelational. Or it may come from the scientific side in saying that the Bible teaches little or nothing when it speaks of the cosmos. Or it may come from the cultural side in saying that the moral teachings of the Bible were merely expressions of the culturally determined and relative situation in which the Bible was written and therefore not authoritative today (GED: 50).
> Evangelicalism is not consistently evangelical *unless there is a line drawn* between those who take a full view of Scripture and those who do not (GED: 51).

At times it seems that Schaeffer felt so strongly on this issue that he came close to incorporating submission to the Bible in his definition of what it means to be Christian:

> The real chasm is between those who have bowed to the living God and thus also to the verbal, propositional communication of God's inerrant Word, the Scriptures, and those who have not (GED: 77).

Not bowing to Scripture is not bowing to God. Other texts, however, make it clear that Schaeffer felt that it was indeed possible to be a Christian and to reject biblical inerrancy:

> . . . one of the leading men of the weakened view of the Bible who is called an evangelical, and who certainly does love the Lord, . . . (GED: 52).

> . . . this is not to say that those who hold [weaker views of Scripture] are not often brothers and sisters in Christ, nor that we should not having loving personal relations with them (GED: 89).

Schaeffer understood the situation of the 1980s to be both the consequence of the events of the 1930s and a parallel to them.

> *Within the evangelical circles things are moving rapidly in the direction of what happened fifty years ago in the denominations.* But there still is time to head off a complete takeover of the leadership and key organizations within evangelicalism by those who hold a weakened view of Scripture and have been infiltrated theologically and culturally by the surrounding world view—if we have the courage to clearly but lovingly draw a line (GED: 88).

Balancing Holiness and Love

In his advice to the church at the start of the seventies, Schaeffer had advocated confronting error, disciplining before it was too late, and doing so with compassion and love. As he began to draw lines publicly within the evangelical camp, he tried to follow his own advice to speak clearly but lovingly:

> *Truth carries with it confrontation.* Truth *demands* confrontation; loving confrontation, but confrontation nevertheless. . . . We must say no to [the attack on Scripture], clearly and lovingly, with strength (GED: 65).

Schaeffer's focus on holiness with love tied directly with the indelible effects that the events of the thirties had on him. He had seen the church of his Lord split in great bitterness. He deeply felt that those who had stood for the holiness of God had failed to reflect the love of God. No one who knew him for any length of time had any question of the seriousness of his conviction that both God's love and his holiness need to be shown in the actions of his people.

Schaeffer's personal contact with people diametrically opposed to all that he stood for was consistently marked by a visible love for them as people. As a matter of course he declined invitations to debate because the debate format placed men in an antagonistic posture. A visible exception to that rule was his debate with Bishop James Pike. Schaeffer's deep concern for the debate was that "a clear Christian position" be presented and that the debate would end "with a good human relationship between the two." His books and personal conversations often mentioned his pleasure that both goals were clearly achieved in the debate (GED: 83).

The balance of holiness and love that Schaeffer sought in his debate with Bishop Pike was important to him in other areas as well. Faced with a clear move among some evangelicals away from a "full" or "strong" view of Scripture, Schaeffer called for loving action and sought to explain it clearly.

Practicing the Purity of the Visible Church

Francis Schaeffer came from the conservative wing of the Presbyterian church which lost the battle for control of the denomination in the 1930s. The liberal power structure of the denomination defrocked the conservative leaders who challenged their departure from the confessional documents and historic Christian beliefs. The result was an exodus of conservatives who founded what they regarded as a *continuing* Presbyterian church. Those who withdrew from what they considered apostasy have been labeled "Separatists." Well aware of the importance of the connotations of words, Schaeffer was always unhappy with the "separatist" label.

> Names are funny things, and especially in the connotations they are given. Names can be used either to enhance or to destroy (GED: 95).
> It is important to notice the principle we are speaking about here and the language we use to express the principle. It is not the principle of *separation*. It is the *practice of the principle of the purity of the visible church*. Words are important at this point, because we make attitudes with the words we choose and use year after year. . . . The church belongs to those who by the grace of God are faithful to the Scriptures. Almost every church has in its history a process for exercising discipline, and when needed this should be used in the practice of the positive principle . . . (GED: 85).

The negative connotations of the word "separatism" offended Schaeffer. He was not interested in separating from the church, but in purifying it. It was Schaeffer's conviction that the church is Christ's bride and that its members are called upon to maintain the purity of the body, by practicing discipline if necessary. To fail to do so would be an affront to the divine Bridegroom:

> . . . we are not dealing with a merely human organization but with the church of Christ. Hence, the practice of the principle of the purity of the visible church first means discipline of those who do not take a proper position in regard to the teaching of Scripture.
>
> We should first of all, of course, do all we can on a personal, loving level to help the liberal; but if he persists in his liberalism he should be brought under discipline, because the visible church should remain the faithful bride of Christ (GED: 86–87).[3]

This call to confront and to discipline liberalism was a central theme of Schaeffer's closing years. He did not want the mistake of the thirties to be repeated. He wanted discipline before it was too late. After personal discussion, formal discipline was the first step toward the purity of the church. True to his Calvinist Reformation heritage, Schaeffer considered that if a church or Christian organization would not exercise discipline, true believers might ultimately have to leave it.

> . . . once Christ is no longer King and Lord in a church, then that church cannot have our loyalty. . . .
>
> When a church . . . comes to the place where it can no longer exert discipline, then with tears before the Lord we must consider a second step. If the battle for doctrinal purity is lost . . . it may be necessary for true Christians to leave the visible organization with which they have been associated. But note well: If we must leave our church, it should always be with tears—not with drums playing and flags flying (CBWW: 74–75).

It is interesting to note that, while Schaeffer devoted a lot of space to the necessity of discipline, he goes no deeper than what is said above as to how or when to separate from a body that will not discipline. He does, however, plead for a manner of leaving that will show the love of God, even for the opponents being left (GED: 89). Schaeffer's call for love at the time of leaving is a direct response to the bitterness that surrounded the split in the northern Presbyterian church.

It is my opinion that Schaeffer was not as successful at making loving contact with his opponents in his writing as he was in his speaking. A look at his concrete illustrations of liberalism within evangelical circles shows the drawbacks of his method of communication when addressing issues within the church as opposed to issues between the church and the culture.

Schaeffer's Illustrations of Evangelical Liberalism

Earlier in this chapter I commented on Schaeffer's strategy of choosing dramatic examples to make his point. His illustrations of evangelicals who have left their moorings are no exception. His examples include abandonment of the historical nature of the first chapters of Genesis, support of socialist causes, the feminist movement, lax obedience to biblical standards on divorce, approval of homosexuality, devaluation of the distinctiveness of the Reformation, and renewed relations with the World Council of Churches. These are all volatile issues within the evangelical world. It is worth considering some of his examples.

Socialistic Mentality

Schaeffer was troubled by the way in which "a large section of evangelicalism is confusing the kingdom of God with a socialistic program" (GED: 111). His actual evidence is limited to one quote from the *Evangelical Newsletter* describing the Evangelicals for Social Action (ESA). According to the article, the ESA considers issues such as crime, abortion, lack of prayer, and secular humanism to stem from "unjust social structures in the United States" and these in turn stem from national and international poverty and maldistribution of wealth.

Schaeffer is quick to challenge this sort of thinking from both theological and political perspectives. Commenting on the article that reviewed the position of the ESA, he explains:

> Do you understand what is being said here? Remarkably, the ESA is saying that "unjust social structures" and in particular "the maldistribution of wealth" are the real causes of evil in the world. . . . on a factual level this is foolish. . . .
>
> [The ESA has] made a complete confusion of the kingdom of God with basic socialistic concepts . . . [and] back of this stands the idea of the perfectability of man if only cultural and economic chains are removed. . . .

The basic problem is much deeper than social structures, and by not recognizing this, ESA ends up with an understanding of salvation which is very different from what the Scriptures teach. Sin is the problem. . . .

[The ESA] is equally wrong in its naive assessment of the redistribution of wealth and its consequences. . . . To understand this all we need to do is look at the repressive societies which have resulted from attempts to radically redistribute wealth along socialistic . . . lines.

. . . when we look more carefully at what is involved [in the evangelical accommodation to socialists], we find that the socialist mentality ends up in a completely different place, with disasterous consequences theologically and in terms of human life (GED: 112–14).

I find myself in agreement with Schaeffer's criticism of the ESA position as presented in the article. It is, however, worth asking what effect the critique is designed to have and to whom it is addressed. It is certainly not an apologetic to win the ESA. It is a prophetic herald's warning of danger on the left side of the right wing. If I were a defender of the ESA I would lodge a number of complaints:

1. *Unfair secondary sources:* Schaeffer has treated only an article by a third party summarizing the views of the group without actually dealing with the substance of those views.

2. *Emotional word choice prejudices the reader:* Schaeffer has chosen a number of very dramatic words and phrases which, on the basis of very slim "evidence," will polarize the audience emotionally. The groups views are "foolish," "the Marxist line," "a complete confusion of the kingdom of God and socialism," "teach a different salvation from Scripture," "naive," and "can be corrected merely by looking at other societies."

3. *Guilt by association:* While admitting that the ESA is not communist, Schaeffer goes on to attack its socialist views by arguing that "radical redistribution" has always wrecked economies, and Marxist revolutions have always led to bloodbaths. This is guilt by association. The group claims only to be "trying to acquaint biblical Christians with crucial areas and the need to change them."

4. *Unfair extension of ideas:* Schaeffer has (typically) taken ideas that he perceives as foundational to the ESA view and shown how, if extended, they might lead to disaster. While he claims to do so by "looking more closely at what is involved," he actually looks only at his fears that the socialistic flavor and programs of the ESA will in practice

operate as the Marxist programs have. The basic problem is
that he does not look closely at what is involved!

The very characteristics that made Schaeffer so effective in
galvanizing the evangelical church for the fight against liberalism make his effort to lovingly draw a line within evangelicalism a difficult task. His broad brush strokes, dramatic illustration, dependence on secondary sources, and polar language
communicate very effectively with his audience. Those persuaded by him will be solidly aligned against the "liberals." I
personally share Schaeffer's view that radical redistribution of
wealth by government fiat or Marxist revolution is catastrophic
for social structures. I am not convinced, however, that that is
what most evangelicals with leftward leanings are promoting.

For his critiques to be effective with those who are
knowledgeable and are moving to the left, Schaeffer would
have had to really get into the details and critique the
arguments of the left. This he did not do. His treatment of
social injustice and socialism is simply too broad and too
simplistic to persuade those influenced by socialism. Evangelicals moving toward socialism will be left with the feeling that
they have received less than full consideration and will
certainly not be won over by his approach.

Devaluation of the Reformation

The Reformation heritage of northern Europe was an
important part of Schaeffer's apologetic. He felt that the balance
of structure and liberty (form and freedom) in post-Reformation
Europe demonstrated that the biblical teaching would lead to a
better lifestyle because it describes man as he was made to be.
All his later works—films and books—stress the loss of this
"balance" as a result of embracing relativistic, humanist ways
of thinking. As his works became better known, they began to
attract scholarly attention and critique.

Ronald Wells has criticized Schaeffer's view of the Reformation.[4] Wells considers the Protestants' appeal to the Bible as
the only authority binding the conscience to be the religious
expression of the humanistic independence of the Renaissance.
Wells' view is certainly not beyond debate, but it is also
certainly worthy of debate. In an article on Schaeffer's position,
Wells comments that Schaeffer "refuses to see [the Protestant
Reformation] as an aspect of the humanistic movement itself."[5]

Schaeffer grasped the implications of Wells's view for his own work and produced a vehement paragraph criticizing it. The paragraph is one of the weakest in all of Schaeffer's work. It does not show a clear grasp of Wells's point itself, nor does it provide a specific answer to him. Schaeffer wrote:

> Do you understand what is being said here? . . . Everything the Reformation stood for is swallowed up in a morass of synthesis and relativity. Exactly the same line is taken by the relativistic, non-Christian, secularized historians of our day. This is not a dispute over the facts of history; in fact, many non-Christian historians would disagree with this radically disparaging view of Reformation ideas. . . . we must stand against those who accommodate to the spirit of this age under the guise of scholarship and in the process not only distort the facts of history but Christian truth as well (GED: 118).

Wells's point, if conceded, would undercut some of Schaeffer's confidence in the Reformation heritage. It is not clear that it necessarily leaves "everything in a morass of synthesis and relativity." Schaeffer's actual response to Wells borders on self-contradiction. On the one hand, Schaeffer faults Wells for taking the same line as relativistic, non-Christian, secularized historians; on the other hand, he appeals to other non-Christian (presumably equally relativistic and secularized) historians who concur with him to show that the dispute is not over facts.

Schaeffer's two appeals demonstrate that some secular, non-Christian historians support Wells while others support Schaeffer. That is a weak basis on which to accuse Wells of accommodating to the world spirit under the guise of scholarship and of distorting the facts of history and Christian truth. Such language will motivate audiences, but will not win scholars who disagree. It is a criticism rather than a confrontation. Wells developed his point and criticized Schaeffer. Schaeffer did not clearly grasp the critique, developed no case, and criticized Wells.

To be fair to Schaeffer, the context of each author's remarks must be taken into account. Wells wrote in an article devoted to an analysis of Schaeffer's views. Schaeffer referred to Wells as an illustration in a book devoted to other issues. Even so, Schaeffer has not really answered Wells. His criticism seems to be an objection to the impact of Wells's point rather than a response to Wells's content. Several of the criticisms of Schaeffer's treatment of the ESA apply here as well:

1. *Prejudicial word choice:* Schaeffer has chosen dramatic, emotional words that will prejudice readers without providing a content base for their reaction to Wells.

2. *Unfair extension of ideas:* Schaeffer warns against a dangerous possible extension of Wells's thought, but does so as though it were the content of Wells's argument.

3. *Guilt by association:* Schaeffer faults Wells for importing the ideas of relativistic, secularized historians under the guise of evangelical scholarship, yet appeals to similar historians for his own case.

I believe the intensity of Schaeffer's opposition to liberalism and relativism has clouded his judgment, that his response to Wells falls short of his goal of a loving confrontation, and that he will fail to win those in the other camp.

Feminism

Schaeffer was deeply troubled over the confusion within evangelical ranks over issues such as adultery, divorce, and homosexuality. In his writings these topics receive much more attention than the ones mentioned above. He develops a basic theology of marriage in his treatment of adultery and apostasy (CETC, CBWW, GED). In *The Great Evangelical Disaster* he employed it to show that certain feminist directions are flatly contrary to biblical teaching. As usual, he warned against the extremes, showing their consequences. Schaeffer's discussion focused on those who entirely deny distinctions between men and women and on those who promote homosexual marriage.

While acknowledging that "few would go as far as the extremes mentioned" (GED: 138), Schaeffer argued that many evangelicals are influenced by the world spirit which, when carried out, leads to the extremes that he criticized. He conceded that many are unwittingly being influenced, but argued that conscious choice to accommodate the extremes and unreflective acquiescence produce similar, destructive results.

Despite the fact that Schaeffer spent more than his usual time on biblical texts in the discussion of feminism, his work is a better illustration of the case he might make than a presentation of it. Schaeffer's treatment of the feminist or pro-homosexual positions consists almost entirely of selecting the extreme examples.

What is completely missing from his treatment of the feminists is a development of their point of view in a manner

Schaeffer on Evangelicalism | 295

that might help the reader understand the motives or even the specific positions held by people who are to the left of Schaeffer without being at the extremes he documented. Readers favorably influenced will come away from the discussion convinced that they must stand against feminism that undercuts biblical teaching. They will not, however, have any understanding of how such a view is being promoted or defended. Schaeffer called for the drawing of lines, but did not really say where to do so. His illustrations were of the extremes. He wanted the line to be drawn far short of the extremes, but did not explain how to do so. His discussion gave virtually no attention to separating "feminist" issues that may be legitimate from those that are not.

This is a serious flaw, because it leaves his readers without the tools necessary to engage in discussion with feminists or even to make personal decisions about where to draw the line he calls for. This situation is not uncommon in Schaeffer's writing.

THE LIMITATIONS OF PAINTING
WITH A BROAD BRUSH

Great strengths can also be great liabilities. Certain gifts that made Francis Schaeffer a great spokesman for evangelicalism were also liabilities when he began to address specific applications of biblical faith or liberalism within the evangelical ranks.

Earlier in this chapter I proposed that Schaeffer was at his best as an evangelist and as a popular communicator. His gifts and his work at L'Abri placed him in a position in which he could be used to catalyze a generation of evangelicals. His ability to lay out a vivid, broad-brush picture of the "flow" of ideas and concepts through Western history, and his ability to infect others with his own passionate sense of the urgency of choosing between biblical Christianity and the secular relativism of the modern world were powerful tools. God used them to raise up an army of enthusiastic evangelicals, many of whom have gone into scholarly fields and are making significant contributions. These distinctives helped him rise to a position of enormous influence as a spokesman for evangelical Christianity.

The Critic As Activist

In a certain sense, Schaeffer the critic was a tour-guide leading evangelicals through past Western history. His method was wonderfully suited to that task. But his role changed during the last years of his life. As a critic of the past development of relativism, Schaeffer had always argued that Christianity produced better options. In the last decade of his life he became an activist promoting action to change the direction of contemporary society as it moves away from Christian values. His initial focus was on the abortion issue and the implementation of what he called "sociological law"—law based on current consensus without reference to absolute values.

Schaeffer worked steadily to encourage evangelicals to enter the political arena and to resist the drift of the culture. His films, conferences, and personal appearances with figures such as Jerry Falwell and on the "700 Club" television program contributed to the shaping of the political right wing of the evangelical world.

Schaeffer emphasized the need for positive action to halt abortion, to curb sociological law, and to prevent the euthanasia programs that he felt were in the offing. The central thrust of his political program was nevertheless negative and conservative rather than positive. To some extent that was inevitable, as he was calling the nation to return to Christian values in its roots and was critiquing points at which the humanist basis of modern culture cut deeply into them.

Yet it is hard to think of a point at which Schaeffer promoted a Christian answer to new problems. This is really not surprising in that new answers to new questions generally require persons who are thoroughly acquainted with and personally involved in the issues. Schaeffer was not directly involved in matters of government, employment, defense, or even world hunger. Those sorts of involvements simply were not his role.

When Schaeffer came to address the political scene, the target was new, but his methodology was essentially the same as before. His political material is filled with dramatic presentations, life-setting vignettes, and urgent choices between polar alternatives. As before, he beckoned audiences to a commitment to opposing secular thought. As before, it worked. The current pro-life movement owes much of its success to Schaeffer. His contribution to the evangelical right is less. In each case, however, Schaeffer's role was not to follow through or to set up an apparatus. Others had to do that.

Schaeffer was aware of his limits and spoke of the need for others to go beyond him in areas where he had blazed a trail. When asked why Christians had not produced great artists or musicians in the recent past, he talked about the emergence of Pele, the great Brazilian soccer star. He noted that virtually every Brazilian boy kicked soccer balls around from childhood. Out of the millions of boys, one Pele emerged. Christians, he said, need to start kicking soccer balls—or doing music. He sometimes made similar point about politics. Christians have not been involved and lack experience. Many need to get involved.

Schaeffer the critic-exhorter should not be criticized for not having answers on every matter. Nor should he try to give answers on every matter. Many Christians working at many levels will be needed to begin producing Christian answers.

The Critic Confronts Defecters

In the last years of his life Schaeffer formed a new combination of his critical and activist roles. He became a critic of "evangelical liberalism," calling for action to stop encroaching liberalism within evangelicalism.

I personally believe that he was right to call attention to the significant debate within evangelicalism over the nature and authority of Scripture. I also believe that his method and resources left him with liabilities as he spoke on the subject. On the positive side of the ledger:

— His personal past made him sensitive to the need to speak to the issue before historic orthodoxy has again become a minority;

— His past also gave him a sensitivity to the need for loving confrontation;

— His communication skills made him a powerful spokesman who could inform an ignorant audience and gain their support;

— His established position provided him a wide hearing among evangelicals of all sorts.

On the negative side of the ledger:

— His tendency to trace the flow of a train of thought led him to point out where he feared people would go rather than where they were;

— His broad-brush approach and lack of time for or access to scholarly resources meant that he did not engage on the details of issues;

— His urgent, polar approach led him to select extreme examples and to pose them as polar opposites of positions that he favored; people between the extremes sometimes felt pushed or wrongly treated.

As Schaeffer approached shifts away from traditional evangelical positions with regard to Scripture, he employed the methodology that he had used before. His "watershed" concept is a good illustration of the assets and liabilities of his method as applied to the controversy:

> Not far from where we live in Switzerland is a high ridge of rock with a valley on both sides. One time I was there when there was snow along the ground along that ridge. The snow was lying there unbroken, a seeming unity. However, that unity was an illusion, for it lay along a great divide; it lay along a watershed. One portion of the snow when it melted would flow into one valley. The snow which lay close beside would flow into another valley when it melted. . . .
>
> . . . when it melts, where [the snow] ends in its destination is literally a thousand miles apart. . . . A watershed divides. . . .
>
> . . . Evangelicals today are facing a watershed concerning the nature of biblical inspiration and authority. . . . like the snow lying side-by-side on the ridge, the new views [of Scripture] when followed consistently end up a thousand miles apart (GED: 45).

The illustration is clear and arresting. Every reader sees the ridge and the snow. What looks unified is not. Lines must be drawn to mark the divide, because the final results end up far apart. Readers will immediately see the importance of marking the divide.

The watershed analogy is not only a good illustration; it also has a structuring effect on the mind of the reader. The reader will begin to ask which side of the line people are on. People will be placed in two camps, polar opposites.

It is worth asking whether people are really as clearly in two camps, as Schaeffer believes. With regard to intellectual positions, Schaeffer is largely right: one is committed to

Scripture as verbal revelation that is correct when it speaks of God's creation, or one is not. But the battles to maintain or abandon the position are not generally fought at the theoretical level. They are fought in terms of specific issues and often at points where traditional theology has endorsed one of several possible positions as *the* Christian view.

Dealing with such issues requires a fresh assessment of biblical teaching and detailed conclusions for change without abandoning biblical foundations. The feminism issue, for example, is generally fought out in terms of specific expressions of sexual bias or chauvinism. As Schaeffer notes, most people are not as extreme as his examples. Many people fall between. This is an issue on which our culture and the church have been more narrow than the Scripture requires. Much rethinking is taking place.

Schaeffer has pointed out that presuppositions about Scripture do influence where people come out. Other things too will enter into the final equation. Many people are confused, seeing new options and trying to discern whether the options violate Scripture. These people need both help to work through the details and exhortation to keep their biblical foundation. Schaeffer's "watershed" approach may force them to one side or another while they are not yet sure what side they are on. They may prematurely close options or feel that their genuine concerns are being pushed aside. How are these to be won? Let me play with the watershed analogy in order to explain.

In Schaeffer's watershed, the unity of the snowfield is only apparent, superficial. The snows will really end up far apart. Observers need to know this and mark the line. But I am not sure that the snowfield of the church is really divisible by a line. Many people are in fact on both sides of the line, confused or inconsistent. The snowfield may be one field. If nothing is done, it is the underlying divide that will finally separate the snows when they melt (i.e., when theological positions work themselves out to their logical conclusions). If, however, we draw lines between individuals prematurely, we will alienate many who could be won. It may be impossible to draw a precise line. Schaeffer too may have had this problem. His actual examples are not from those near the divide; they are drawn from situations or individuals whom he believed had clearly moved down the wrong slope.

I propose that we conceive of Schaeffer's watershed as a bumpy plateau with valleys on either side rather than as a ridge. Under Schaeffer's conditions, when the snow melts (positions are worked out to their logical conclusions), the ridge will cleanly divide them. Under the conditions of my plateau, the melt will produce confusion, puddles, and water that will ebb and flow before going over the edge.

Schaeffer's "watershed thinking" calls for drawing the line. "Plateau thinking" calls for a modification in the plan. While it is important to have people like Schaeffer clearly pointing out the consequences of moving in one or another direction, it is also important to have people who will be able to work on the plateau itself. These people would need to be clear themselves about which side they wanted and would then begin to deal with the snow or the thaw. They would need to begin to deal with the believers who are confused. To do this successfully, they must be prepared to concern themselves with details as Schaeffer did not.

The Need for Follow-Up

Schaeffer's broad brush and lack of scholarly detail are appropriate to his role. He sounded a call to engagement. It was not really his goal to provide detailed answers to questions that he raised. If his work stands alone, it is rather like a watchman on a wall who announces the arrival of an enemy, only to find that the troops are asleep.

Those who agree with Schaeffer will have to follow his lead and begin to work out the answers that he felt would "flow" from biblical truth. Those who share his concern about socialist political tendencies will need to produce alternative positions that can deal with the injustices the socialists are seeing, either to develop alternative approaches or to show that they are not injustices. Historians sharing his view of the Reformation will need to do the scholarship the show that his sketch can be substantiated in the traceable facts of history. Wells, for instance, demands an answer rather than rhetoric. Those who share Schaeffer's view of the roles of men and women must grapple with the chauvinism of our culture and work out the implications of biblical truth in the context of the present debate.[6]

SCHAEFFER'S LEGACY TO THE EVANGELICALS

It will be interesting to see how future historians treat Francis Schaeffer. I am sure that he will not be remembered for his contributions to theology or philosophy. I am quite sure that he will be remembered as one of the great shapers of evangelicalism in the mid-twentieth century. The data for a final evaluation of the three phases of his work are not yet available.

I think it is quite likely that Schaeffer will be remembered for his catalytic role in the emergence of an intellectually aggressive evangelical church in the 1970s. This is the fruit of his early work. The fruit of his call for political activism is harder to assess. Those influenced by him and by others to enter the abortion controversy and political action are still at work in the battles.

Schaeffer's call to purify the church as liberalism threatens is also difficult to assess. Scholars in the International Council on Biblical Inerrancy and various seminaries are zealously engaged in defending the traditional view of Scripture that he embraced. Churches continue to face pastors and teachers who are in fact moving away from traditional views but wish to remain and to call themselves evangelical. Will they be won over? Will they be disciplined? It is hard to say.

Whatever the final verdict on his success, it is inevitable that Francis Schaeffer will be counted as one of the most powerful influences on the evangelical church at the end of the twentieth century.

NOTES

[1] CBWW: 64–82 presents this with typical forcefulness.

[2] Ronald A. Wells, "Francis Schaeffer's Jeremiad," *Reformed Journal* (May 1982): 18; cf. also Wells's chapter in this volume.

[3] Cf. CBWW: 72ff.

[4] Wells, "Francis Schaeffer's Jeremiad," p. 18.

[5] Ibid.

[6] My own work on role relationships represents a start in this direction; cf. *Man and Woman in Biblical Perspective* (Grand Rapids: Zondervan, 1981).

APPENDIX
A Guide to the Subjects of Schaeffer's Writings

TOPIC	EFR	GWIT	HIT	Book HSWTL	Film HSWTL	WHHR	CM	GED
History								
Roman Age				1	1			
Middle Ages	1a			2	2			
Renaissance	1b			3	3			
Reformation	2			4	4		5	
Revolutionary Age				5, 6	5		2	
Disciplines								
Science	3a			7, 8a	6			
Philosophy	3b	I:2		8b, 9a	7a			
Art		I:3		10a	8a			
Music/General Culture	6	I:4		10b	8b			
Theology	4	II:1–5		9b	7b			
Theistic Proofs								
Metaphysical		III:1	1					
Moral		III:3, 4	2					
Epistemological		III:2	3, 4					
Historical						5		
Evangelism		IV, V, VI						
Western Culture								
Humanism				11	9	4	4	
Authoritarianism				12	10			
Ethics								
Abortion						1		
Infanticide						2		
Euthanasia						3		
Evangelicalism								All

BIBLIOGRAPHY ON FRANCIS SCHAEFFER*

I. BOOKS BY SCHAEFFER

Escape From Reason. Downers Grove, Ill.: InterVarsity, 1968.
The God Who Is There. Downers Grove, Ill.: InterVarsity, 1968.
Death in the City. Downers Grove, Ill.: InterVarsity, 1969.
The Church at the End of the Twentieth Century. Downers Grove, Ill.: InterVarsity, 1970.
The Mark of the Christian. Downers Grove, Ill.: InterVarsity, 1970.
Pollution and the Death of Man. Wheaton, Ill.: Tyndale, 1970.
The Church Before the Watching World. Downers Grove, Ill.: InterVarsity, 1971.
True Spirituality. Wheaton, Ill.: Tyndale, 1971.
Back to Freedom and Dignity. Downers Grove, Ill.: InterVarsity, 1972.
Basic Bible Studies. Wheaton, Ill.: Tyndale, 1972.
Genesis in Space and Time. Downers Grove, Ill.: InterVarsity, 1972.
He Is There and He Is Not Silent. Wheaton, Ill.: Tyndale, 1972.
The New Super-Spirituality. Downers Grove, Ill.: InterVarsity, 1972.
Art and the Bible. Downers Grove, Ill.: InterVarsity, 1973.
No Little People. Downers Grove, Ill.: InterVarsity, 1974.
Two Contents, Two Realities. Downers Grove, Ill.: InterVarsity, 1974.
Joshua and the Flow of Biblical History. Downers Grove, Ill.: InterVarsity, 1975.
No Final Conflict. Downers Grove, Ill.: InterVarsity, 1975.
How Should We Then Live? Old Tappan, N.J.: Fleming H. Revell, 1976.
Whatever Happened to the Human Race? Old Tappan, N.J.: Fleming H. Revell, 1979.
A Christian Manifesto. Westchester, Ill.: Crossway, 1981.

*Section I includes all books listed in Schaeffer's *Complete Works*, arranged chronologically, as well as two items that appeared subsequently. At the end of section I there is a table that indicates in which volume of the *Complete Works* each book by Schaeffer is located. Section II lists many, but not all, articles written by Schaeffer. Section III contains books about Schaeffer. Finally, sections IV and V list articles on Schaeffer and reviews of his books. Items that are judged to be of interest to the readers of this collection of essays are noted with an asterisk.

Who Is for Peace? (with Vladimir Bukovsky and James Hitchcock). Nashville: Thomas Nelson, 1983: 11–31, "The Secular Humanist World View Versus the Christian World View."

The Great Evangelical Disaster. Westchester, Ill.: Crossway, 1984.

Schaeffer's books have recently been collected in *The Complete Works of Francis A. Schaeffer: A Christian Worldview* (Westchester, Ill.: Crossway, 1982, 5 vols.). Since most readers will have the individual editions, the references in this collection of essays are to those editions. However, the following table will enable the reader to find the appropriate book in the *Complete Works.*

The God Who Is There	I: 1-202, 385-90
Escape From Reason	I: 205-270, 390-91
He Is There and He Is Not Silent	I: 273-352
Back to Freedom and Dignity	I: 355-84
Genesis in Space and Time	II: 1-114, 415
No Final Conflict	II: 117-48
Joshua and the Flow of Biblical History	II: 151-316
Basic Bible Studies	II: 319-70
Art and the Bible	II: 373-413
No Little People	III: 1-191
True Spirituality	III: 193-378, 423
The New Super-Spirituality	III: 381-401, 423
Two Contents, Two Realities	III: 403-22, 423
The Church at the End of the Twentieth Century	IV: 1-110, 301
The Church Before the Watching World	IV: 113-79, 302-4
The Mark of the Christian	IV: 181-205
Death in the City	IV: 207-99, 304
Pollution and the Death of Man	V: 1-76, 503
How Should We Then Live?	V: 79-277
Whatever Happened to the Human Race?	V: 279-410, 503-32
A Christian Manifesto	V: 413-501, 532-34

II. ARTICLES BY SCHAEFFER

"Are Christians Headed for Disaster?" *Moody Monthly* 84 (July–August 1984): 18–20.

"Beware the New Super-Spirituality." *Eternity* 23 (November 1972): 15–17.

"Christian Compassion: Have We Lost Our Touch?" *Eternity* 21 (December 1970): 16–18.

"Christian Manifesto." *Moody Monthly* 82 (January 1982): 13–15.

"Christian Revolutionaries." *His* 21 (November 1970): 8.

"Christian's Crucial Choice." *Moody Monthly* 78 (March 1978): 50–52.

"Christianity and Culture." *Themelios* 2 (1962): 5–16.

"Church in Our Age." *Inter-View* 2 (Spring 1973): 13–17.

"Dust of Life." *Eternity* 32 (March 1981): 36–41.

"God—Or Nobody Home in the Universe." *Moody Monthly* 71 (February 1971): 23.

"He Is There and He Is Not Silent," 4 pts. *Bibliotheca Sacra* 128 (April–June 1971): 99–108; (July–September 1971): 195–205; (October–December 1971): 300–315; 129 (January–March 1972): 3–19.

"How To Speak For The God Who Is There." *Eternity* 23 (July 1972): 8–10.

"Humanism: A Threat to Your Liberty." *Moody Monthly* 78 (February 1978): 47–56.

"Irrationality of Modern Thought." *Christianity Today* 15 (December 4, 1970): 10–14.

"Mark of the Christian." *Christianity Today* 14 (September 11, 1970): 7–10.

"The Modern Drift: Is Nobody Home In This World?" *Christianity Today* 4 (June 20, 1960): 3–6.

"No Little People, No Little Places." *Eternity* 25 (May 1974): 18–19.

"Race and Economics." *Christianity Today* 18 (January 4, 1974): 18–19.

"Race and Reason." *The Other Side* (May–June 1974): 12.

"Schaeffer on Scripture." *Christianity Today* 19 (August 29, 1975): 29.

"Schaeffer Reflects on Fifty Years of Denominational Ins and Outs." *Christianity Today* 25 (April 10, 1981): 28–31.

"Shattering the Plastic Culture." *His* 31 (October 1970): 1.

(With Arthur Glasser) "Should Evangelicals Cooperate with the World Council of Churches?" *Christianity Today* 27 (November 11, 1982): 82.

"A Suggested Strategy." *Christianity Today* 9 (February 12, 1965): 26.

"Tragic Loss of Our Era." *Christianity Today* 5 (May 22, 1961): 3–5.

"True Spirituality." *His* 32 (June 1972): 17–24.

"Universe and Two Chairs." *Christianity Today* 13 (April 25, 1969): 8–11.

"Watershed of the Evangelical World." *United Evangelical Action* 35 (Fall 1976): 19–23.

"What Did the Shepherds See? What Did the Shepherds Do?" *His* 35 (December 1974): 15–19.

"When a Christian Leader Sins." *Charisma* 7 (January 1982): 50–51.

"When a Christian Leader Sins." *Moody Monthly* 76 (January 1976): 81–83.

"Why and How I Write My Books." *Eternity* 24 (March 1973): 64f.

"Why You Can't Understand Your Children." *Moody Monthly* 70 (December 1969): 38–39.

III. BOOKS THAT DISCUSS SCHAEFFER

Catherwood, Christopher. *Five Evangelical Leaders.* Wheaton, Ill.: Harold Shaw, 1985. Pp. 113–61.

Dennis, Lane T. "Conversion in an Evangelical Context: A Study in the Micro-Sociology of Religion." Ph.D. diss., Northwestern University.

————. *Francis Schaeffer: Portraits of the Man and His Work*. Westchester, Ill.: Crossway, 1986.

————. *Letters of Francis A. Schaeffer*. Westchester, Ill.: Crossway, 1985.

Fowler, Robert Booth. *A New Engagement: Evangelical Political Thought, 1966–1976*. Grand Rapids: Eerdmans, 1982. Pp. 61–76.

Hall, Timothy D. "Rutherford, Locke, and the Declaration: The Connection." Unpublished Th.M. Thesis submitted to Dallas Theological Seminary, 1984.

Lewis, Gordon R. *Testing Christianity's Truth Claims*. Chicago: Moody, 1976. Pp. 296–300.

Morris, Thomas V. *Francis Schaeffer's Apologetics: A Critique*. Chicago: Moody, 1976.

Parkhurst, L. G. *Francis Schaeffer: The Man and His Message*. Wheaton, Ill.: Tyndale, 1985.

Reymond, Robert L. *The Justification of Knowledge*. Nutley, N.J.: Presbyterian and Reformed, 1976. Pp. 136–48.

Schaeffer, Edith. *The Tapestry*. Waco, Tex.: Word, 1981.

IV. ARTICLES ABOUT SCHAEFFER

Bechtel, P. "Civil Disobedience: A Necessary Option?" *Christian Life* 43 (February 1982): 16–17.

"Beyond Personal Piety." *Christianity Today* 23 (November 16, 1979): 13.

*Blomberg, D. G. "Apologetic Education: Francis Schaeffer and L'Abri." *Journal of Christian Education* 54 (December 1975): 5–20.

Board, Stephen. "An Evangelical Thinker Who Left His Mark: Francis A. Schaeffer IV: 1912–1984." *Christianity Today* 28 (June 15, 1984): 60–61.

————. "The Rise of Francis Schaeffer." *Eternity* 28 (June 1977): 40–42.

*Brown, Harold O. J. "Kierkegaard's Leap or Schaeffer's Skip?" *Christianity Today* 28 (December 14, 1984): 82.

Buckles, Peter. "Schaeffer's Shelter away from the Swiss." *Christianity Today* 24 (July 18, 1980): 54.

*Clark, Gordon H. "A Semi-defense of Francis Schaeffer." *Christian Scholar's Review* 11 (1982): 148–49.

Cleath, R. "Schaeffer on Film and in Person." *Christianity Today* 21 (April 1, 1977): 50.

*Cunningham, Stuart. "Towards a Critique of Francis Schaeffer's Thought." *Interchange* 24 (1979): 205–21.

Dennis, Lane T. "The Family Loses a Powerful Advocate." *Focus on the Family* 8, no. 7 (July 1984): 2–5.

Fiske, Edward B. "L'Abri." *Moody Monthly* 76 (October 1975): 70–72.

*Geehan, E. R. "The 'Presuppositional' Apologetic of Francis Schaeffer." *Themelios* 8, no. 1 (1972): 10–18.

*Gill, D. W. "Jacques Ellul and Francis Schaeffer: Two Views of Western Civilization." *Fides et Historia* 13 (Spring 1981): 23–37.

Grounds, Vernon C. "A Friend of Many Years Remembers Francis Schaeffer." *Christianity Today* 28 (June 15, 1984): 61–63.

Haack, D. "Francis August Schaeffer, RIP." *National Review* 36 (June 15, 1984): 20.

*Harper, Kenneth. C. "Francis A. Schaeffer: An Evaluation." *Bibliotheca Sacra* 133 (April 1976): 130–42.

Henry, C. F. H. "Mission In the Mountains." *Christianity Today* 8 (July 3, 1964): 37–38.

*Hill, Kent R. "Francis Schaeffer (1912–84): An Evaluation of His Life and Thought," in *Faith and Imagination: Essays on Evangelicals and Literature,* ed. Noel Riley Finch and Richard W. Etulain (Albuquerque, N. M.: Far West Books, 1985), 137–71.

Houston, J. "Behind Those Best Sellers." *Moody Monthly* 72 (November 1971): 28–29.

Hurley, J. "Notes on the Philosophy and Writing of Francis and Edith Schaeffer: A Bibliographic Essay." *Christian Librarian* 20 (July 1977): 15–16.

Kucharsky, David E. "A Barrier to Christian Belief." *Christianity Today* 21 (February 4, 1977): 38–39.

Marsden, George. "Francis A. Schaeffer." *Reformed Journal* 34 (June 1984): 2–3.

Phillips, M. "Francis Schaeffer: The Man behind the Manifesto." *Moody Monthly* 82 (January 1982): 10–12.

*Pierard, Richard V. "The Unmaking of Francis Schaeffer: An Evangelical Tragedy." *The Wittenburg Door* 78 (April–May 1984): 27–31.

*Rogers, Jack. "Francis Schaeffer: The Promise and the Problem," 2 parts. *Reformed Journal* 27 (May, June 1977): 12–15, 15–19.

*Ruegsegger, Ron W. "Francis Schaeffer on Philosophy." *Christian Scholar's Review* 10 (1981): 238–54.

*————. "A Reply to Gordon Clark." *Christian Scholar's Review* 11 (1982): 150–152.

*Wells, Ronald A. "Whatever Happened to Francis Schaeffer?" *Reformed Journal* 33 (May 1983): 10–13.

Whitehead, John W. "A Challenge to Confront the World." *Christianity Today* 26 (February 5, 1982): 44–45.

Woodward, Kenneth L. "Guru of Fundamentalism." *Newsweek* 100 (November 1, 1982): 88.

Yancey, Philip. "Francis Schaeffer: A Prophet for Our Times?" *Christianity Today* 23 (March 23, 1979): 14–18.

*————. "Schaeffer On Schaeffer," 2 parts. *Christianity Today* 23 (March 23, April 9, 1979): 19–21, 21–26.

V. REVIEWS OF SCHAEFFER'S BOOKS

Art and the Bible

Jayne, DeWitt W. *Christian Scholar's Review* 5 (1975): 67–68.
Review for the Religious 33 (1974): 246.

Back to Freedom and Dignity

Bube, R. H. *Journal of the American Scientific Affiliation* 25 (September 1973): 124–26.
Kennedy, J. R. *Christianity Today* 17 (December 22, 1972): 26.

A Christian Manifesto

Barker, W. S. *Presbyterion: A Journal for the Eldership–Covenant Seminary Review* 9 (1983): 98–104.
Bernbaum, J. A. *Eternity* 33 (June 1982): 33–34.
Cutchins, M. A. *Creation Research Society Quarterly* 19 (September 1982): 106–7.
*Forbes, W. M. *Grace Theological Journal* 4 (Fall 1983): 303–9.
Gill, D. W. *Journal of the American Scientific Affiliation* 35 (1983): 53–54.
Kageler, L. *Alliance Witness* 117 (March 31, 1982): 22.
McCulley, M. *Journal of Church and State* 25 (Spring 1983): 354–56.
*Wells, Ronald. "Francis Schaeffer's Jeremaid." *Reformed Journal* 32 (May 1982): 16–20.
Wenig, S. *United Evangelical Action* 41 (Spring 1982): 34–36.
Wilburn, Stephen Sallis. "Blaming the Courts." *Reformed Journal* 32 (March 1982): 2–3.
Wimbish, D. *Charisma* 7 (Fall 1982): 70.
Woodruff, M. J. *Christianity Today* 26 (September 3, 1982): 106–7.
*Zens, J. *Searching Together* 11 (Winter 1982): 41–48.

The Church at the End of the Twentieth Century

Covell, R. *Evangelical Missions Quarterly* 8 (Fall 1971): 56–57.
Daane, J. *Eternity* 22 (July 1971): 50–51.
Hoekema, A. A. *Calvin Theological Journal* 7 (April 1972): 68–70.
Hood, L. *Church Teachers* 9 (January 1972): 28–29.
Kane, J. H. *Occasional Bulletin of Missionary Research* 2 (July 1978): 100.
*Pinnock, C. H. *Christian Scholar's Review* 1 (1971): 370–72.
Segler, F. M. *Southwestern Journal of Theology* 13 (Spring 1971): 122.
Stanger, F. B. *Asbury Seminarian* 28 (April 1973): 25–26.
Wagner, J. E. *Christianity Today* 15 (May 1971): 15–18.

The Church Before the Watching World

Battenfield, J. R. *Grace Journal* 13 (Spring 1972): 35.
Books and Bookmen 17 (April 1972): R2.
Lightner, R. D. *Bibliotheca Sacra* 129 (April 1972): 150–51.
Tinder, D. *Christianity Today* 16 (November 1971): 21.

Death in the City

Breisch, F. *Eternity* 20 (October 1969): 50–51.
Bube, R. H. *Journal of the American Scientific Affiliation* 22 (June 1970): 72–73.
Johnson, A. *Moody Monthly* 70 (October 1969): 59–60.

Escape From Reason

Bube, R. H. *Journal of the American Scientific Affiliation* 21 (June 1969): 54–55.
Johnson, A. F. *Moody Monthly* 69 (June 1969): 96–98.
*Lakey, P. *Gordon Review* 11 (Summer 1969): 241–45.

Everybody Can Know

Breisch, F. *Eternity* 26 (January 1975): 36.

Genesis in Space and Time

Bube, R. H. *Journal of the American Scientific Affiliation* 25 (September 1973): 124–26.
Choice 10 (March 1973): 125.
Klug, E. F. *The Springfielder* 36 (March 1973): 313–14.
Laughlin, D. E. *Journal of the American Scientific Affiliation* 25 (September 1973): 126–27.
Mixter, R. *Christian Teacher* 10 (May–June 1973): 27.
Rybolt, J. E. *Catholic Biblical Quarterly* 35 (April 1973): 273–74.

The God Who Is There

Bube, R. H. *Journal of the American Scientific Affiliation* 21 (June 1969): 54–55.
Cressey, M. H. *The Churchman* 83 (Spring 1969): 55–56.
Dye, D. L. *Journal of the American Scientific Affiliation* 21 (June 1969): 55–56.
*Franz, H. J. *Westminster Theological Journal* 32 (November 1969): 114–16.
Holmes, A. F. *His* 29 (February 1969): 26.
Johnson, A. F. *Moody Monthly* 69 (June 1969): 96–98.
Johnson, J. F. *The Springfielder* 33 (Spring 1969): 55–56.
Lakey, P. *Gordon Review* 11 (Summer 1969): 241–45.
Pinnock, C. H. *Christianity Today* 13 (January 3, 1969): 24.
Pogue, V. C. *Exposition Times* 80 (February 1969): 143–44.
Reist, J. S., Jr. *Foundations* 12 (April–June 1969): 183–86.
Witmer, J. A. *Bibliotheca Sacra* 126 (July–September 1969): 253–54.

The Great Evangelical Disaster

Barlow, Jack. *Christian Scholar's Review* 14 (1985): 181–83.
Christian Century 101 (May 16, 1984): 529.

He Is There and He Is Not Silent

Blum, E. A. *Bibliotheca Sacra* 130 (January 1973): 74.
Brown, H. O. J. *Christianity Today* 17 (September 14, 1973): 18.
Hendricks, W. L. *Southwestern Journal of Theology* 15 (Fall 1972): 139.
Marchant, G. J. C. *The Churchman* 88 (January–March 1974): 63.

How Should We Then Live?

Barr, W. R. *New Review of Books and Religion* 1 (March 1977): 13.
Bube, R. H. *Journal of the American Scientific Affiliation* 29 (December 1977): 185.
Daane, James. *Christian Century* 94 (October 12, 1977): 922–23.
*Davis, S. T. *Evangelical Quarterly* 50 (April–June 1978): 109–12.
Danton, D. W. *Theology Today* 35 (October 1978): 341.
Foos, H. D. *Moody Monthly* 77 (March 1977): 98.
*Giacumakis, George Jr., and Gerald. C. Tiffin. "Francis Schaeffer's New Intellectual Enterprise: Some Friendly Criticisms." *Fides et Historia* 9 (Spring 1977): 52–58.
Kaufman, P. L. *Journal of Psychology and Theology* 5 (Winter 1977): 73–75.
Mano, D. K. *National Review* 29 (1977): 345.
Matson, R. W. *Wittenburg Door* 37 (June–July 1977): 28–29.
Moritz, E. *Church and Synagogue Libraries* 11 (January 1978): 9.
*Pinnock, C. *Sojourners* 6 (July 1977): 32–35.
*Reid, W. S. *Westminster Theological Journal* 40 (Spring 1978): 379–84.
Scadding, S. *Journal of the American Scientific Affiliation* 29 (December 1977): 185.
Van Der Haag, E. *National Review* 29 (March 1977): 345.
West Coast Review of Books 3 (1977): 38.
Wieremga, P. A. *His* 37 (June 1977): 21–22.
Woodfin, Y. *Southwestern Journal of Theology* 19 (Spring 1977): 130–31.

Joshua and the Flow of Biblical History

Vannoy, J. Robert. *Westminster Theological Journal* 38 (Spring 1976): 423–25.

The New Super-Spirituality

Bube, R. H. *Journal of the American Scientific Affiliation* 25 (September 1973): 124–26.

No Little People

Crighton, J. *His* 35 (Fall 1975): 11–12.
Ponstein, Lambert J. *Reformed Review* 28 (Winter 1975): 98.

Pollution and the Death of Man

Baer, R. A., Jr. *Christian Scholar's Review* 2 (1971): 84–87.

Bube, R. H. *Journal of the American Scientific Affiliation* 23 (June 1971): 70–71.
Bullock, W. L. *Christianity Today* 15 (April 23, 1971): 20–24.
Nevin, P. *Moody Monthly* 71 (November 1970): 45–46.
Tuinstra, K. *Eternity* 22 (March 1971): 61–62.
Scudder, C. W. *Southwestern Journal of Theology* 13 (Spring 1971): 123.

True Spirituality

Buehler, W. W. *Christian Scholar's Review* 3 (Spring 1973): 91–92.
Christianity Today 16 (March 31, 1972): 25

Whatever Happened to the Human Race?

Kiwiet, John J. *Southwestern Journal of Theology* 23 (Spring 1981): 107.
Litfin, A. D. *Bibliotheca Sacra* 137 (January–March 1980): 81–82.
Palmer, B. *Eternity* 31 (October 1980): 92.

Who Is for Peace?

Christian Century 101 (February 29, 1984): 227.
Library Journal 109 (January 1984): 101.
Reflections 3 (Winter 1984): 20.
Williamson, C., Jr. *National Review* 35 (December 23, 1984): 1629.

INDEX

Abortion, 38, 217, 223, 227, 237–38, 246, 248, 259, 281–83, 290, 296
  acceptance by evangelicals, 40
  as leading naturally to euthanasia, 252, 253, 262, 263, 264
  linked to racism, 257
  as product of humanism, 37, 38, 107, 260, 264
  Schaeffer arguments against, 250–51
Absolutes, 30, 163, 177
  as universals, 122, 135, 136, 202
  See Truth: as absolute
Adams, John, 232
Alexander, Archibald, 46–47
Allis, Oswald T., 53
Altizer, Thomas, 174
American Civil Liberties Union, 226
American Council of Christian Churches, 58, 59, 64
Anabaptists, 216
Antithesis, 13–14, 84, 229–31, 234–35, 242, 270, 276, 277, 282, 283, 298–300
  between truth and error, 12, 13
  See also Synthesis
Apologetic points of comparison
  basis of faith, 72, 73–74, 85–86, 102
  common ground, 56–57, 64, 72, 73, 80–81, 90, 92, 101, 177
  criteria of truth, 72, 73–74, 82–83, 101
  logical starting point, 72, 73–74, 78–80, 101
  role of reason, 72, 73–74, 84–85, 102
Apologetics, 33–34, 49, 56, 245
  See also Evidentialism; Presuppositionalism; Verificationalism
Aquinas, Thomas, 28–29, 36, 111, 112–15, 120, 126, 185–86, 203, 215
  on nature and grace, 29, 215
  on particulars and universals, 29, 113–14, 120, 202, 215
  on reason, 28–29, 112, 114, 120, 175, 178, 185–86, 202, 215

Aristotle, 111, 112, 113, 114
  on particulars, 29, 36, 112, 202
Art
  fragmentation in modern, 137–39, 169
  human creativity in, 161, 163
  meaning in, 168–71
  principles for evaluation of, 151–53
  as product of world view, 134–35, 153–56, 157–59
  as search for a universal, 136, 138
  See also Impressionism; Naturalism
Art and the Bible, 132–33, 150–56
Auburn Affirmation, 51
Augustine of Hippo, 46, 114
Augustus Caesar (Octavian), 201
Authoritarianism, 39, 206, 211, 216
Ayer, A. J., 109

Bach, Johann Sebastian, 144, 146, 150, 159
Bacon, Francis, 205
Barmen Declaration, 216
Barth, Karl, 36, 55, 60, 175, 176, 178, 187, 192, 216
Beatles, the, 149–50
Beauty, 159–60
  equation with truth, 134, 135, 155, 159–60
Beethoven, Ludwig van, 145
Bible
  and higher criticism, 48, 49, 52, 55
  as propositional, verbal revelation from God, 270, 277, 278, 285
  and science, 48, 49
  See also Inerrancy of the Bible
Bible Presbyterian Church, 54, 58, 61
Bioethics, 249–53
  See also Abortion; Infanticide; Euthanasia
Boccaccio, 202
Bonaventure, 114
Bonhoeffer, Dietrich, 192
Briggs, Charles A., 50–51, 54
Bronowski, Jacob, 197
Brown, Colin, 88, 93, 185
Brunelleschi, Filippo, 202